The Four Workarounds

The Four Workarounds

HOW THE WORLD'S SCRAPPIEST
ORGANIZATIONS TACKLE
COMPLEX PROBLEMS

PAULO SAVAGET

JOHN MURRAY

First published in Great Britain in 2023 by John Murray (Publishers)
An Hachette UK company

1

Copyright © Paulo Savaget 2023

Text design by Steven Seighman

A CIP catalogue record for this title is available from the British Library

Hardback ISBN 9781529346039
Trade Paperback ISBN 9781529346046
eBook ISBN 9781529346060

Typeset in Fournier MT Std

Printed and bound in Great Britain by Clays Ltd, Elcograf S.p.A.

John Murray policy is to use papers that are natural, renewable and recyclable
products and made from wood grown in sustainable forests. The logging and
manufacturing processes are expected to conform to the environmental regulations
of the country of origin.

John Murray (Publishers)
Carmelite House
50 Victoria Embankment
London EC4Y 0DZ

www.johnmurraypress.co.uk

To Janjan, Miltão, and Ju,
with much love, appreciation, and admiration

Contents

Author's Note

My first workaround occurred before I could even walk. When I was ten months old I developed life-threatening diarrhea. Unable to absorb food and water, I suffered from severe malnutrition and dehydration and experienced rapid weight loss and hair loss. My parents had to figure out how to save my life. There were two ways to treat my condition: formula or breast milk.

The problem was that my mother was no longer able to breastfeed me, and where I lived in Brazil, formula was unavailable and breast milk banks were on strike. My family needed a workaround—and fast. Through word of mouth, they located young mothers living in favelas who generously fed me alongside their own babies. My parents knew that there was a risk of transmitting diseases such as HIV through breast milk. But they had to take a chance and make a choice, even if it was an imperfect one. And it worked. If not for this workaround, I would have lost more than 10 percent of my body fluid and died—just like the roughly 1.7 million children under the age of five who died of diarrhea worldwide that year.

The remarkable yet unconventional approach that my parents pursued speaks to a larger issue.

We constantly encounter complex problems at home, in our places of work, and in society at large. Even if we had all the time and money in the world, sometimes no good solution can be found. So what should we do, especially when we can't wait? The answer: a workaround.

Workarounds have helped me with my problems and, after reading this book, you'll be able to use them, too. What you are about to read describes how we can use workarounds to effectively address problems with minimal fuss. While gracefully circumventing our obstacles, we can explore unconventional alternatives to the status quo in situations that range from everyday problems to some of the world's toughest challenges.

The Four Workarounds

Introduction

I didn't plan to study workarounds; I bumped into them as I searched for resourceful ways to tackle complex problems. I'm now an associate professor at the University of Oxford's Department of Engineering Science and Saïd Business School, working on applied research that focuses on transforming unjust systems. Before I became an academic, my background combined a bundle of seemingly disconnected activities. I pursued paths that combined my excitement for entrepreneurship with my concerns about social and environmental challenges, such as poverty, inequality, and climate change. I co-founded companies, taught executives, engaged with nonprofits, and worked as a consultant to projects in different settings, ranging from high-end offices of large companies and intergovernmental organizations to remote regions in the Amazon and scattered across Brazilian favelas.

Consulting gave me the opportunity to peek into realities that were very different from mine. Yet whether I was making recommendations for science and technology policy in high-income countries or evaluating social projects with traditional populations in the rain forest, my reports (and, in fact, all the studies I had read) included similar types of recommendations, such as "collaborate more actively," "improve coordination and alignment," and "engage in long-term planning." These recommendations aren't wrong, but they are too generic. They fail to suggest next steps, particularly in situations where we can't afford to wait for a solution to a tough problem.

I also became increasingly disillusioned with management practitioners. It seemed that the business gurus tended to ignore the groups that weren't directly paying them. Worse, over the past decade large companies have been trying to convince nonprofits to be more like them. But my work with nonprofits had taught me that there was a lot that corporations could learn from small organizations that make outsized impacts. I call these small organizations "scrappy" because they're feisty, resourceful, and operate at the fringes of power. Scrappy organizations have to think quickly out of necessity, and despite some apparent clumsiness they often persist and succeed *because* of their unconventional methods. But in the business world, learning from the innovative wit and practical ingenuity of these "ugly ducklings" was uncharted territory.

This inspired me to look at deviants—even criminals—who made impactful changes. Once while procrastinating at work I stumbled upon the blockbuster-ready story of a computer hacker and cybercriminal, Albert Gonzalez, in *The New York Times*. By the age of fourteen he was the ringleader of a group of mischievous computer geeks who had hacked into NASA, drawing the attention of the FBI in 1995. Just about thirteen years later, and after very little additional formal training, Gonzalez was being prosecuted in one of the world's largest and most complex identity theft cases. At final count, he and his colleagues had stolen more than 170 million credit card and ATM numbers.

Don't get me wrong, I wasn't particularly interested in Gonzalez's malicious motivations, but I was astonished by how he, and many other hackers with meager resources and training, were able to crack computer systems. I knew nothing about coding, but hackers intrigued me, and I couldn't find much information about them at the time. Management scholars seemed to be interested in hackers only when it came to cybersecurity, and journalists seemed more interested in reinforcing negative stereotypes about hackers than in revealing *how* they hacked. Despite the fascinating things they did behind computer screens, we knew very little about their methods.

So I knew I had to learn more about hacking.

I started my PhD at the University of Cambridge, as a Gates Scholar, with one question in mind: Can we learn from hackers and deploy their methods to address our world's most urgent and high-stakes socio-environmental challenges?

Prior to my research, academics had never considered hacking as a means to understand or expedite real-world change. I began by interviewing hackers to find out how they do what they do. I realized that it's human nature to tackle obstacles head-on, but that this often results in banging our heads against the wall. The secret of hackers is that they weave through uncharted territory and, instead of confronting the bottlenecks that lie in their way, they work around them. These workarounds may not solve problems all at once, but they enable hackers to obtain good enough immediate outcomes—and quick wins can sometimes pave the way for big, unpredicted change.

The way hackers get things done also made me realize that people often follow conventional wisdom, which streamlines our responses to daily tasks. Consider how you have "the way" to do a bunch of things: the way you make pasta, the way you use a hammer, the way you respond to authorities, the way you write an email . . . Although these explicit rules or customary practices help us get stuff done without overexerting ourselves, they also numb us, limiting the realm of possibilities that we see and pursue. We inadvertently don't explore other ways to make pasta or use a hammer, and we subconsciously dismiss new ways of addressing authorities and creative ways to write an email.

As I dove deeper into online hacker communities, I also found that hacking isn't limited to the world of computing. As Paul Buchheit, creator and lead developer of Gmail, once wrote, "Wherever there are systems, there is the potential for hacking, and there are systems everywhere."

This finding was a turning point in my work. I realized that my original premise was wrong; oftentimes organizations the business world tends to think of as "scrappy" were essentially hacking their own problems—even though they didn't use this term. From working around their obstacles, they addressed critical issues and were sometimes able to leave a powerful legacy, especially when it came to issues that, despite best efforts, seemed intractable.

I then pivoted my research to explore how change makers—entrepreneurs, academics, companies, nonprofits, community groups, and even policymakers—work around obstacles, both on- and off-line, to "hack" all sorts of problems, ranging from global responses to some of the world's toughest challenges, such as global pandemics, gender inequality, and poverty, to everyday inconveniences. This pivot took me to unexpected places, where I had the privilege of learning from scrappy organizations that don't get the widespread credit they deserve.

All great exploratory research starts with unabashed prying. Researchers just want to peek into the unknown. So, with the help of research grants and awards from the Gates Foundation, the University of Cambridge, the Ford Foundation, Santander, and the IBM Center for the Business of Government, I traveled on various occasions for three years across nine countries to study cases of mavericks adopting hacker-like approaches to pressing problems such as healthcare, education, abortion rights, caste prejudice, sanitation, and corruption. In the quest for smart fixes, I learned from an unlikely A-team of lateral thinkers, ranging from physicians to indigenous tribe leaders to activists.

After engaging with these mavericks, it was time for me to do what researchers do best: find patterns. This was a much more tedious task than fieldwork. Boosted by high doses of caffeine and pain au chocolat, I spent months reading, synthesizing, categorizing, and comparing the data that I had gathered from the field.

What did these trailblazers have in common? How did they approach their respective problems? These questions helped me find some reoccurring themes: the workaround masterminds tend to mistrust authorities, thrive on urgency and immediacy, think unconventionally, and act resourcefully. However helpful these early observations were for my dissertation, they felt like an introduction rather than a conclusion. The more I thought about these patterns, the more I wanted to focus on and learn about the workaround *method*. I dove into the transcripts of my interviews to "let the data speak" (a technique that researchers tend to love), hoping to find patterns across the cases. Unfortunately, the conversation was one-sided, and I didn't want to torture my data into an unreliable confession. So I stepped back and reapproached each case as its own story. Starting from the beginning, what happened? Then what? And what came after that?

To my surprise, I realized that despite their different settings, characters, and plot devices, the stories unraveled in similar ways. As I stepped back from the data and looked at each case individually, patterns arose. All of my stories' protagonists used at least one of four workaround methods, which I have termed piggyback, loophole, roundabout, and next best.

Once I identified these four approaches, I started finding workarounds everywhere. Sure, scrappy mavericks might be especially well positioned to use these flexible tactics, but it began to occur to me that workarounds happen not just in creative organizations with tight budgets but also everywhere from influential legal cases to fairy tales—I even found them scattered around the very corporations I was determined *not* to learn from. To my surprise, some of the world's most powerful organizations resort to scrappy strategies when the stakes are high and there's no time for the usual drawn-out decision-making processes.

Workarounds are effective, versatile, and accessible methods for tackling complex problems. Together, we'll explore each of the four workarounds, fleshing out their key principles by weaving together different and sometimes unexpected stories whose protagonists vary from housekeepers to influential policymakers. We'll travel from international waters to clandestine digital terrain; from the boardrooms of large companies to inventors' laboratories; and from urban Delhi to some of the hardest to reach places on Earth, like rural Zambia. These chapters will give you an opportunity to dive into new settings and learn from unconventional stories. They will challenge how you think about problem-solving and show how workarounds can help you with the obstacles you repeatedly bump into.

Part I covers what workarounds are and how to come up with them. In Part II I dig into how to cultivate a workaround attitude and mindset, including how to reflect on the ways you typically see, judge, and approach your obstacles. Then, on the more practical side, I'll show you how you can systematically conceive workarounds to your problems and how your workplace can become more workaround friendly. I conclude with a reflection on how workarounds can ultimately help you with your daily, sometimes messy life.

As much as this book shares my research, my goal is that you'll be able to identify workarounds that you've already used, consider how a different approach might've changed how you looked at and addressed challenges, and learn the fundamentals of assessing and interacting with new obstacles that cross your path. So if you're interested in plunging into unconventional stories, challenging yourself to think differently about decision-making and management strategies, and defying the status quo to address your problems, then please read on.

Part I

The Four Workarounds

The workaround is a creative, flexible, imperfection-loving, problem-solving approach. At its core, a workaround is a method that ignores or even challenges conventions on how, and by whom, a problem is meant to be solved. It is particularly suitable when traditional problem-solving methods have systematically failed or when you don't have the necessary power or resources to pursue the conventional approach.

There are four workarounds, and each uses a different attribute. The piggyback capitalizes on pre-existing but seemingly unrelated systems or relationships. The loophole relies on selectively applying or reinterpreting the rules that traditionally define a situation. The roundabout disrupts or disturbs self-reinforcing behavior patterns. Finally, the next best repurposes or recombines readily available resources in order to find different ways to get things done.

Anyone can stumble into a workaround, but knowing the approaches will enable you to intentionally pursue them.

The Piggyback

As a consultant I once visited a remote region in the Brazilian Amazon that could only be reached by boat. Locals lived in an environmentally protected area, and, because they were cash-strapped and isolated from urban areas, they had access to only a few industrial products. When I arrived, they generously invited me to lunch. I was given a meal of local delicacies, including tasty fish from the Amazon River that were completely new to me, alongside a bottle of Coca-Cola.

No matter where I've traveled, I've always seen bottles of soft drinks like Coca-Cola and Pepsi. What had never occurred to me was the role a crate of Coca-Cola could play for people seeking to work around critical obstacles to bring lifesaving medicines to communities in need of them. Luckily, there was a couple who had been trying to tackle the problem of access to medicine by tapping into the existing flows of Coca-Cola bottles. In their creative approach, they have provided an example for a type of workaround that I'll refer to as piggybacking.

We are often burdened by the inertia of patterns and habits and forget to look for untraditional connections; piggyback workarounds can help us find opportunities across silos. It's a remarkable strategy that is suitable for use by everyone from nonprofits in low-income countries to big corporations in Silicon Valley. Before we dive deep into what I learned from this couple, let's take a look at what a piggyback workaround entails.

WHAT IS A PIGGYBACK WORKAROUND?

The piggyback workaround enables us to circumvent all sorts of obstacles and address our problems by using seemingly unrelated relationships. Because a piggyback is based on the interactions of multiple actors or systems, the relationships vary from case to case. This type of behavior isn't only found in human interactions—it can happen anywhere in nature.

In biological terms, symbiotic relationships leverage what is "already there" in an ecosystem. These relationships can be mutualistic, commensalistic, or parasitic.

A mutualistic relationship benefits both species. For instance, think of goby fish and shrimp, two species that spend a lot of time together in and around the sand burrow that the shrimp both builds and maintains. The burrow provides the goby fish a refuge to hide from its predators and lay its eggs, and the goby fish, in return, touches the nearly blind shrimp with its tail as a warning to retreat to the burrow when a predator approaches.

A commensalistic relationship is one in which a species benefits and the other is unaffected. For example, the remora is a small fish that attaches itself to the fins of bigger animals, such as sharks. The shark barely feels the remora's presence, but the remora benefits from "free rides," food leftovers, and protection from predators—who wouldn't dare to get too close to a shark.

As most of us know, a parasitic relationship is one in which a species benefits at the expense of another. Think briefly of roundworms: the parasites use hosts for food, water, and a space to reproduce. Their hosts are harmed in the process, though, presenting symptoms such as fever, cough, abdominal pain, vomiting, and diarrhea.

Piggyback workarounds can be similar: relationships between organizations can be mutualistic, commensalistic, or parasitic, sometimes in surprising ways. As we go through the next few examples of scrappy organizations, we'll see the flexibility of piggybacking, in terms of both the relationships it employs and the goals it pursues.

PIGGYBACKING ON COCA-COLA

Now back to Coca-Cola and the British couple, Jane and Simon Berry, who figured out a remarkable way to put the distribution of soft drinks to use. The couple founded a nonprofit organization, ColaLife, that has successfully bypassed the bottlenecks that hamper access to diarrhea medicine in remote regions of Zambia by piggybacking on pre-existing networks of fast-moving consumer goods such as Coca-Cola.

I stumbled across their story when the Berrys were featured in a BBC article after winning the Product Design of the Year award from London's Design Museum. The award was presented in 2013, but the idea that led to it was conceived much earlier. In the 1980s Simon worked with a British aid program on an integrated development project for rural farming communities in Zambia. At the time, he was surprised to see that Coca-Cola was readily available but lifesaving medicines weren't. That was the case even for affordable over-the-counter medicines that treated some of the most prevalent causes of mortality in the country, such as diarrhea.

Simon's idea was clever and simple: work around the systemic issues facing medicine access and literally piggyback on Coca-Cola's distribution by inserting a package containing a cheap and simple diarrhea treatment for children between the bottles in Coca-Cola crates. Simon and Jane Berry were keen to put the piggyback to the test, but first they had to understand the obstacles they wanted to work around.

Why Was the Problem Still a Problem?

Simon and Jane didn't know much about why diarrhea was such a persistent problem when they first conceived a piggyback workaround to tackle it. They knew diarrhea killed a lot of children, and treatment didn't reach remote regions in Zambia. As they researched the viability of piggybacking on Coca-Cola flows to make treatment available in remote regions, they found out that childhood diarrhea is one of the direst problems of our times: it is the second leading cause of death among children under the age of five in Sub-Saharan Africa. At the time the Berrys co-founded ColaLife in 2011, according to the CDC, diarrhea killed about 800,000 children yearly worldwide, which was a higher rate of mortality among children than AIDS, malaria, and measles combined.

Public-sector responses to diarrheal infections generally require a high level of coordination, with comprehensive policies and investments from multiple fronts. However, governments of low-income countries like Zambia face multiple constraints, including lack of funding, poor infrastructure, and inadequate governance. Only 50 percent of rural households had a healthcare facility within about three miles in the early 2000s, and the Zambian Ministry of Health recognized that insufficient infrastructure; sparsely distributed population in rural settings; inadequate resources for outreach, like vehicles; and poor scheduling were all factors that limited the public sector's ability to provide accessible medical treatment across the country. Even in cases where healthcare facilities existed, they often faced medicine supply shortages. Improving infrastructure, such as building better roads or more healthcare access points, might help in the long run, but it would be very costly and difficult to implement due to potential social, political, and economic barriers. The situation was too dire to sit and wait for long-lasting public solutions.

So what about distributing the World Health Organization's recommended remedy, oral rehydration salts (ORS) and zinc, through the private sector? ORS together with zinc is an over-the-counter treatment, can be administered at home, and is very inexpensive. Even in remote regions, distribution networks already existed: shopkeepers sold products like sugar, cooking oil, and the ever-present Coca-Cola. So why weren't ORS and zinc available in these shops?

Unfortunately, there were quite a few hurdles in the private sector, too. Despite the demand for medicine, the treatment of disease in low-income regions isn't a top priority for global markets due to the low profit margins earned from selling directly to the poor or because of the low purchasing power of underfunded governments. Furthermore, retailers like pharmacies are also too few and far between. In 2008 there were only fifty-nine pharmacies in Zambia, forty of which were concentrated in the capital, Lusaka. Local regulations mandated that pharmacies employ a pharmacist, but there were fewer than a hundred pharmacists in the country, thus stifling pharmacy expansion. Meanwhile, poor infrastructure and limited transportation services hampered the flow of products between pharmaceutical companies, wholesalers, and retailers.

There were many obstacles preventing access to diarrhea treatment in Zambia, which meant that there were many opportunities to find workarounds.

Putting the Piggyback to the Test

Workarounds require changing how we typically approach our problems. A piggyback workaround involves shifting our attention from "what lacks" to "what exists" in a given situation. This was precisely Simon and Jane's approach: they valued contextual potentialities and recognized the need to maintain local autonomy. In the 1980s Simon was employed by the UK Department for International Development (DfID) and lived in Zambia, working on a then-revolutionary program that transferred management to the local community. Even in the early 2000s,

Simon noticed that international development organizations implemented programs that created dependence, aiming to "fill voids," treating low-income regions as places of scarcity instead of building on local capabilities and activities.

When the Berrys decided to put their piggyback work-around to the test, they built it on the ethos that, in Simon's words, "every single problem in developing countries can be solved by the people and the systems that are already there. It's not a question of bringing in new people or parallel systems . . . It's about making what is already there work better and in a more coherent way." So how could they benefit from the flow of Coca-Cola and other fast-moving consumer goods that worked so well in Zambia so that they could address the pressing health issue? And how could they get started?

Simon posted the idea of fitting medicines between Coca-Cola bottles on Facebook. The idea gained traction through Facebook post likes and shares and led to a BBC feature. After the feature, Jane and Simon gained access to Coca-Cola's European headquarters, which led them to SABMiller, the beverage's bottler in Zambia. They also designed the medicine's triangular packaging that fit between bottles in Coca-Cola crates, and their creative design made it possible to raise funds and test their idea in an exploratory trial in two districts in Zambia.

They soon discovered that this piggyback method was commensalistic: it would neither harm nor benefit Coca-Cola and SABMiller, but it would help sick children. Coca-Cola's distribution is decentralized, so even Coca-Cola's managers don't usually know where the bottles travel—their flow is very demand driven. Distribution in countries like Zambia involves a bunch of local players, ranging from large supermarkets to owners of micro shops in sparsely populated regions. Many distributors help move bottles between urban and rural regions, including those who transport Coca-Cola crates strapped to their bikes with rubber bands. Each of these autonomous actors, big and small, plays an important role in the bottles' journey between producer and consumers all over the country.

SABMiller connected the couple to wholesalers that purchased Coca-Cola, and those connections made it possible for Jane and Simon to identify other key players in the supply chain who made soda accessible in every corner of the country. They engaged with many small shopkeepers who started selling the treatment, as well as with different actors throughout Coca-Cola's distribution chain, such as grocery stores, retailers, and distributors, to understand how they interacted with each other and how each benefited from those interactions. As part of this exploratory trial, ColaLife also worked with caregivers to design Kit Yamoyo, an anti-diarrheal treatment kit that co-packaged ORS and zinc.

While pursuing its greater vision, ColaLife bumped into a series of small hurdles, but the Berrys worked around those, too. They learned how difficult it was for people to properly administer the medicine if they lacked easy access to measuring cups. Because caregivers couldn't precisely measure the water needed to dissolve the ORS on their own, Kit Yamoyo's triangular package also functioned as a measuring cup.

Local regulatory constraints posed additional challenges. ColaLife had added a bar of soap to the package, so that caregivers would wash their hands before dispensing the medicine. But the Zambian medicines regulator advised that soap could not be placed in the same container as medicine because the two items belonged to different product classes. Instead of confronting the rule or conforming to it, Simon and Jane cleverly employed their piggyback mentality: they designed a soap tray to fit into the top of the package, separating the soap from the ORS and zinc. That way, they made both product classes available separately but simultaneously. The regulator was satisfied, and they got what they wanted.

Following a series of workarounds like these, the results of the trial were impressive. Within the span of one year, the uptake of the combination therapy increased from less than 1 percent to 46.6 percent across the intervention districts. No similar change was detected in other parts of the country, which they monitored for comparison.

The results of the pilot program also demonstrated that in order to expand their reach and to ensure a continuous and resilient flow of medicine, Jane and Simon had to move away from a model that used only Coca-Cola's distribution networks. Despite the success of the trial, the tactic of fitting medicines in Coca-Cola's crates wasn't the core of ColaLife's success—in fact, distributors often wouldn't "waste time" fitting kits between bottles, but rather strapped them in with the other things they transported.

Furthermore, that initial distribution model relied on Jane and Simon's physical presence in Zambia, but the couple had no plans to remain part of the medical supply system. As Jane told me: "We are not going to be there forever. There are lots of programs that start, five-year programs, and they transform the landscape for five years, and then they go, and things go back to what they were before if not worse than before . . . Everything we do is about what happens when we leave: it is about planning for your own demise."

Scaling the Piggyback

Jane and Simon knew they had to ensure that the flow of medication would be self-sustainable, profitable, and resilient; for that, they had to adopt a more integrated and mutualistic approach to emulate the value chain of Coca-Cola. They had to guarantee that all players involved in the flow of the treatment, from the pharmaceutical industry at the beginning to the retailers at the end, would profit; otherwise, they would likely opt out and compromise the flow of the medicine. In other words, they had to move from merely physically piggybacking on the crates of Coca-Cola to making use of the entire system of relationships that made distribution possible.

In the four years following their successful trial, they scaled up their impact through an approach that benefited the entire chain. ColaLife provided a free, nonexclusive license of the intellectual property of Kit Yamoyo to Pharmanova, a local pharmaceutical company. They also helped Pharmanova with the design and packaging of the product, even importing machines for the company and funding some of their marketing efforts. With that, they increased the chances that the company would profit from the production of Kit Yamoyo and become robust enough to offer the quality and quantity of treatment needed to meet the country's needs.

ColaLife also worked with agents in the middle of the distribution chain. This included, for example, liaising with supermarkets, pharmacies, and wholesalers to ensure they procured the treatment directly from Pharmanova and stocked the product. These players were critical: they sold the treatment directly to caregivers and to other small retailers and distributors, such as the ones who took the medicine to shopkeepers in remote regions. Small shops were the primary point of contact for most caregivers in rural regions, but they were also the most fragile. With the support of a local nonprofit, ColaLife trained thousands of shopkeepers to instruct caregivers how to administer diarrhea treatment. The nonprofit supported the shopkeepers with business skills to build their capacity to continuously stock and offer the product.

ColaLife also worked around funding constraints, tapping into the resources and efforts from bigger players. For example, when promoting Kit Yamoyo through the private sector, Jane and Simon came across a program funded by the US Agency for International Development (USAID) that had an allocated budget for marketing medicines. They piggybacked onto USAID's marketing budget and training program to promote Kit Yamoyo alongside other medicines in USAID's portfolio.

Many seemingly small workarounds similarly contributed toward making diarrhea treatment available in Zambia by creating a flow of medicine wherein everyone benefited. When all players had an interest in maintaining the flow of the treatment,

ColaLife knew it had successfully expanded access to treatment to almost twenty districts, with better results than those of the initial trial.

The workarounds that ColaLife implemented in the private sector also created momentum to tackle some of the systemic issues preventing access to the medicine through the public sector. Jane and Simon were particularly interested in expanding their approach to the public sector because it had the ability to treat an even larger number of children across the country. They knew that they could help the government to work around issues of funding and infrastructure. So they helped Pharmanova to create a government-branded version of Kit Yamoyo, which could be procured by the Zambian Ministry of Health and provided for free at healthcare facilities and by community health workers in fourteen districts. Again, ColaLife supported and connected resources from all agents involved in the distribution chain, ranging from the pharmaceutical company to those who dispensed the treatment, such as doctors, nurses, and community health workers.

Approximately four years after ColaLife began, the organization had piggybacked on existing flows of products, like Coca-Cola, to deliver locally produced, widely accessible, and affordable diarrhea treatment through both the public and private sectors. When I visited Zambia in 2017, Pharmanova was selling an average of fourteen hundred kits per day, making it one of the best-selling and most promising products in its portfolio, and use across intervention districts had increased from an average of 1 percent to 53 percent.

Piggybacking on the World Health Organization

Jane and Simon returned to the UK, leaving a self-sustaining flow of diarrhea treatment in Zambia. Now that they had become more familiar with "how things work" in healthcare, they recognized an opportunity for another game-changing workaround, but this time it could be implemented from their sofa in London. They knew that if they were successful they could spread ColaLife's impact to people in many other low-income countries who, like the population of Zambia, lacked access to adequate diarrhea treatment.

In Zambia, Jane and Simon learned that governments tend to procure and dispense ORS and zinc separately, even though both are needed to treat diarrhea. This meant, for example, that healthcare facilities often lacked one of the two or that doctors would prescribe ORS without zinc because they weren't aware of the WHO's recommendation for the combined therapy. Co-packaging ORS and zinc helped to avoid these kinds of problems, and Jane and Simon had the evidence: in 2016, they collected data that showed that even when healthcare facilities in Zambia had both ORS and zinc in stock but they were packaged separately, only 44 percent of cases received both, but 87 percent received the combined treatment when ORS and zinc were packaged together.

So how could Jane and Simon make co-packaged ORS and zinc a norm instead of an exception?

Toward the end of their stay in Zambia, Jane and Simon started paying attention to the WHO's Essential Medicines List, a sort of checklist of basic medicines designed to be adopted by national governments everywhere. The list contains medications that the organization considers critical for meeting the basic needs of any national healthcare system, and it's frequently used by policymakers to help develop their own local lists of essential medicines (which they use for prioritization in the public procurement of medicines). Not all countries follow the WHO's lead and mimic this list, but low-income ones often do because they depend on funds from international organizations, which in turn tend to prioritize medicine on the WHO's list. So Simon and Jane thought of piggybacking onto the list. Backing up their claims with plenty of data, ColaLife worked with a team of global health experts and successfully applied to add the word "co-packaged" to a treatment that was already on the list: ORS + zinc.

This new idea involved minimal effort: Simon and Jane wouldn't need to convince governments to make the combination treatment available if they piggybacked on WHO recommendations that drove government procurement decisions. It's still too early to know the full impact of this workaround, but it is highly likely that the correct diarrhea treatment reached exponentially more children in the world's poorest countries.

MUTUALISTIC RELATIONSHIPS

We've already seen one example of how piggybacks can be symbiotic: ColaLife started with the goal of fitting medicines between bottles of Coca-Cola to give medicines a free ride to children in need in remote regions. As they scaled the intervention, they started working toward a more mutualistic approach, ensuring that the pharmaceutical company, local distributors, wholesalers, and retailers would be connected to work around deep-rooted obstacles preventing access to medicines and that they would all profit from it. This type of mutually beneficial relationship is possible even when the cause isn't as noble as saving children's lives. Let's turn to a somewhat unexpected example: advertising.

Rice with M&Ms

Piggybacks in advertising date back to the 1950s, when television commercials in the United States were a full minute long. TV advertising was an effective way to reach a valuable and growing group of consumers—the number of people who owned a television grew from 9 percent to 87 percent over the course of the 1950s, and families with TVs tended to be larger and younger. They owned more telephones and refrigerators, and they bought more new cars than families without TVs. Television advertising revenue jumped from $41 million in 1951 to $336 million in just two years.

Despite this boom, regulators such as the National Association of Broadcasters (NAB) did not keep pace. The NAB designed and enforced the Television Code, which aimed to reduce advertising clutter and prevent stations from overwhelming users with commercials. It allowed for a standard break, which consisted of one 60-second advertisement, and a TV broadcaster could sell each minute-long time slot to a sponsor. This rule was originally designed for radio, not for TV, and as the television industry grew, 60-second time slots became expensive and ineffective for a single sponsor.

The only "by-the-book" way to share time slots, as regulated by the NAB, was with an integrated commercial, where two brands selling related products (e.g., butter and bread) advertised together. These advertisements shared the same story and actors but simultaneously promoted multiple products. Integrated commercials were much less effective for brand assimilation, and they didn't provide companies with flexibility to adapt to geographies. If one company sold bread in California and New York but the other sold butter exclusively in New York, it would be unfeasible for the two companies to advertise together.

Then, in 1956, Uncle Ben's Rice and M&Ms invented what became known as piggyback commercials: two or more individual commercials for unrelated products were plugged back-to-back in a single time slot. This meant that one company purchased from the broadcaster, and the other(s) piggybacked onto the time slot and shared costs with the official sponsor. These workarounds stirred quite a controversy among regulators, but the sponsors weren't violating rules. With these piggybacks, sponsors worked around the regulatory hurdles of the NAB, maximizing product exposure per dollar spent. Piggyback commercials transformed marketing tactics, making it possible for companies of different sizes and sectors to boost their brand exposure and client base.

Sponsors understood that they had to find the most effective balance between the number of times each product was advertised and the length of individual messages. They observed that in TV, frequency trumped length. An ad would be quickly forgotten if the consumer wasn't continually exposed to it. Besides, most households had only one television at the time, so advertisements had to appeal to the entire family. These advertisements conveyed simple themes with a unique selling proposition and a plain visual demonstration. Then repetition linked the simple slogans to a product—like "M&Ms melt in your mouth, not in your hands." Sponsors didn't need 60 seconds to convey these kinds of messages. The benefit of this mutualistic workaround was so clear that ten years after the first Uncle Ben's and M&Ms spot, an average of 350 piggyback commercials appeared each week on network television (an estimated average of 20–25 percent of all spot commercials).

Frequent piggybackers included manufacturers selling high-volume, low-unit-value goods, like Procter & Gamble, Bristol-Myers, General Foods, and Colgate-Palmolive. But this workaround was beneficial to smaller businesses, too. The Alberto-Culver company—a cosmetics company founded in 1955 that grew to a revenue of $1.6 billion in 2010, when it was sold to Unilever—was a prominent defender of piggyback commercials in their early days. The company argued that piggyback commercials helped smaller companies like them, which would never be able to independently afford an entire 60-second slot, to receive television exposure and compete with larger businesses.

Piggybacking in the Cloud

Let's fast-forward to our current hyperconnected times, when we have seemingly infinite content on many blue light screens.

While traditional TV ad spending in the United States is still growing—thanks to event-based programming like the Olympics, presidential elections, and the Super Bowl—broadcast TV viewership, such as cable TV, is falling in demographics between the ages of two and forty-nine. Digital media have become the dominant players in terms of advertising dollars spent. Naturally, when viewership shifts, so do marketing strategies.

Using piggyback tactics, companies have creatively responded both to the speed and to the growing number of channels for the creation and diffusion of content on digital platforms. In the early days of the internet, companies with complementary products used their online media channels to promote each other instead of paying for expensive ads. These small or medium-sized companies had similar market demographics, but their products, such as coffee and milk or suits and formal shoes, did not compete.

The piggyback has become much more sophisticated and targeted over time, as online companies started to obtain more data: instead of targeting "American businessmen who buy suits," they progressively started to target each one of us individually based on our web searches. You probably have noted how when you visit an e-commerce site and search for a product without purchasing it, you'll later see an ad for related items on different websites or social media. This is a sort of mutualistic workaround used by online platforms. Domain-specific cookies, which are small pieces of data that are used to identify your computer as you use a network, restrict companies' ability to collect information and display relevant ads to customers, reducing their reach. By piggybacking on each other, however, multiple platforms can synchronize their cookies to work around these kinds of limitations, flooding you with offers for what you're already tempted to buy.

COMMENSALISTIC RELATIONSHIPS

With the rise of digital media advertising, many other opportunities to piggyback have become possible, and not all of them have been mutualistic or agreed upon. Some were commensalistic, meaning one party benefits while the other experiences no effect. Advertisers are often perfectly happy to piggyback in a commensalistic way, making use of current events without causing harm. But if they're not careful, companies can risk being sucked into a vortex of bad PR. Let's examine a few advertising examples, some of which brought success to companies and others that dragged companies into the undertow.

Oreo Wins the Super Bowl

Oreo's most retweeted tweet in 2013 was a successful response to an unexpected event. Within ten minutes after a power outage caused lights to go out for 34 minutes in the third quarter of the 2013 Super Bowl, Oreo's social media team tweeted an ad that read, "Power out? No problem," with a solitary Oreo and this caption: "You can still dunk in the dark." Mondelēz, the multinational company that owns Oreo, had a fifteen-person social media team ready to respond to whatever happened during the Super Bowl. The president of the digital marketing agency that handled game-day tweeting for Oreo said in an interview with *Wired*: "Once the blackout happened, no one was distracted—there was nothing going on." With the power out, many people turned to their phones to waste time until power was restored in the stadium—it was the perfect opportunity for consumers to take in Twitter-based advertisements. As a result, if you searched #SuperBowl or similar hashtags on Twitter in those 34 minutes, you'd find Oreo trending, leading to substantially increased brand exposure. Whereas Oreo benefited directly from the piggyback, the Super Bowl neither won nor lost anything from Oreo's ad.

SpongeBob Gets a Free Ride

The promoters of *The SpongeBob Movie: Sponge Out of Water* used another stroke of piggybacking genius. Paramount released the SpongeBob movie one week before its rival Universal was set to unveil a film that was gaining a lot of traction among an older audience. You may remember the teaser posters for *Fifty Shades of Grey*: an enigmatic figure in a high-rise office stands with his back to the camera, with a caption reading, "Mr. Grey will see you now." The SpongeBob marketing team mimicked the poster of Christian Grey, but with the recognizable SpongeBob silhouette and the caption, "Mr. SquarePants will see you now." You can imagine the cheeky smiles of parents who watched *Fifty Shades of Grey* and were reminded to bring their kids to see the SpongeBob movie. SpongeBob benefited, and *Fifty Shades of Grey* was unharmed since the two movies weren't competing for the same audience.

Pepsi's PR Fumble

When advertising is done well, companies can achieve an enormous amount of publicity for a very small investment with this commensalistic approach. But if a strategy is executed poorly, these types of fast-response advertisements can backfire, and the company can look mercenary or desperate. That's what happened when Pepsi jumped on the bandwagon of the Black Lives Matter protests in 2017. Pepsi's video ad on YouTube borrowed imagery from the movement and shows young protesters smiling, clapping, hugging, high-fiving, and holding signs that say, "Join the conversation." The climactic scene shows Kendall Jenner, a white woman, offering a police officer a can of Pepsi, which evokes an appreciative smirk from the officer and the approval of the protesters.

Pepsi tried to piggyback on Black Lives Matter using a commensalistic approach, hoping to gain PR without adversely affecting BLM. Yet this video missed the mark so badly that it was straightaway condemned for trivializing the danger of police brutality, minimizing the frustration that protesters feel, and cynically trying to co-opt the movement against the killing of Black people by the police. Activists say Pepsi portrayed precisely the opposite of their lived experiences of police brutality, and some of their comments went viral. Bernice King, the daughter of the Reverend Dr. Martin Luther King Jr., tweeted a picture of her dad being pushed by the police and said, "If only Daddy would have known about the power of #Pepsi." DeRay Mckesson, a civil rights activist who is one of the leading voices in the Black Lives Matter movement, tweeted, "If I had carried Pepsi I guess I never would've gotten arrested. Who knew?"

What Pepsi had hoped would strengthen its brand instead led to a flood of negative comments on social media and boycott campaigns that tarnished the company's reputation. Pepsi wasn't the first company to misjudge the repercussions of a lack of moral judgment in commensalistic piggybacking. Pepsi could have learned from the negative repercussions of American Apparel's tone-deaf ad for a "Hurricane Sandy Sale" in 2012. The retailer sent out an email blast that highlighted the region where Sandy, one of the deadliest, most destructive hurricanes of the 2012 Atlantic hurricane season, hit the hardest, offering 20 percent off "in case you're bored during the storm." The storm killed 233 people across eight countries and inflicted nearly $70 billion in damage.

American Apparel tried to piggyback on the media attention to the hurricane. But its email instead came across as cringy and opportunistic, trying to capitalize on a national crisis.

Commensalistic piggybacking on current events to gain publicity may be a good strategy for seeming vibrant and plugged in, but it has its risks, too. While these companies' piggyback ads were designed to be commensalistic, the audience perceived them as parasitic, harming those affected by the events. So, before implementing a commensalistic workaround, ask yourself: How will others perceive it?

PARASITIC RELATIONSHIPS

Piggyback interventions may also be *designed* to be parasitic. Some of these piggybacks, like malware, are employed for cybercrime, attempting to gain access to users' systems by piggybacking on legitimate software in disguise. Likewise, phishing emails piggyback on the credibility of a trustworthy organization, such as a government body or a company, to attempt to obtain personal data such as usernames, passwords, or credit card details. Counterintuitively, not all cases of parasitic piggybacks are frowned upon—and these are the ones we will delve into.

The Productive Parasite

Airbnb implemented a transformative parasitic piggyback marketing technique that, while ethically dubious, proved to be a stroke of genius, helping the start-up to grow its user base exponentially.

In 2017 Airbnb had more listings worldwide than the top five hotel corporations combined. This is an astonishing accomplishment for a company that started in August 2010 when two designers offered lodging with three air mattresses in their loft in San Francisco. They went on to create a platform to connect people who have rooms and houses to rent with potential customers who want a place to stay. The founders of the start-up knew they offered a promising service, but because they were cash-strapped they needed to build their marketplace cheaply.

At the time, the traditional marketing route of paying for advertising was unfeasible because they lacked a budget, so the creators of Airbnb searched for a workaround. They knew that their target audience—people who needed lodging but didn't want to stay in hotels—was on Craigslist, which already had a massive user base but fell short when it came to user experience.

The inflection point of Airbnb's growth happened around 2010–2011, exactly when the company started to poach Craigslist users by parasitically piggybacking on its rival's platform. Every time an Airbnb host created a listing, Airbnb sent them an email with a publishable link that enabled the user to automatically cross-post the same listing on Craigslist. Airbnb justified this to its users (people who listed their homes) by reasoning that the increased exposure would lead to higher earnings. When someone surfing on Craigslist found a listing that originated on Airbnb, they would click on a link that rerouted them to Airbnb's platform. This meant free site traffic and new sign-ups for Airbnb, both for new listings and for prospective lodgers. Airbnb's listings were far superior: it offered professional photography services for its listings, a more user-friendly experience, and personalized ads. Eventually users started going straight to Airbnb, ignoring Craigslist for their lodging needs. Airbnb quickly gained a portion of Craigslist's market share.

While this integration afforded much-needed traffic and boosted the company's user base, Airbnb also allegedly emailed prospective property letters who were already using Craigslist and encouraged them to try Airbnb. The emails told individuals who posted vacation rentals on Craigslist how easy it was to post on Airbnb and that their listings would be automatically cross-posted to Craigslist. When Craigslist finally realized what was going on and disabled Airbnb's cross-posting, the new upstart had already outcompeted its rival. Airbnb had taken off without dropping a dime on ads. Hundreds of thousands of people had discovered Airbnb, a once scrappy organization, through these ingenious parasitic piggyback tactics, which have become legendary in the Silicon Valley.

THE GOAL OF PIGGYBACKS

Just as piggyback interventions can make use of different types of relationships, they can also work toward different goals: they can be employed to improve current practices, diversify and expand existing services, or create entirely new avenues for development. Next, we'll explore an example of each of these approaches to give you an idea of how you can benefit by looking for untapped and underutilized connections.

Improving Current Practices

Let's start with a basic question: How can piggybacking build upon current practices? You may have heard about micronutrient deficiencies, also known as "hidden hunger," which can impair the intellectual and physical development of a person, largely without signs or symptoms, and can affect all population groups. Less known, however, is that a common solution to this problem is piggybacking on foods that people eat regularly.

Nutrient deficiencies, which have long-term effects on health, education, productivity, life span, and overall well-being, are most prevalent and have the most consequences in economically vulnerable households. Additional factors alongside wealth, including locale, food scarcity versus availability, food education, and cultural norms, can also play a role in levels of nutrient deficiencies.

The task of changing all these factors that, combined, shape diet and health can feel daunting. Dietary habits are incredibly tough to change, especially on the scale and at the speed necessary to save lives. Approximately 9 percent of the global population is chronically undernourished, 22 percent of children experience stunted growth because of poor nutrition, and about two billion people are overweight. Nutrient deficiency is an acute issue, and we need swift action.

So why not piggyback nutrients onto people's existing dietary patterns to work around these constraints?

The food fortification process consists of adding micronutrients to food items that the population is already eating. This piggyback tactic is successful because it's quick, cost-effective, and doesn't require big, systemic changes to personal habits nor to the food industry. This practice isn't new. Iodine deficiency is a serious health problem; between 1994 and 2006, according to the WHO, it affected approximately 30 percent of the world's population. About 740 million people had goiter—a swelling of the thyroid gland often caused by chronic iodine deficiency.

People in the United States suffered from goiter in great numbers before the advent of a micronutrient piggyback intervention. In 1924 iodized salt was first introduced in Michigan, and it was adopted in the rest of the country shortly afterward. Because iodine was piggybacked on salt, the prevalence of goiter quickly fell, and by the 1930s goiter caused by iodine deficiency had been virtually eliminated from the country's healthcare concerns.

Following the success of the iodine piggyback initiative, fortification practices have continued to grow in popularity and have been adopted by most countries. In 2021, UNICEF estimated that over six billion people consume iodized salt (about 89 percent of the world's population). Many countries in South America offer good examples of large-scale government programs that spurred fortification of cereals. In the 1990s Chile mandated that wheat flour be fortified with folic acid. After the mandate's implementation, the country experienced a 40 percent decrease in rates of neural tube defects, which occur in the first months of pregnancy. When current food practices were improved through piggybacking, fewer health complications occurred.

Sometimes, when the intervention's target population has different dietary habits or only a specific segment of the population is affected by a nutrient deficiency (e.g., children, the elderly, or pregnant women), it may be better to select more than one food vehicle or to design programs tailored to specific groups. Many programs have tried to piggyback on food distributed in context-specific circumstances, such as school meals to address illnesses that are more prevalent in children. These focused programs can be very beneficial since fortification can focus on the needs of specific target groups and add the amount of the nutrients needed by people with similar body masses. A randomized trial involving adding iron to school meals in India, for example, showed a reduction in the rate of anemia in children ages five to nine by more than 50 percent.

Policymakers are key players in implementing micronutrient fortification programs. Through regulations, public agencies can impose fortification mandates on food manufacturers. The WHO, for example, has a set of guidelines for implementing food fortification programs that are largely supported by pediatricians and global health experts. According to the Global Alliance for Improved Nutrition, today over a hundred countries have national salt iodization programs, and eighty-six countries mandate at least one kind of cereal grain fortification with iron and/or folic acid—and the alliance suggests that many others could benefit from the implementation of new programs to fortify foods.

But governments aren't the only interested players who have leveraged this sort of workaround. Just think of ready-to-eat breakfast cereals, marketed as containing a wide range of vitamins and minerals that children need. These practices have also stirred up controversies, with critics claiming that companies add micronutrients into highly processed foods that are sugary and addictive and then advertise them as if they were healthy. Whether their practices are ethical or not, the impact is outstanding. A study from 2010 estimated that if it were not for fortified ready-to-eat cereals, 163 percent more American children between the ages of two and eighteen would consume less than the recommended intake of iron.

Many food manufacturers have begun to voluntarily fortify their products, both to increase their nutritional value and to promote their products' appeal. For example, in 2009 Nestlé began to implement fortification strategies. By 2017 about 83 percent of Nestlé's most purchased brands were fortified to address at least one of the "Big 4" micronutrient deficiencies as defined by the WHO: iron, iodine, zinc, and vitamin A. Despite controversy, this piggyback tactic provides much-needed nutrients to some of the world's most vulnerable populations, who can't afford to wait for a complex problem to be solved. For food companies such as Nestlé this tactic offers the opportunity to build on current portfolios to increase sales while simultaneously addressing pressing social problems.

Diversifying and Expanding Existing Services

Whereas piggyback interventions such as food fortification programs improve upon processes that already exist, other piggybacks leverage resources across seemingly disconnected industries, giving companies the opportunity to diversify their business models and create new sources of revenue.

That's the case of M-Pesa, a Kenyan money transfer service that was launched in 2007 by telecommunication giants Vodafone and Safaricom. It makes it possible for people to store money on a mobile phone and transfer it to other users via text message. Soon after its launch M-Pesa became one of the world's most effective financial services for those who do not have bank accounts, successfully working around the costly infrastructures of traditional banks.

The story of M-Pesa is well known in business schools around the world as a successful example of corporate sustainability and innovation and of how a company created a positive social impact, addressing needs of vulnerable populations, while profiting from the diversification and expansion of its services. But this description overlooks the most fascinating part of the story: how M-Pesa's journey was rife with workarounds.

M-Pesa began with Nick Hughes, an executive who worked on corporate social responsibility at Vodafone, the British multinational telecommunications company that owns 40 percent of Safaricom, a mobile network operator in Kenya. He was particularly interested in microcredit because he thought it was a promising approach to tackling poverty and barriers to upward social mobility.

Social entrepreneurs and organizations working with international development were increasingly convinced that access to financial services facilitates entrepreneurial activity, creates wealth and jobs, and stimulates trade. Hughes thought telecommunication could play an important role in microcredit, too, especially in places like Kenya, where less than 20 percent of the population had bank accounts but many more had mobile phones.

Instead of looking to traditional banking systems, he came up with the idea of working around them through a win-win approach. He wanted to create a service that would permit microfinance borrowers to conveniently receive and repay loans using the network of Safaricom airtime resellers that already existed in Kenya. The new program could offer more loans and at better rates.

To put his idea into motion, Hughes had to work around a first obstacle. Why would Vodafone back a project like this? Financial services weren't part of Vodafone's core business: they had little to do with the voice and data services that comprised the company's revenue streams, and Kenya was a relatively small market in the company's terms.

Hughes had to convince Vodafone's shareholders that this

risky route was worth the investment. This was a tough sell. But what if the company used somebody else's capital? That's how Hughes thought to tap into a government fund.

The time for this was ripe. In the early 2000s, state organizations, nonprofits, and intergovernmental agencies had realized that social and environmental goals would be unachievable without engaging the private sector, and many started to actively cooperate with the private sector with the goal of pursuing ambitious sustainability targets. The so-called challenge funds from the UK Department for International Development (DfID) were an instance of such an effort. The DfID granted about $20 million for private-sector projects that would improve access to financial services in emerging economies. The money was awarded on a matched basis, and Vodafone could contribute its half of the costs in the form of nonfinancial assets, like human resources. With DfID's money, Hughes found a way to work around internal barriers to investment. By outsourcing the financial risks, Hughes dodged internal competition for capital, thereby making it possible for his high-risk idea to move ahead. He leveraged resources across seemingly unrelated industries to diversify and expand on Vodafone's existing services.

After securing the grant and gaining buy-in from his company and Safaricom colleagues in Kenya, Hughes kick-started a pilot to put his idea to the test. In 2005 Hughes and his collaborators teamed up with a Kenyan microfinance institute and a commercial bank. During the pilot program that took almost two years, Hughes and his colleagues realized that Vodafone saw itself as young and fast-moving, and it saw banks as old, traditional, and slow-moving. So why should Hughes's superiors agree to team up with slow-moving partners to provide financial services in a relatively small market to address an issue that wasn't at the core of their company's business?

Rather than invest in marrying these different business models, Hughes and his team realized that financial institutions were not necessary to the project: the financial partners were adding unnecessary complexity to the simpler services that customers actually wanted.

There was a much simpler and more efficient avenue that did not rely on financial institutions at all. In the pilot, Hughes's team noticed that customers were loading more money into their wallets than what was needed for loans. After assessing the pilot data and watching users' behavior, Hughes and his colleagues discovered that customers adopted the service for a variety of alternative uses that seemed more important than accessing credit, for instance, for saving and transferring money to others. These findings weren't new: a few years earlier, researchers had found that unbanked people were piggybacking on mobile phones' airtime as a proxy for money transfers in Botswana, Ghana, and Uganda.

Hughes's trial demonstrated that the core challenge in Kenya wasn't shortage of funds, as Hughes had initially thought, but rather moving money. So the team opted to strip microcredit from the platform and launch M-Pesa as a service to simply transfer money.

Some trial partners became unnecessary, but Hughes's goal from the outset was to create benefits simultaneously for Vodafone, Safaricom, and the unbanked. Vodafone and Safaricom then simplified the model to provide basic financial services that piggybacked on Safaricom's own platforms and network of re-sellers, so users could turn cash into e-money (and vice versa) and use their phones to transfer e-money to others.

This piggyback tactic worked around key hurdles to the moving of money:

- *Instability*: In 2005 the informal sector constituted about 80 percent of the population, and 70 percent of the country's population lived in remote regions; therefore the great ma-jority of people couldn't open or manage bank accounts. Cash transfers used to be managed through physical par-cels of cash delivered by nearby friends or family or even via local buses or the post. Naturally, none of these ways was reliable, safe, or practical.

- *Inaccessibility*: Even in urban centers where financial insti-tutions operated, few people could access official banking channels, and therefore over 80 percent of Kenya's popu-lation remained unbanked. Because banks profited from fewer transactions with higher margins, they charged ex-orbitant fees, which disproportionately affected vulnerable populations.

But mobile phones, like the ever-popular Nokia model, were becoming ubiquitous, and because M-Pesa piggybacked onto the mobile pay-as-you-go network structure, users only had to present an identity card and have a phone number, circumvent-ing the hassles of informality. With M-Pesa and their mobile phones, users could then easily move e-money to other people who were unbanked, regardless of distance, and recipients could either keep the money in their e-wallet and use it for their own payments or cash out at a local Safaricom airtime reseller.

M-Pesa was not only more practical; it was also cheaper. In fact, before M-Pesa was launched, opening and maintaining a bank account in Kenya cost at least $123 per year. M-Pesa users didn't need to keep cash in an account or pay fees for deposits or withdrawals. They paid only when sending money, and, even then, the fee was far less than that charged by traditional banks.

Because it could circumvent all these hurdles, M-Pesa was successful quickly—even faster than Hughes expected. Within only two years of its launch, Safaricom had registered 8.6 million M-Pesa customers in Kenya and had a transaction volume of over $328 million per month.

In addition to the revenue created for Vodafone, Safaricom, and others, M-Pesa addressed a market void that hampered social and economic well-being. It is estimated that nearly ten years after its launch, M-Pesa had increased per capita consumption levels and lifted 194,000 households out of poverty. The success of M-Pesa in Kenya also led to the expansion of the model to other low- and middle-income countries, like Afghanistan, Tanzania, Mozambique, the Democratic Republic of the Congo, Lesotho, Ghana, Egypt, and South Africa. M-Pesa is an example of how a piggyback workaround can lead to a new business model, one that allows an organization to benefit from seemingly unrelated connections, which can in turn be replicated and adapted to different contexts.

Creating Entirely New Businesses

As we know from ColaLife, when using piggyback tactics, people can respond to demand in new and creative ways, but this approach is not limited to the nonprofit sector. Many start-ups have explored disruptive opportunities and used piggyback workarounds to compete against their sectors' incumbents—and make a lot of money.

As a loyal user of TransferWise, now a multibillion-dollar company that specializes in sending money across borders, I was excited to learn about one of its founders, Kristo Käärmann, when I stumbled across a BBC profile of the entrepreneur. Back in 2008, the then twenty-eight-year-old Estonian was working in London as a consultant and received a Christmas bonus of £10,000, approximately US$14,200, which he decided to transfer to Estonia to benefit from the country's higher interest rates. He checked the exchange rate online, the one that shows up in a Google search, assumed he was paying his UK bank a £15 (approximately US$20) international transfer fee, and sent the money. But to his surprise, the amount that actually arrived in his Estonian account was £500 (approximately US$710) less than what he had expected. When he dug into what happened, he realized that he had foolishly believed his UK bank would give him the real exchange rate. Unbeknownst to him, the bank had added a hefty markup.

Those of us who have lived abroad can sympathize. When possible, we find ways to work around these hidden fees by finding someone we trust who wants to transfer the same amount in the opposite direction. That's exactly what Käärmann did. He started to swap British pounds and Estonian kroons with his friend Taavet Hinrikus: Käärmann transferred British pounds to Hinrikus's account in the United Kingdom, while Hinrikus transferred the equivalent amount in Estonian kroons to Käärmann's account in Estonia. They used the formal official exchange rate and saved on the fees and hidden markups that their banks would have charged. Soon they built up a network of Estonian friends with ties to the United Kingdom who, like Käärmann and Hinrikus, needed to transfer money and could benefit from piggybacking on each other.

The problem was that this workaround was very limited in scale: it's difficult to find someone you trust who wants to transfer the same amount in the opposite direction at the same time you do. That's when Käärmann and Hinrikus realized they could make a business out of this; after all, international money transfer is a huge and growing market in our globalized world. In 2011 they founded TransferWise, a platform that provides international remittance services. It offered the real exchange rate, with no hidden markups, and charged only a 0.5 percent fee per transaction.

Here's how it works: the platform operates on a peer-to-peer basis, so most of the money doesn't actually cross any borders. Just like Käärmann and Hinrikus did with their exchanges in Estonian kroons and British pounds, the platform matches up millions of people in different countries who want to change money with those who want their money to go in the opposite direction. TransferWise can do it more efficiently and on a much larger scale because of the platform's enormous user network and a large store of different currencies scattered around the world.

This workaround threatened an enormous market of big players in the financial sector. An internal memo of Santander—one of the world's largest banking institutions—leaked to *Guardian Money* in 2017 implied that international transfers generated about 10 percent of the bank's profits. The memo sparked controversy because it illuminated the extent to which consumers are overcharged by traditional banks when sending money overseas and how untransparent banks are when informing consumers of their often-hidden markups. In Hinrikus's words: "It's a massive consumer rip-off, but the Santander document doesn't surprise me. What does surprise me, is how long they've been able to get away with it. This is a major issue—three-quarters of consumers who regularly send money abroad can't work out the final cost when fees are factored into the exchange rate. Consumers and businesses are losing £5.6 [billion] a year in the UK because of rate mark-ups." This is about $7.7 billion in US dollars.

The TransferWise start-up was an ingenious workaround to banks. Note that it was not a bank; it was designed as a scalable peer-to-peer platform that works around commercial banks' international transfers. It secured clearance and licenses from the UK's Financial Conduct Authority to avoid legal problems, but it didn't actually provide banking services. Instead it piggybacks on the existing structures of banks around the world. Both the platform and its clients use their respective banks for local transactions. By benefiting from free or cheap local transfers and pairing transactions globally, TransferWise enables customers to bypass the steep international remittance fees charged by large commercial banks—and takes away a lot of their business in international transfers. Piggybacking allowed TransferWise to create an entirely new business model.

TransferWise has challenged the banking industries by offering their users international transfers that are up to eight times cheaper. Piggybacking opened up a path for an innovative business that defied the status quo of cross-boundary financial transactions. The founders of TransferWise started with a small workaround (exchanging money between friends), which inspired them to do more through piggybacking on a network of people who were in similar circumstances but in different countries. The company has gained so much traction that it received investments from magnates like Virgin Group's Richard Branson (a bank owner himself) and PayPal co-founder Max Levchin. Almost a decade after its creation, the platform is saving its customers over $4.1 million in bank fees every day. In 2020 TransferWise was worth over $5 billion, and in 2021 the company changed its name to Wise as it expanded its financial services beyond money transfers.

WHEN DO WE USE A PIGGYBACK WORKAROUND?

As we've seen through several examples, the piggyback is a workaround that makes use of relationships—social, commercial, technological, or otherwise—that already exist. Scrappy organizations operating from the fringes of power tend to have an advantage when it comes to spotting unconventional pairings. Managers, policymakers, and other "insiders" tend to look at the systems they represent and see them as they believe they're supposed to be seen, but they fail to see how different pieces can be broken apart, reassembled, and used to their advantage.

The piggyback workarounds in this chapter, like using Coca-Cola bottles to deliver diarrhea treatment, aren't trivial, but similar opportunities often go ignored. In addition to being a great example of a piggyback, because it involves giving a product a literal piggyback ride, ColaLife also exemplifies the mindset most conducive to piggyback workarounds: there's always possibility. Even in the most remote locations, systems are in place. Your challenge is to identify these opportunities and leverage them.

There's much missed value that falls between the cracks in our siloed structures. In addressing your own challenges, I suggest you identify and pursue symbiotic and unconventional relationships, be they mutualistic, commensalistic, or parasitic: look between silos rather than in them, and think of how the successes of others can be used for your own benefit. In other words, be a goby fish, a remora, or a roundworm and think laterally about what, and who, is at your disposal.

2

The Loophole

It was through a loophole that a friend who works as a housekeeper in Brazil got herself out of deep trouble. Joanna (a pseudonym), who lived on a minimum-wage job and had recently put her savings toward buying a house, started accumulating credit card debt after her husband had a stroke. Not only did her husband have to stop working, meaning that the couple had to rely on one income instead of two, but he also needed special medicines.

In Brazil, the public healthcare system is supposed to provide free access to all. But medicines for chronic diseases aren't always covered, and sometimes people with limited information can be swindled into paying for treatments that the state actually does provide for free. Joanna, under pressure to keep her husband alive, hastily purchased the medicine, assuming that she could gradually pay her debt in installments. She didn't know that her bank would charge her approximately 20 percent interest every month.

Compound interest rates are devious and especially dangerous for low-income populations and those who don't, from the outset, grasp the depth of trouble these rates can bring. In the first month the total balance owed isn't too bad relative to your income. But if you can't promptly pay off your debt, the interest accumulates, and suddenly your debt exceeds your ability to repay. When she called me, my friend's debt was eighty times her credit card purchase. By that time it was almost equivalent to the value of her house.

In the year of that call, the average interest rate for credit card debt in Brazil was 323 percent per year. The rate charged to someone like my friend, who had a low income and little collateral, went up to 875 percent. When she incurred the debt to buy the medicine, the country's inflation rate was 6 percent per year, and there had been no hyperinflation in two decades. An average rate of 323 percent was unfathomable even compared to other low- or middle-income regions—in fact, the second-highest rate in Latin America that year was 55 percent, in Peru. Even the Code of Hammurabi, the Babylonian code of law dating to 1755–50 BC, stipulated that a lender couldn't charge yearly rates that exceeded 33.3 percent for a grain loan and 20 percent for a silver-based loan. What justifies these surreal numbers then? The only answer I can come up with is that it's, unfortunately, a lawful extortion of the poor.

But my friend didn't know that when she paid for the medicines. She could never imagine that what she needed to keep her husband alive would turn into a nightmare. The more she tried to save up to pay off her debt, the more it snowballed. When she realized her inability to liquidate what she owed, she tried to renegotiate it, offering the bank five times the amount she had spent using her credit card. The bank didn't accept her offer; instead it started sending threatening letters to remind her of the devastating effects that debt could have in the long term.

What I find particularly exasperating about her story is that the law was on the bank's side. The bank was technically right. But how could this be acceptable?

When my friend told her story, I kept thinking of it as a modern-day version of Shakespeare's *The Merchant of Venice.* Long story short, Antonio borrows 3,000 ducats from the moneylender Shylock for his friend Bassanio, who intends to travel to Belmont to marry Portia, a wealthy heiress. The contract pledges that, if the debt isn't liquidated by the specified deadline, Shylock can carve out one pound of Antonio's flesh. Unexpectedly, Antonio can't pay off the debt and Shylock brings him to court. Antonio pleads for mercy, offering an overdue payment of twice the amount of the loan, but Shylock steadfastly refuses, claiming that he stands for the law.

The contract can't be nullified; after all, Shylock is technically correct. As ruthless as it sounds, the law is on Shylock's side and he goes for the flesh. But then Portia (the rich, smart heiress who just married Bassanio), disguised as a man, comes to Antonio's rescue. At the trial, she turns around the wording of the contract to claim that it allows Shylock to remove one pound of Antonio's flesh, but exactly one pound—no more, no less, and not a single drop of blood could be shed in the process. Portia's workaround is clever and effective precisely because it doesn't confront the brutality of the contract as a reason to nullify it. Instead it makes enforcement practically impossible.

Just like Shylock, the bank harassing my friend was inflexible but technically right. I knew her contract couldn't be nullified. But was there any sort of workaround that could void it?

When my friend and I sought legal advice, the lawyer said that banks know how to best formulate their contracts to avoid wording turnarounds like Portia's. But there was another way of working around the contract.

According to Brazilian law, a debt expires in five years. In the meantime, the bank could take my friend to court to "carve out her flesh"—in modern-day usury, that means grabbing all the belongings in her possession. The exception was her house: the only asset interpreted by the law as uncarvable from a debtor. So what if she left no flesh for the bank to confiscate?

Here's what the workaround entailed for her. She kept her house in her name and donated her few remaining assets to her son. Her monthly income wasn't confiscated because she worked informally and asked her employers to pay her in cash. Until her debt expired, she couldn't purchase anything in her name and couldn't use any kind of financial service from her own account. Fortunately, she had relatives to do that on her behalf: her son opened a bank account in his name to become her de facto account. A hassle? Yes, but it was very small when compared to what she had to lose if she kept using the bank account in her name.

In the beginning of the fifth year, knowing that it would end up with nothing, the bank called to offer a settlement: she would pay five times the original amount she owed. The bank made it sound like a great deal when compared to her debt, which at that time was approximately 9,100 times what she had spent with her credit card. But the tables had already turned. For her, the best way out was still around. She knew that within a few months her life would go back to normal.

In the end she got herself out of deep trouble and didn't even have to pay back the money she had spent on her husband's medical bills. Should she feel remorse? Maybe, maybe not. Was she "technically right"? Yes, just as right as the bank that attempted to legally extort her.

WHAT IS A LOOPHOLE WORKAROUND?

We often think of loopholes as inherently negative schemes that benefit the powerful. Most of us have heard about the tricks the richest one percent in the world use to avoid taxes, such as hiding fortunes in tax havens like the Cayman Islands—a country that houses more offshore companies than people. What we fail to note is that loopholes also work for those of us who are neither rich nor famous.

A loophole workaround can be particularly useful when there are formal or informal rules that may be unfair or that create a barrier to reaching a goal. The loophole either capitalizes on an ambiguity or uses an unconventional set of rules when they aren't the most obviously applicable. In this chapter we will delve into stories of scrappy organizations and feisty individuals who with great ingenuity found ways to defy an undesirable status quo. From them we will learn how with some creativity and close attention to what rules do (and don't) say we can benefit from their inadequacies to circumvent or otherwise avoid their purpose.

USING AMBIGUITY

When we think about loopholes in rules, we naturally start with lawyers. We have all come across movies, TV shows, and novels that feature charismatic lawyers sailing through legal breaches. Personally, I loved watching the character Saul Goodman use every dirty trick in the book to defend crooks and gangsters in *Breaking Bad* and *Better Call Saul*.

What intrigues us the most about these legal breach cases is that even when the lawyers stumble into blurred ethical territory the methods they deploy are "technically right": they stand by the law and cleverly exploit ambiguities for their clients. In fact, all sorts of loopholes make use of ambiguities or use one set of rules to circumvent another. They don't always solve larger societal issues, but they do address a client's most pressing needs.

Sometimes societal injustices do, in fact, need to be addressed, since being technically or legally right does not always mean being morally right. Finding the right loophole can help both an individual and a community. One such case was the defense of Arthur Ewert, a German communist who came to Brazil in the 1930s to take a leading role in an insurgency against the dictatorship of Getúlio Vargas. Following an unsuccessful uprising, Arthur was arrested and kept for more than two years in cramped confinement and repeatedly subjected to all sorts of horrific torture.

Ewert's arrest happened thirteen years before the Universal Declaration of Human Rights. Not only was there no reason for secrecy about torture back then, but the regime also wanted would-be dissidents to know about Ewert's treatment, hoping it would intimidate them into submission.

People knew what was going on, and there was nothing technically wrong with it according to the Brazilian civil law of the time. But when the lawyer Sobral Pinto agreed to represent Ewert, he came up with the ingenious idea of tapping into Act n° 24.645 for the protection of animals, instituted one year before Ewert's arrest. The act stated that all animals living in the country shall be protected by the state and that anyone who privately or publicly treated animals with cruelty could be fined and arrested. The act prohibited, for example, keeping animals in unhygienic spaces and imperiling them with a dearth of air, rest, space, and light.

Putting a loophole to the test, Sobral Pinto filed a petition that claimed that Ewert's body should also be protected by the state under Act n° 24.645. He described how Ewert's treatment was a clear violation of the act, comparing the conditions of his imprisonment to the cruel treatment of animals in farms and slaughterhouses that the act outlawed. The lawyer even referred to a precedent from a judge who had sentenced to prison an individual who violently beat his horse to death.

Sobral Pinto's petition not only exploited a legal breach; it exposed the incoherencies of a dictatorial regime. The grotesque association of torture in prisons with animal welfare in farms and slaughterhouses spawned public outrage. People realized and openly criticized the fact that the regime treated horses better than humans. Thanks to this loophole, Arthur was transferred to a more humane cell; the president, who wanted to put a halt to the negative comments about his administration, allegedly requested the transfer. In addition to improving Arthur's condition, this petition also triggered public commotion and mobilization that gradually pushed the boundaries of human rights in the country.

Even if the dictatorship didn't immediately crumble and Arthur wasn't freed, his condition improved. The loophole wasn't perfect, but Pinto explored possible solutions rather than the perfect path. By applying a seemingly unrelated set of rules to the problem, we can explore possibilities that are feasible and deliver on our most urgent needs.

There's no reason to think of a single intervention as the unique inception or total culmination of a big change in laws; norms reflect our expectations, and our expectations shift as we learn, struggle, and recognize new possibilities.

TYING THE KNOT

Studying historical cases can shed light on the notion that even today the law can be unfair, making us more sympathetic toward workarounds used to sidestep oppressive laws so that we can attend to urgent needs while we gradually push for legal changes.

You may remember from history classes that in the sixteenth century, the Roman Catholic Church forbade Henry VIII, the king of England, from divorcing Catherine of Aragon to marry Anne Boleyn. So he broke ties with the Church in Rome and created a church of his own: the Church of England. That may have been the optimal solution for an absolute monarch, but most people don't have the same power to antagonize powerful institutions.

In fact, Henry VIII's problem remained prevalent for centuries. Divorce—especially no-fault divorce, where marital ties can be dissolved without evidence of wrongdoing by either party—is a very recent legal instrument in many jurisdictions with large Christian populations. For example, Malta allowed it only in 2011, Chile in 2004, Ireland in 1997, Argentina in 1987, and Brazil in 1977. In the United States, where rules on marriage dissolution vary across states, the first to allow no-fault divorce was California in 1969, and the last was New York, only in 2010.

Before that, many ordinary folks—those without a king's powers—turned to loopholes. Yet again we see people without power to change the rules leveraging loopholes to get what they need. Even when it doesn't change entire systems of law, a loophole can benefit large groups of people directly when the tactic is applied in a situation that affects the masses, or indirectly by providing inspiration for new workarounds in similar contexts.

The Elizabeth Taylor Loophole

In the twentieth century, the most common and effective loophole to obtain a no-fault divorce was to go to a foreign country for the divorce and then validate the certificate in the country where the couple resided. This loophole was viable for two reasons. First, some countries granted legal, administratively straightforward no-fault divorces to foreigners. Second, most jurisdictions honor legal instruments agreed to abroad.

Of all destinations to get a divorce, Mexico became the go-to country, especially for Americans during the 1940s–1960s. The so-called quickie Mexican divorce took as little as three hours, and in some cases divorce certificates were obtained via mail order. Approximately 500,000 couples in the United States alone obtained a quickie divorce in Mexico between 1940 and 1960. Notable examples of couples who used this loophole include Elizabeth Taylor from Eddie Fisher in 1964, Marilyn Monroe from Arthur Miller in 1961, and Paulette Goddard from Charlie Chaplin in 1942.

Many couples also tapped into a similar loophole to remarry. For example, until 1977 Brazilians could officially separate from a spouse, but they were barred from fully dissolving their marital ties. The practical implication was that even if they no longer shared a home and assets, the state didn't allow them to remarry. But by crossing the border into Bolivia or Uruguay, ex-spouses turned their "separation" into a "divorce" and then the individuals were free to marry someone else. With their new marriage certificates in hand, they could return to validate their papers in Brazil. Some took an even simpler route: through a double proxy wedding in Mexico, couples worldwide got married without having to leave their home country; they were represented at their weddings by other individuals, such as local lawyers, who would then mail the marriage certificate to the couple's home address. The certificate would be subsequently notarized and validated in the couple's country with no legal impediment.

These cases of couples, both historical and contemporary, remind us that many people can benefit from the same loophole; we don't have to be the ones who spotted a loophole to be able to benefit from it; and we can be inspired by loopholes from the past to find analogous opportunities in the present.

The Adam and Steve Loophole

The logic of using a loophole to marry continues to help the millions of same-sex couples who are disenfranchised from the institution of marriage (in 2021, this meant couples in 164 of the 195 countries in the world). The first legislation legalizing same-sex marriage took effect in 2001 in the Netherlands, and many countries, especially in western Europe and in the Americas, have since followed the Dutch.

The legislation changes in these countries created opportunities for same-sex couples in the twenty-first century to repurpose loopholes used by twentieth-century heterosexual couples. In Israel, for example, one can easily find wedding planners offering packages for same-sex couples to marry in western European countries, like Portugal. Even though Israel grants homosexual couples the same pension, inheritance, and medical rights as heterosexual couples, it won't let them marry because marriage is seen as a religious institution in the country. This is a limitation not only for same-sex couples but also for mixed-religion heterosexual couples or for anyone who doesn't wish a religious marriage. For this reason, thousands have officially tied the knot abroad and subsequently registered their marriage certificates in Israel with no legal impediment.

Although this is an attractive alternative for couples in Israel, the stakes of using a loophole to arrange for a same-sex marriage can be much higher in other countries, where nonheterosexual relationships are outlawed and punishable by incarceration or even death. But even in Russia—a country that has actively encouraged hate crimes against same-sex couples and LGBTQIA activists—there is a loophole that has been put to the test. The country's law states that marriages conducted abroad are legitimate so long as they aren't between relatives or people who are already registered as married in Russia. It doesn't mention that same-sex unions should be disqualified. Through this loophole, a gay Russian couple who reside and got married in the United States sent their documents to the Russian Federal Taxation Service to receive social deductible taxes for spouses. The agency apparently had no option but to approve the request and grant them the benefit.

Cases of same-sex couples traveling to a foreign country to get married remain uncommon in Russia, Poland, Uganda, Morocco, and other countries where animosity toward LGBTQIA individuals remains high. Numbers are hard to come by because these countries often make the ridiculous claim that "no homosexual individuals live here"—a statement that's obviously false but convenient for regimes hoping to brush their discrimination under the rug. Most same-sex couples living in these countries either are afraid of repercussions or simply can't afford the costs of marrying abroad. The alternative loophole is for the couple to open a company, turning them into "business partners." Then they can tap into the existing legal structures of the country where they reside at least to safeguard their rights to share assets, income, investments, and bank accounts, while also avoiding the spotlight.

This loophole is of course far from ideal, but it addresses a few of the issues same-sex couples face in most countries in the world. People can work around the rules that hold them back without having to engage in the arduous and time-consuming process of changing oppressive rules in their countries of residence. They can successfully get what they want—with less fuss than Henry VIII.

LOOPHOLES IN UNCHARTED WATERS

While their effects may be monumental, loopholes aren't once-in-a-lifetime opportunities reserved exclusively for experts with a profound knowledge of the law. It was only when I interviewed Dutch physician Rebecca Gomperts as part of my research (following a very lucky cold call) that I realized that loopholes are much more accessible and impactful than we tend to think.

In this section, we will learn about ways that have been found to work around laws that limit abortion access. Our focus is exclusively on (1) legal constraints, disregarding other issues (such as financial and religious impediments and lack of infrastructure) that prevent people from getting an abortion; (2) the health risks that many people face specifically in countries where abortions are illegal; and (3) safe, nonsurgical abortions that can be provided during the first ten to twelve weeks with abortive pills.

Unsafe Abortions

"It is unequivocal that abortion bans cost women's lives." This was one of the first things Dame Lesley Regan—an obstetrics and gynecology professor at Imperial College London, one of the world's leading experts on reproductive health, elected honorary secretary of the International Federation of Gynecology and Obstetrics (FIGO) in 2018—told me when I tried to understand the magnitude of this problem. A common mistake is to think that antichoice laws prevent abortions: instead abortions keep occurring but in unsafe ways.

Safe abortions are carried out using a method that is recommended by the WHO: they can be done using abortion pills or a surgical procedure provided by a person who has the necessary medical skills, depending on the stage of the pregnancy. The WHO defines unsafe abortions along a spectrum: "less safe," when done with outdated surgical methods or without the patient receiving proper information and support; and "least safe," when the procedure involves ingestion of hazardous substances or when untrained individuals use unsafe surgical methods like the insertion of foreign bodies.

Data from the WHO show that between 2015 and 2019 on average 73.3 million people worldwide had induced abortions, and approximately 25 million of those were carried out in unsafe conditions. Worldwide, about 22,000 people die from complications related to unsafe abortions every year, and another 2 million to 7 million sustain serious health problems, such as sepsis, uterine perforation, or injury to other internal organs. Furthermore, out of the average 60 million abortions performed each year, approximately 45 percent are unsafe as defined by the WHO, and 97 percent of all unsafe abortions take place in low- and middle-income countries, especially in Southeast Asia, Sub-Saharan Africa, and Latin America.

Abortions that are performed unsafely represent one of the

leading causes of maternal mortality, accounting for about one in eight pregnancy-related deaths worldwide. Nevertheless, performing an abortion on the basis of a pregnant person's request is allowed in only 30 percent of countries. A critical step forward to prevent unsafe abortions is to change the laws of countries where abortions are illegal. Yet antichoice laws reflect moral, religious, and regulative factors that are pervasive and difficult to change. Is there a way around these laws—one that addresses this urgent issue in the present while also pushing for structural changes in the future?

Sailing to International Waters

In the mid-1990s Dr. Rebecca Gomperts volunteered for Greenpeace as a ship's doctor. She came from the Netherlands, a country where pregnant people had access to safe abortions upon request. But while working for the organization in countries where abortion was illegal, she saw people suffering the consequences of botched backstreet abortions when they could have been offered safe abortions with pills. Noticing the legal constraints preventing access to safe abortions, Gomperts asked the captain of Greenpeace's ship, "How can we create a space where the only permission a woman needs is her own?" The captain's response spurred action: "If you had a Dutch ship, you could take women aboard and sail to international waters, legally helping them with a safe abortion." The reason: when a vessel is in international waters and at least twelve miles offshore, only the laws of the flagship country apply.

Gomperts was already a maverick, but this idea was a catalyst. She founded a nonprofit organization, Women on Waves, in 1999. Run by a group of activists and volunteers, the organization provides safe abortion services to people residing in countries where abortions are illegal. People who choose to terminate their pregnancies board one of the Dutch ships rented by Women on Waves and sail to international waters accompanied by health professionals, and there they can have safe and legal abortions.

The organization uses the fact that what constrains people's access to a safe abortion is not their nationality but the law in the jurisdiction where they live. On board the ship, Women on Waves provides patients with a combination of two pills: mifepristone and misoprostol. Both have been on the WHO's Essential Medicines List since 2005. When combined, these pills are 95 percent effective and can potentially save thousands of women from dying from an unsafe abortion. In fact, only 1 in 500,000 people die from these medicines: "That is way safer than giving birth and equally safe to a miscarriage," says Gomperts.

The ship's mobile clinic—a shipping container outfitted on the inside with a treatment room—was another sort of loophole that Gomperts found. The Dutch government wouldn't grant a medical license if the ship didn't have a clinic. As she told me, they "didn't need a full clinic to give abortions with pills, but we built it to help us get the Dutch medical license." This means that Gomperts and her colleagues built an unnecessary clinic only to get the license they needed to provide abortion services.

Women on Waves' first campaign took place in 2001 in the Republic of Ireland, at that time the country with the most restrictive abortion laws in Europe. In that instance they failed in the mission of providing abortion services on board because they hadn't realized they needed a license from the Dutch government. Yet Women on Waves stirred up controversies and gained worldwide awareness when it was described by conservative and liberal media as the "Abortion Boat." Since then, the organization has launched several successful campaigns, with volunteers sailing to several other countries where abortion is illegal, such as Poland, Portugal, Morocco, and Ecuador, to provide safe abortions.

Despite pushback on these campaigns, Gomperts says, "There is no such thing as bad press, except for an obituary." That's why Women on Waves often antagonizes antichoice groups, openly adopting a fierce and controversial approach to raise awareness and mobilize local pro-choice grassroots movements. In Ecuador, for example, Women on Waves partnered with grassroots groups that had previously had little press coverage. They hung a banner on the Virgin (a statue of the Virgin Mary in Quito), written in Spanish, that read "Your Decision: Safe Abortion," followed by a hotline number. This was a way to advertise the ship's services and create media attention that could be leveraged by grassroots groups pushing for changes in abortion legislation.

In Portugal the backlash Women on Waves faced was unpredictable and even stronger than in Ecuador. When sailing toward the Portuguese coastline, the captain of the "Abortion Boat" was informed that the local government had sent two warships to prevent them from entering national waters. The government's response was a clear violation of international agreements: the Portuguese government couldn't refuse access, especially to a ship coming from a country within the European Union, where there is freedom of movement.

One of Gomperts's colleagues who volunteered for Women on Waves told me, "In the beginning we were very pissed off, thinking the campaign was failing, because the ship could not get in. But then, at a certain point, we realized that that was the best thing that could ever happen. We got media coverage from everywhere. The warship was even more spectacular than the Abortion Boat itself."

From Waves to the Web

After the media coverage in Portugal, Gomperts realized another loophole that could be used to work around law enforcement: using the media to spread word about Women on Waves and educate the general public on safe abortion access. Following the attention the organization garnered, Gomperts went on an open Portuguese TV channel to provide step-by-step instructions on how locals could autonomously use misoprostol, which induces contractions, to safely terminate their pregnancies. Women on Waves also uploaded the instructions to its website and shared them with all sorts of media.

Gomperts's approach was very clever for two reasons: First, the law in Portugal wouldn't let her provide abortion services in the country, but there was nothing that legally prevented her from providing *information* on how to get an abortion. Second, whereas mifepristone is often unavailable outside hospitals, misoprostol is found in the pharmacies of most countries, including many countries where abortion is illegal, because pregnancy termination is a side effect of the medicine, whose therapeutic indications are for stomach ulcers and postpartum bleeding. It can be used alone and off-label to safely induce abortions, and the success rate is 94 percent if the drug is taken within the first twelve weeks of pregnancy. Even if the pill causes worse side effects than expected or too much pain, the patient can still go to a doctor and say she has had a miscarriage, since the doctor cannot detect the difference between a miscarriage and an abortion induced by misoprostol: the symptoms are exactly the same.

This was an important moment for the organization, and its momentum could be attributed to the utilization of various loopholes. To be able to reach more people, Gomperts then created a sister organization, Women on Web, which helps people receive information and access abortive pills when there are no safe and legal options available where they are. On the website, people hoping to terminate their pregnancy first go through an interactive web-based questionnaire, followed by interactions with nonmedical volunteers. The questionnaire responses determine whether patients are referred to an online consultation with a doctor or not. If there is an indication of risk, a doctor will meet the patient online to identify whether (and in what circumstances) the person can obtain a safe abortion; if no counterindication was flagged in the survey, respondents could receive the abortive pills with instructions on how to use them without talking to a doctor.

If no complications (like notoriously nosy customs officers or unreliable postal services) are identified, people receive a gratis package containing mifepristone, misoprostol, and a pregnancy test, most often delivered by courier or mail. In order for the medicines to get through customs, the packages are sent with a prescription from a Dutch doctor; sending medicines from the Netherlands isn't illegal. But if the medicines are held at customs, Women on Web's volunteers tell the patients how to purchase misoprostol where they live and how to safely use it off-label.

The Benefits of Bypassing Laws

With the twin organizations Gomperts and her colleagues have worked resourcefully, adapting their approaches within different contexts. The impact of these organizations has been impressive. When I spoke with Gomperts in 2018, the team at Women on Web had replied to over 100,000 emails and sent more than 6,000 packages yearly. Approximately 99 percent of people who have used the service have reported high satisfaction with the support they have received.

Furthermore, in some cases, the organization had a more permanent impact than just providing abortions to people in need. For example, two years after the Abortion Boat sailed to Portugal, the country legalized abortion. After military forces attempted to prevent Women on Waves' ship from entering Portuguese waters, the abortion discourse in Portugal became mainstream. Policymakers and grassroots movements were outraged by the disproportionate reaction of the government. In Gomperts's words: "We know that bypassing [laws] is actually facilitating legal change as well . . . It catalyzed the possibility for the mainstream political organizations to take a stance."

By being adaptable and learning to look for opportunities, Gomperts created initiatives that demonstrate how loopholes can be both accessible and consequential. There is much to learn from scrappy organizations like Women on Waves, precisely because they lack access to funds and power structures to change entire rules systems. Instead, they approach problems resourcefully and unconventionally, through piecemeal interventions that lead them to explore uncharted territories and find opportunities that could not have been conceived from the outset. Gomperts didn't have a law degree, but she used innovation and creativity to work with and around national and international conventions; she didn't set out to reframe the narrative around abortion, but she learned to take advantage of opportunities that nevertheless transformed her simple mission of providing a service into something much bigger.

She is now an experienced mastermind of finding loopholes, but this is an ability that she developed over time, and which we can all cultivate, too. She doesn't just provide us with great examples of how we can identify and pursue loophole workarounds; she also shows us that the continued impetus to explore lots of workarounds can be more beneficial (both in the short term and in the long term) than trying to dream up a single, earth-shattering intervention.

LOOPHOLES TO SHARE PROTECTED INFORMATION

Loopholes—like Gomperts's—might make a bang, but they can also be quieter than a whisper. For instance, when the government comes to a communications service provider for user data, many tech companies warn the world by going silent. The so-called warrant canary is a sort of workaround of government surveillance that tech companies use to address challenges before they arise.

This workaround was named after the bird that was taken down mine shafts to alert workers to the presence of carbon monoxide and other undetectable toxic gases: if the canary got ill or died, workers knew they had to leave quickly. A "warrant canary"—a company's statement that it has *not* received secret requests for user data by law enforcement agencies—is similar. When the statement disappears and the company goes silent, users can assume that the platform received a warrant.

A Little Birdie Told Me

Through warrant canaries, tech companies use a loophole to keep their users aware of what is happening behind the scenes, thwarting the nondisclosure requirements from law enforcement agencies in the United States. Under the US Patriot Act, law enforcement agencies can subpoena tech companies with a court-imposed gag order. In these cases, companies are not only forced to provide user data; they are also legally barred from disclosing to third parties that they have been served with the warrant. Tech companies detest national security letters even more: these can be issued without court orders, allowing law enforcement agencies to conduct investigations with no interference, including from the judicial system. With these sorts of legal instruments, agencies including the NSA, FBI, and CIA aim to keep their targets in the dark while watching them.

Governmental surveillance goes against the most basic ethos of geek communities and the tech companies they have founded. There's not much that tech companies can do to oppose the law, but they can work around it by exploiting a loophole: under US freedom of speech laws, the companies are allowed to state that "the government has not been here" and to remove these statements when a warrant comes in. Law enforcement agencies can't censor what companies say before they are served with a warrant.

A warrant canary is a good enough and legally safe approach that provides users some leeway to safeguard their data and, ultimately, their privacy. Tech giants such as Adobe, Apple, Medium, Pinterest, Reddit, and Tumblr have already employed this workaround to indicate that it was "all clear" for users, cultivating customer loyalty and a positive corporate reputation.

The case of Reddit—an American company valued at $6 billion in 2021 that aggregates news and provides a platform for web content rating and discussions—was particularly emblematic. Until 2014, Reddit had a statement informing users that it had "never received a National Security Letter, an order under the Foreign Intelligence Surveillance Act, or any other classified request for user information." It also explicitly said, "If we ever receive such a request, we would seek to let the public know it existed."

When the statement was removed in 2015 and Reddit posted a cryptic message saying that it couldn't comment on the disappearance of the canary, users knew exactly what it meant and could act accordingly. The company-executed loophole was effective not despite but because of its quiet compliance.

Reddit's silence in 2015 was important not only because it successfully informed users, but also because it was implemented a couple of years after the death of one of its co-founders, Aaron Swartz. The circumstances surrounding his death encouraged many academics and activists to pursue loopholes that work around paywalls that bar access to and dissemination of academic knowledge.

Around the Paywall

Swartz was one of the world's most renowned hacktivists and an avid member of the open knowledge movement—which is guided by the principle that knowledge should be free to use, reuse, and redistribute without restrictions. He was arrested and risked thirty-five years in prison after allegedly trying to circumvent a paywall by downloading academic articles from JSTOR through an MIT account in order to make the articles publicly available. He committed suicide after the prosecution rejected a counteroffer to his plea bargain. For his fight for open knowledge, he became an icon among computer geeks, tech giants, academics, and activists, but he has been frowned upon in the entertainment, publishing, and pharmaceutical sectors.

He inspired those who are still trying to push the boundaries of knowledge access, but who will do so without risking going to jail. While Swartz adopted a more confrontational approach toward intellectual property rights and suffered major pushback, some have since found and used legal loopholes for which the law cannot easily prosecute them. Law enforcement would have to stretch to categorize these loopholes as contributory infringement—that is, when a defendant knows of the ultimate infringement and induces or materially contributes to it. But even in the very unlikely case that such people were prosecuted, their actions would be highly contested and hard to prove.

For example, the same year Aaron Swartz was arrested, the hashtag #icanhazpdf came into use to request access to academic journal articles behind paywalls. This is how it works: someone who wants access to an article makes a request by tweeting the article's title or other linked information, along with their email address and the hashtag #icanhazpdf. Someone who has access to the article (for example, through a university affiliation) and sees the tweet can download and share the article directly with the requester. This loophole works because even though we can't make such articles publicly available without infringing on copyright, scholars are typically allowed to share articles directly and non-commercially with individuals—the same way you can borrow a book from a friend. If the article isn't made available to everyone and if you aren't charging for sending it, then you'll most likely be safe from prosecution.

Interestingly, the authors of papers have used loopholes, too. Authors make their copyright-protected articles accessible as PDF files in social networks, like ResearchGate, without the logo or layout of the academic journal. This is possible because even though the journal article has a copyright, the knowledge and content from the article can be freely shared as a "preprint." This isn't directly infringing on the copyright of the journal publisher, and everyone in the academic community understands what it means: read the free one but cite the published version.

The people who publish journals aren't fans of this strategy because it ruins their business model, which relies on keeping research behind paywalls and subscriptions. But academics pursue this workaround for different reasons. The first is a selfish one: being published in a journal provides the reputation they need among their peers; freely available content helps them diffuse their knowledge, grants them more citations, and therefore boosts their careers. This means that by having both published journal articles and openly shared knowledge, scholars can have their cake and eat it, too.

Second, just like Swartz, many academics believe in open knowledge, especially when the research is funded with taxpayer money. Many scholars vehemently oppose the business models of academic publishers, which charge for access to articles yet do not fund research and do not pay authors and reviewers for their contributions. Through loopholes, academics can defy these publishers and cut into their profits, without risking going to jail or compromising their careers. Furthermore, academics can pursue these loopholes autonomously and scrappily through diffused networks, which do not require the support of the institutions with which they are affiliated.

The loopholes that support knowledge sharing differ from previous examples for a couple of reasons. First, they present a blurrier case. Those who make use of workarounds like #icanhazpdf aren't entirely in the clear, but the boundaries of what is "permissible" are less well established, and enforcement is unfeasible. Second, this case also illustrates how the impact of a loophole can snowball to create change: as the case of the open knowledge movement shows, when a major group of stakeholders (like academics) flock to a workaround, they can challenge the dominant power (publishers, in this case) and spur the creation of alternative models.

HOW LOOPHOLES SAVED LIVES DURING THE COVID-19 PANDEMIC

Similar to Gomperts and nerds in tech companies, many people at the fringes of power have found and used loopholes to openly antagonize powerful forces within government. But power is relative, and loophole workarounds can be used by government officials, too. In fact, one of the most ingenious workarounds I have seen came from Flávio Dino in Brazil, who was re-elected governor of Maranhão the same year his rival Jair Bolsonaro was elected president of the country.

With approximately half of its population living on less than $5.50 per day, Maranhão faced severe difficulties early in the pandemic to provide healthcare to the growing number of patients suffering from COVID-19. At the beginning of the outbreak, the estimated cost of fighting the virus in the state was approximately $160 million. The federal government had provided only about $10 million, and the state urgently needed ventilators to care for the growing number of COVID-19 patients.

Local businesspeople then offered approximately $3 million

to the state government to promptly purchase ventilators for public hospitals. Even though the state government had secured the money, it couldn't successfully obtain the ventilators because they had to come from China—and there's no direct flight from China to Brazil. In the first attempt, the state government procured ventilators from China with a stopover to refuel in the United States, but the US government intercepted the shipment and offered the company more money for the equipment. The second attempt was via Germany, where the same thing happened. The third time, they tried to purchase ventilators from a Brazilian company based in São Paulo, but the company couldn't sell them because the federal government had requested all the ventilators so that it could redistribute them to states according to the federal government's own centralized plan.

Governor Dino was a former federal judge, so he had a good understanding of what rules do and don't allow. With his staff and local businesspeople—including executives of one of Brazil's largest supermarket chains and its largest mining company—he came up with a series of ingenious workarounds that leveraged all sorts of legal loopholes. In contrast to Gomperts, who used many loopholes on different occasions, Governor Dino needed to stack loophole workaround on top of loophole workaround in order to meet a single goal: promptly purchasing and installing ventilators after the COVID-19 outbreak. What the governor and his business partners achieved is noteworthy because it shows how a series of loopholes can be stacked together, in a specific sequence, and how loophole workarounds can result from the unlikely collaboration of different actors in urgent situations, such as saving lives in a global pandemic.

Loophole After Loophole

First, instead of donating money to the government to purchase ventilators through the typical public procurement process, businesspeople donated the majority of the funds directly to the supermarket chain Grupo Mateus, which already had a system in place to procure goods from China. By doing so they bypassed the government's bureaucratic procurement processes, which would have taken up to three months. Employees of Grupo Mateus and the mining company Vale not only purchased the equipment; they also leveraged their networks in China to monitor the fabrication of 107 ventilators and ensured that they wouldn't be sold to other customers.

Then they came up with the second loophole: instead of hiring a cargo service to fly the ventilators via Germany or the United States, the group escorted the ventilators from the manufacturing facility to the nearest airport, where a cargo airplane rented by Vale was waiting to fly them to Brazil—preventing others from knowing what cargo was being transported. But the plane still needed to stop somewhere for fuel. Avoiding Dubai, the US, and Europe, the flight traveled via Ethiopia because the cargo would be scrutinized less and Ethiopia had fewer resources to dedicate toward confiscating the equipment.

After the plane landed in São Paulo, Governor Dino's team faced another critical obstacle to their workaround: the federal government could still confiscate the ventilators as they went through customs. So the cargo was to be kept secret while traveling from São Paulo and going through customs in the state of Maranhão.

Nevertheless, even in Maranhão, the federal government was the employer of the Revenue Customs officers, and they could still confiscate the cargo and ship the ventilators back to São Paulo. Then came the third and last loophole of the series: the plan was for the plane to land at nine p.m.—outside the working hours of customs and revenues employees at the airport. Using this last loophole, a state secretary signed a document ensuring that he would return the following day to fulfill all the legal requirements of customs (which was, in fact, done), and a committee of employees of the state government took the equipment directly to hospitals to intubate patients.

When they went back to the airport the next day to go through customs, they knew that the federal officers wouldn't confiscate ventilators that were already being used to save lives. With this series of workarounds, all 107 ventilators were successfully transported and installed for use at local hospitals.

Not Guilty

When I spoke to a federal judge about this case, he explained that the federal agency responsible for tax collection and customs in Brazil opened an administrative proceeding against the state of Maranhão and one of the companies involved in the workaround, fining them for disobeying laws of international trade and customs when taking the ventilators from the airport without clearing them first. The state appealed, and a couple of months later a court found them not guilty. The judge understood that the parties had no intent of evading taxes or smuggling prohibited products into the country, and that the state of emergency trumped the imperative of strictly following a bureaucratic process for clearing imported products through customs.

According to the judge I spoke to, the federal government could still appeal or open other lawsuits against Governor Dino and the others involved in the workaround, but the chance of a guilty verdict would be close to zero. Mustering institutional capacity and creativity for finding and using loopholes, the state government and businesses collaborated—each entity capitalized on its own strengths, but both groups were necessary for assembling the string of loopholes that saved thousands of lives.

CONFRONTING THE MORALITY OF LOOPHOLES

Whereas many of us view loopholes for sharing academic knowledge or for purchasing ventilators during a global pandemic as fairly inoffensive, people with different agendas can make use of the moral ambivalence surrounding loopholes. In this section, we'll delve into the morality of loopholes and how it's almost always easier to use them than to prevent others from doing the same.

Make Your Own Medicine

Let's look at a more extreme part of the open knowledge community. There is a controversial group pushing to defy the intellectual property rights of pharmaceutical companies and the authority of public departments of health, such as the United States Food and Drug Administration (FDA).

Dr. Mixæl Laufer, a math professor at Menlo College in California, is the chief spokesperson of Four Thieves Vinegar, an autonomous and informal collective of individuals who share a strong do-it-yourself ethos and a loathing for intellectual property rights in healthcare. He quickly became a controversial figure in the biohacking space by teaching the poor to make medicine. His efforts have been seen as subverting capitalism and intellectual property rights, which by their nature constrain access to medicine and overall healthcare treatment.

I had a thought-provoking chat with Dr. Laufer about Four Thieves Vinegar, which was named after a possibly apocryphal story from the time of the bubonic plague in the Middle Ages. The anecdote illustrates the aim of the collective: to liberate healthcare knowledge from the people or companies who benefit from the spread of disease. As the story is told, thieves looted plague-ridden areas while wearing masks containing vinegar and herbs with antimicrobial properties. They were captured but subsequently freed after agreeing to reveal the formula that, when made public, saved many lives. That's what the contemporary collective metaphorically aims to do: share the "vinegar" owned by those who profit from others' illness.

Laufer became prominent in 2017, when he worked around the intellectual property rights of Mylan, the pharmaceutical company that held the patent to the EpiPen, an epinephrine autoinjector that saves people from life-threatening allergic responses. The company inflated the price of the EpiPen two-pack from $100 in 2007 to over $600 in 2016 to spike its profit margins. Those actions stirred the frustration of people like Laufer who believe that the right to access medicines morally trumps any justification for corporate profits, and naturally of the many who could no longer afford the medicine they needed to live.

In response, Laufer recorded a video and published a step-by-step manual showing how to make an "EpiPencil," an obvious reference to the EpiPen, using products that can be bought from Amazon for about $30. His legal loophole is that since he is only sharing knowledge, not commercializing the EpiPencil, he shouldn't be liable for intellectual property rights infringement—unless Mylan attempts to make the difficult case that the video constitutes a sort of contributory infringement. Laufer is aware of the risks, but he also knows that pharmaceutical companies aren't particularly keen on pursuing the judicial avenue in these cases. Taking him to court could do more harm than good; after all, a lawsuit would unintentionally promote Laufer's cause because more people would become aware of his workaround and, ultimately, of the reasons that motivated him to defy the company.

That's how he keeps pushing the boundaries. Laufer thinks that access to healthcare products can eventually become a matter of assembly if we know how to put the pieces together, as with the EpiPencil. "It shouldn't be harder than Ikea furniture," he told me. At the time we spoke, he was developing an open-source Apothecary MicroLab: a general-purpose chemical reactor built from materials cheaply purchased online, which could be used to synthesize drugs at home. His plan was to freely publish how to build this MicroLab along with recipes for manufacturing medicines. He was keen to produce a batch of Sovaldi: a drug owned by the biotech company Gilead Sciences that cures hepatitis C. In 2017, Sovaldi cost approximately $84,000 for a twelve-week course of treatment, but, according to Laufer, his recipe to make the drug could cost at least a hundred times less if you buy the components from trusted suppliers and assemble the drug yourself.

When I told this story over lunch to my uncle, a medical doctor with a PhD in cardiology, he said: "Well, if you synthesize the medicine correctly, great, but if you mess it up, you may die. Would you take the risk?" Even if you disagree with Laufer's philosophy, you have to give him credit for his ingenuity. His logic is that even though science is reproducible, we have created powerful artificial barriers preventing us from replicating and benefiting from it. He says that pharmaceutical companies and governments often use these barriers, such as intellectual property rights and "quality control," to legitimize the accumulation of wealth by a few while neglecting the needs of the many.

Bypassing these barriers is something that Laufer considers natural and morally justifiable because he thinks quality control shouldn't take priority over promptly making lifesaving treatments accessible to people who need them. It's clear that Four Thieves Vinegar works to the detriment of big pharmaceutical companies and to the benefit of those who need access to cheaper medication.

Whether you consider this loophole "good" or "bad" will depend on what (and whom) you prioritize. Are you prioritizing safety over access? Do you consider patenting unfair because it prevents people from getting medicines that could be more widely and cheaply available? Or do you think patents ensure inventors are rewarded for their discoveries—and, if society doesn't reward them adequately, they will be deincentivized to invent new drugs, thus negatively impacting socioeconomic progress?

One of the beauties of controversial workarounds is that they push us to think about our values, and to realize how our values diverge from the status quo. They allow us to reflect on the formal rules and customary norms that are enforced upon us and push for change.

The Filthy Loophole

Next, we look at a case of e-waste dumping that I strongly oppose, to explore a bit further the ethics of loophole workarounds, and then we reflect on how loopholes are resilient and can be used for years and by many.

The Basel Convention is an international treaty signed in 1989 to prevent transboundary movement of hazardous waste from rich to poor countries. Yet over thirty years later, countries such as Malaysia still have to send containers of waste back to the rich countries that shipped their trash there, because some low- and middle-income countries are still being treated as the world's garbage dumps.

Electronic and electrical waste disposal are particularly problematic. This type of waste contains a laundry list of chemicals that are harmful to people and the environment. When inadequately disposed of, e-waste can severely contaminate the soil, water sources, air, and entire food chains. Trying to escape the costs of handling the growing amount of e-waste in their home countries, companies in rich countries have systematically worked around the Basel Convention through a loophole and are dumping their e-waste in the landfills of countries such as Ghana while claiming they are actually "exporting secondhand products."

Companies do this because it is significantly more costly to properly dispose of an old computer monitor in Germany or the United States than it is to export it elsewhere. By 2016 the world's population had discarded 44.7 million metric tons of e-waste, of which an estimated 150,000 tons were imported by Ghana alone. Most of these so-called secondhand products end up in Agbogbloshie, a vast urban area in Ghana that houses a massive e-waste recycling dump.

When Greenpeace examined the soil in Agbogbloshie, investigators found levels of contamination that were a hundred times higher than safety regulations recommend. Long-term exposure to these chemicals harms almost all organs and bones, fertility, and even IQ levels. There are about 80,000 inhabitants in the area, and they're trapped in a vicious cycle of poverty, forced to cook circuit boards and burn computer tops to salvage their traces of gold, copper, and iron to resell. They breathe in the poisonous fumes and can barely make ends meet. Because of its harsh living conditions, the area has been nicknamed "Sodom and Gomorrah," after the two condemned biblical cities.

In the case of e-waste dumping, the use of loopholes is controversial, especially because it exposes rampant global inequalities and unbalanced power relations. Whether the impact of using a loophole is positive or negative depends on your moral views on the specific circumstance. I see e-waste dumping in

Ghana as morally reprehensible and the provision of safe abortions as a public good, but I also recognize there are many different opinions on these topics. Regardless of our stances and the controversies, however, using loopholes is a legally valid way of accomplishing your goals. You don't have to be categorically for or against loopholes. You can think of them as a means for achieving your desired outcome.

Cases in this chapter also illustrate the resiliency of loophole approaches. It's been over thirty years since the Basel Convention was signed, and the loophole for dumping e-waste abroad is still wide open. Many have tried to close it, but it isn't an easy task; changing the rules involves a lot of negotiation among a wide range of players with different priorities and agendas. The bandwidth of the loophole may change, but a lot of e-waste will pass through until it closes.

WHEN DO WE USE A LOOPHOLE WORKAROUND?

The situations described in this chapter remind us that we often find ourselves constrained or even trapped by pre-existing rules. But there's often more than one way to be right, and simply following or breaking rules isn't always the best way to get something done. Often there is an option that lies in between. This is especially appealing when we don't have the power or resources to change things, or we don't have time to wait for things to change because the need is too urgent.

The challenge to finding loopholes is that we see ingrained

rules as *the* right ones, instead of as *one of* the right options. This happens because rules channel our thoughts, helping us to quickly process an overpowering volume of information, while also limiting our ability to think laterally and see nuances. Thanks to what we learn from scrappy organizations, however, we can identify patterns in how loopholes can be both found and pursued.

In this chapter, nonprofits, companies, collectives, lawyers, academics, tech-savvy individuals, and even government officials found clever ways of working around all sorts of rules that restricted them or the people they cared about. Despite the type of player, obstacle, and goals in these stories, these people have found loopholes in only two ways.

First, many cases in this chapter made use of a different, more favorable set of rules than the status quo. That's how, for example, couples got divorced and remarried in a foreign land, a man was moved from his cramped confinement when his lawyer tapped into animal rights law, abortion services have been legally and safely provided on board a Dutch ship in international waters, and tech companies found effective ways to inform their users of government surveillance by relying on US freedom of speech laws. When they zoomed out of what constrained them and focused instead on less common types of rules or paths less taken, they found loopholes that empowered them to get what they wanted in a technically right but unconventional way.

The second angle was to look more closely at the "specific performance" of the rules they found restrictive to either void them or make their enforcement impossible. For example, that's how my friend never paid off her credit card debt, Portia voided the contract between Shylock and Antonio, e-waste labeled as "secondhand" products floods Ghana, a governor purchased ventilators during a healthcare crisis, a biohacker shares recipes of patented healthcare products online, and academics and users share scientific papers without infringing on intellectual property rights. This task involves the analysis of the ambiguity of the rules and the circumstances under which they can—or cannot—be enforced.

3

The Roundabout

"I came back to India because I missed the freedom to pee on the streets," said the creative head of a popular television channel in Mumbai, justifying quitting his comfortable life and hefty salary in Canada to return to his country of origin. While this expatriate romanticized public urination as a liberating experience, the owners of the walls would disagree. The country's authorities have condemned this unhygienic habit, but for a long time they have struggled to enforce laws against it.

Why are men inclined to pee on public walls? Some have justified the practice, noting the country's lack of public and private toilets, and some have hoped things would change with the improvement of sanitation infrastructure. Nearly half of Indian households didn't have access to a toilet until 2014, when Prime Minister Narendra Modi launched the Clean India program with the goal of eliminating problems like open defecation and manual scavenging. But despite the 110 million toilets built between 2014 and 2020, the problem of public urination persists. This outcome wasn't a surprise to many policymakers who believed public urination to be a gendered behavioral problem rather than an exclusive reflection of the lack of facilities—after all, women seem to find toilets or other adequate places to relieve themselves.

Indian people of all classes and backgrounds describe this behavior as "inevitable." When I went to India and asked ordinary citizens why it is such a common practice for men to urinate on public walls, people evaded with answers like "This is India; this is how things work here." The more men urinate in public spaces, the more the behavior becomes normalized.

Authorities, activist groups, and individuals disturbed by the practice tried a slew of solutions. Many states in India introduced fines for public urination, but these were hardly enforced. Often police officers didn't see the point in fining people for a practice that they considered inevitable.

Frustrated with the lack of law enforcement, activists took matters into their own hands. A group named the Clean Indian posted a video on YouTube of masked activists in a yellow truck driving around a city and blasting public urinators with a water cannon. The video went viral and raised awareness, but it had little or no impact on public urinators, most of whom, in a country of more than one billion people, weren't even aware of the gimmick. Wall owners also tried shaming strategies, such as painting their walls with messages like "The one urinating here is a bastard." This failed, too. In fact, some urinators seemed encouraged, out of a sense of either defiance or humor.

But one tactic employed by the owners of the walls where men peed seems to work well. Throughout the country I encountered square ceramic tiles of Hindu gods wedged into walls, often about knee-high off the ground. Some walls combined Hindu tiles with paintings that portray Muslim, Christian, and

Sikh iconography, in a harmonious integration of the country's dominant religions. At first I thought they were simply manifestations of religious devotion. Then a researcher explained that the watchful eyes of gods seem to give would-be urinators stage fright. After all, urinating in front of or, even worse, on an image of a god is blasphemous. The difference between god-covered and god-free walls across the street from each other is visible. Some wall owners told me that urination incidents decreased by 90 percent after they installed tiles of Hindu gods.

What happened here? Public urination seems to be a deeply ingrained social habit, and providing toilets or levying fines didn't change people's opinions, perceptions, or behaviors. If you can't easily change people's minds, why not tap into their belief systems to prompt them to act differently?

This workaround may be far from ideal, especially because it doesn't fully address the problem: men still cross the street and urinate where a god isn't looking at them. But sometimes all you can hope for is a way to shield your wall from a behavior you can't change. Unsurprisingly, this workaround gained traction, and these deity-adorned walls can be found across India.

Others have creatively applied this logic elsewhere in the country. For example, catering companies started to put images of deities in their kitchens as "godly reminders" to their employees that they must wash their hands before cooking. Even public campaigns have benefited from the idea. In 2016 an India-based production company released a YouTube advertisement called #DontLetHerGo. The video reminds the roughly 80 percent of the country's population who practice Hinduism that Lakshmi, the goddess of wealth and prosperity, resides only where there is cleanliness. The video says, "Before you think of littering next time, remember that the goddess might walk away from you."

Tapping into people's belief systems can spark changes in their behavior, and in this chapter you'll see other scrappy ways to curb behaviors that seem inescapable by using what I call roundabout workarounds.

WHAT IS A ROUNDABOUT WORKAROUND?

Roundabout workarounds disturb and redirect positive feedback loops, which lead to self-reinforced behaviors. Let's look a bit more closely at what feedback loops entail from a systems thinking perspective.

Feedback loops occur when outputs of a system are routed back as inputs of that same system. These loops can be both positive and negative—and these terms do not refer to whether the impact is beneficial or detrimental. A negative feedback loop is like a home thermostat: if the temperature drops below the set point, the thermostat switches the heating on, and when it reaches a higher set point, it switches the heating off, thus maintaining a stable temperature through self-regulation.

A positive feedback loop, alternatively, leads to self-reinforcement. It consists of a series of events that build on and bolster each other, for better or worse. As the example of public urination in India indicates, the more men urinate in public spaces, the more public urination remains a normalized practice. If it's socially acceptable, more men will either urinate in public spaces or disregard measures that punish the behavior. On the other hand, once fewer men urinate in public spaces, the practice will likely become more frowned upon, and fewer men still will use streets as urinals.

Self-reinforcing behaviors can occur at both the community level and the individual level. When I was a child I experienced the impact of this principle every time I fought with my brother. If he flicked me, I would pull him, then he would throw a punch, and the fight always escalated so quickly that instants later we would find ourselves wrestling on the floor trying to choke each other. The self-reinforced nature of a fight escalation is similar to that of a landslide; one rock falling may knock others out of place, which in turn dislodge many other rocks, and the whole hill may end up sliding down, affecting entire communities.

Once in motion, self-reinforced cycles are difficult to disrupt, but disruption is precisely what roundabout workarounds offer, and what you'll learn about in this chapter. I call these workarounds roundabouts because they can disturb and redirect a flow. When we can go in only one direction, a roundabout workaround works as a sort of stopgap, allowing us to slow down and take a different direction.

Just like wall tiles depicting gods, the roundabout workaround may not provide a permanent solution at first, but it enables us to partially take cover from a pervasive problem, buying time until tough issues are resolved, delaying assessment in order to increase the chances of success, or resisting continuous oppression. In rare cases, roundabout workarounds may also drastically shift the status quo, turning a vicious cycle into a virtuous one. In the following pages we will discuss what roundabout workarounds entail, why they matter, and how they take shape and defy what seems unavoidable.

Our first example is one with which everyone has become very familiar: social distancing, a roundabout workaround that has saved many lives across two of the worst pandemics in history.

THE SOCIAL DISTANCING STOPGAP

I had a little bird,
Its name was Enza.
I opened the window,
And in-flu-enza.

This tune, commonly sung by American children from 1918 through 1919, reflected a "new normal"—that a threat, otherwise known as the Great Influenza, was everywhere when they ventured into the world outside their homes.

The Spanish flu was a global calamity with an estimated death toll of fifty to a hundred million people. The devastating spread of this plague overshadowed the celebrations that marked the end of World War I. In fact, the influenza death toll far exceeded casualties of the war.

Because of the virus's airborne transmission, it swept through the United States, upending everyday social interactions. Philadelphia, the country's primary manufacturing hub for ships and steel, was one of the hardest-hit areas. In October 1918, casket prices skyrocketed. In the first six months of the pandemic, the number of influenza deaths was more than twice as high in Philadelphia as in St. Louis (748 per 100,000 compared to 358 per 100,000, respectively).

Why was Philadelphia hit so much harder than cities like St. Louis? Timing mattered: since the city couldn't confront the virus with effective treatment early, aggressive action to limit social interaction would have been a vital measure to curb the death toll. Philadelphia detected its first case of influenza on September 17, 1918. City officials thought that a campaign against coughing, spitting, and sneezing in public would be enough; they didn't want to disrupt the city's daily life. And despite the pandemic at its doorstep, the city hosted a patriotic parade featuring marching troops, bands, Boy Scouts and schoolgirls in white, and crowds of cheering spectators on September 27. An estimated 200,000 people attended the parade. The virus spread, and two days after the parade, public officials acknowledged the pandemic. By then it was too late.

St. Louis, on the other hand, quickly worked around the lack of effective treatment for the disease. It imposed social distancing measures that limited the spread of the virus. Two days after officials detected the first case, the city shut down public gatherings and quarantined those who had fallen ill. Although they lacked knowledge of what exactly was going on and how to treat this new virus, they did know it was highly contagious, killed masses of people, and put insurmountable pressure on healthcare facilities. Social distancing provided a stopgap to disturb the transmission of the virus. When the virus evolved into a less deadly version a few years later, the death toll in St. Louis was much lower than that of Philadelphia.

It took approximately a hundred years for the world to experience another large-scale pandemic. COVID-19 may have caught ordinary citizens by surprise, but scientists had warned about the next big pandemic since the end of the Spanish flu. In 2018 Professor Julia Gog, a mathematician at the University of Cambridge, warned: "It's not 'if,' it's 'when': it's happened a lot of times in the past, it will probably happen again . . . if we can't stop them, the alternative is at least to allocate our resources better to try and reduce the number of cases in each place."

Policymakers were aware that a new pandemic would pose grave threats. The United States devised a plan, commissioned by President George W. Bush, to deal with bioterrorism (terrorist attacks that intentionally use biological agents), which became the heart of a national playbook for responding to a pandemic of the magnitude of COVID-19. Likewise, in 2017 the United Kingdom Risk Register—a government response plan for all national risks to civil society—listed a terrorist attack and a flu pandemic as the two most catastrophic potential dangers. Worldwide, policymakers and scientists alike knew that viral transmission, whether natural or created in the labs of a country's enemies, could turn into a sort of vicious cycle. In Bush's words, "A pandemic is a lot like a forest fire. If caught early, it might be extinguished with limited damage. If allowed to smolder, undetected, it can grow to an inferno that can spread quickly beyond our ability to control it." Barack Obama's government kept and improved the task force, keeping the language the same. "The way to stop the forest fire is to isolate the embers," said Beth Cameron, who served as senior director for the National Security Council's Directorate for Global Health Security and Biodefense.

In 2006, the commission writing this playbook studied contagion models and worked out a plan that faced great criticism: if the country was hit by a deadly pandemic, the government had to tell Americans to stay home. Much of the knowledge about these patterns came from Dr. Robert Glass, a scientist who worked at Sandia National Laboratories. He studied how complex systems work and how we can avoid catastrophes. Inspired by his fourteen-year-old daughter's work on social networks in schools, Glass explored how schools would be dangerous vehicles for contagion and how to break up transmission chains. Glass and his colleagues ran simulations on supercomputers and revealed that by closing the schools in a hypothetical town of ten thousand people, only five hundred people got sick, but if schools remained open, half of the population would quickly be infected. The study concluded that social distancing "would yield local defenses against a highly virulent strain in the absence of vaccine and antiviral drugs."

Social distancing isn't a new workaround for large-scale contagions—it had already saved lives during the Spanish flu pandemic, when closing schools, churches, and theaters and banning public gatherings reduced death rates. After decades of advances in the pharmaceutical sector, however, many consumers in recent years began to expect the impossible from drug developers. We assumed that there must be an immediate fix or solution for any type of disease that could surface. Unfortunately, that was not the case with COVID-19.

After COVID-19 was first reported in 2019, cases rapidly spread around the world, spurring the WHO to declare a public health emergency of international concern on January 30, 2020, and a pandemic about forty days later. Soon after the pandemic broke out, many populist politicians stirred up controversy, claiming, with little or no scientific evidence, that we already had the right medicines to treat COVID-19 (like hydroxychloroquine, an FDA-approved medicine to treat or prevent malaria). Despite historical and epidemiological evidence of its efficacy, social distancing seemed a dystopian workaround to many politicians, including those in the United States, a country that had seemed to understand the importance of social distancing approximately fifteen years earlier, thanks to the work of scientists such as Glass, as well as of politicians and civil servants who had devised science-based pandemic response protocols.

The scientific community quickly underscored that in the midst of a pandemic we simply couldn't move on with our daily lives, and the media eventually amplified these evidence-informed narratives. Scientists largely recognized that we needed social distancing more than ever: since the Spanish flu, the world's population has grown from 1.8 billion to 7.8 billion, and we now live in a much more globalized, hyperconnected context, thus translating into the potential for higher transmission rates and deaths.

When COVID-19 hit Lombardy hard in March 2020, the scenario seemed all too similar to what had happened in Philadelphia less than a hundred years earlier. Social distancing was introduced gradually and unevenly. In some areas, restrictions limited only social gatherings and a few economic activities. In others, full lockdowns took hold, and individuals were allowed out only to purchase essential products or seek healthcare. As a result, death tolls varied substantially among cities in the region.

Locking ourselves away in our homes may have seemed

backward and economically disastrous. Yet, because the virus spreads at an exponential rate, we needed a temporary stopgap measure to disrupt and slow the rate of transmission: we needed to buy time. This roundabout workaround didn't solve the problem, but it allowed us to reduce death rates and to lessen the strain on our healthcare systems while scientists and healthcare experts learned more about the virus, identified effective antiviral drugs, and developed vaccines to put an end to the pandemic.

THE SECRET ROUNDABOUT
WORKAROUND

Sometimes we have to stay locked away to avoid the worst effects of a pandemic; other times we need to work underground to gain the space and time to fully develop a transformative idea.

In most companies, employees need managerial permission to develop new ideas or projects. When an employee's idea is in its early stages, it's particularly hard to convince managers of its potential. Supervisors are often wary of wasting the company's resources. There's an inherent tension between autonomy and accountability in the generation of innovation, especially in large companies, which struggle to find a balance between giving employees flexibility for creativity and setting the boundaries that guarantee that workers' efforts benefit the company's priorities and respect its resource constraints.

Balance between autonomy and accountability is complicated because both control and freedom can be self-reinforcing and spiral out of control. The more people can experiment with their ideas, the more they feel they can contribute, and they tend to continue to explore. The opposite is also true: the more people's ideas are ignored, or the more managers impose rules that constrain creativity, the less employees think they can propose or engage with innovative projects.

What happens when an employee generates a new idea and wants to explore it but is concerned they won't be able to gain early authorization from their supervisors? Some choose to work around the company's rules or direct orders in order to pursue an idea. Innovation management scholars call this bootlegging, a reference to the practice of hiding alcohol in one's boots during the US Prohibition. Bootlegging includes any kind of work on new ideas that has no formal organizational support and is out of sight of senior management.

With scarce resources, companies often prioritize projects that are less costly or align more obviously with the company's vision and core business. Employees working around corporate rules create a clandestine space to work on projects that haven't been authorized. In extreme cases, they flout direct orders, but in most cases, they simply continue on with their project until their work is sufficiently developed and they are ready to reveal their idea. Note that they may ignore the company's rules, but they aren't stealing; bootleggers use company resources to develop ideas because their views of what may or may not benefit the company differ from those of their managers. If they are successful, bootleggers benefit the company. In fact, some of the most transformative innovations of our time have come from these kinds of workarounds.

Defiance in Action

Bootlegging has arguably resulted in the synthesis of a more tolerable variant of pain-relieving salicylic acid, aspirin. Legend says that when the young Bayer chemist Felix Hoffmann noticed that the bitter active ingredient his father took to treat rheumatism, sodium salicylate, caused him to vomit, Hoffmann became a "bootlegger" and worked to develop a better alternative. About a hundred years later, Klaus Grohe, a scientist at the same company, worked clandestinely to devise the structural formula for ciprofloxacin, a broad-spectrum antibiotic that garnered international attention as the first FDA-approved drug for the treatment of anthrax, a biological weapon.

Bootlegging is also prolific in the electronics industry and has had a profound effect on the development of some of our most common gadgets and appliances. In the 1960s Chuck House, a Hewlett-Packard engineer, designed a large-screen display monitor despite direct orders from the company's co-founder and CEO David Packard to abort the project. The device has been integrated into more than half of Hewlett-Packard's products. Packard later awarded the bootlegger the Medal of Defiance "in recognition of extraordinary contempt and defiance beyond the normal call of engineering duty." Other bootlegged innovations in the industry include the liquid crystal display technology at Merck, the blue LED lighting technology at Nichia, the first laptop computer at Toshiba, and the first laser printer at Xerox.

Because these types of roundabout workarounds are clandestine, they aren't easy to find and document. But we have a good idea of why and how they occur. Bootleggers keep their projects secret until their merit is obvious. This is particularly important because innovative projects can come with big promises and possibilities, but their early performance and features are typically crude. Some of our most beloved products, like aspirin, would not exist or would have taken much longer to be developed if roundabout approaches hadn't provided creative and defiant employees the space and flexibility they needed to pursue autonomous projects that were, or would likely have been, vetted by their superiors.

Prohibition Culture

Innovation management studies have shown that in companies where bootlegging is more common, employees are less likely to disapprove of colleagues' deviant behavior and more likely to engage in clandestine innovative group efforts, creating an environment that encourages employees to develop new ideas and reveal them in their own time. The opposite, however, is also true: if managers are very rigid about bootlegging, they create a self-reinforcing culture that discourages creative efforts.

Bootleggers can disturb these self-reinforcing behaviors and inspire changes in corporate culture. When companies recognize the value of bootleggers' creative projects, some start to turn a blind eye, letting them flourish while avoiding conflicts with accountants and controllers. Others, like 3M and Hewlett-Packard, who have both benefited from bootlegging, took things a step further, drastically pivoting corporate culture. They formally allowed employees to devote 10 to 15 percent of their time to the pursuit of their own innovative interests, so employees don't have to work around management's rules to pursue their ideas.

From these cases, we learn that companies can capitalize on successful roundabout workarounds to promote a more flexible corporate culture. With more autonomy and flexibility, employees no longer need to work around their superiors. They can leave the underground and explore opportunities in the open, and that allows them to find complementary opportunities that would go unnoticed if the development had to happen discreetly. By doing so, they can expose their ideas, get feedback, and engage with others to co-create.

THE POWER OF THE ROUNDABOUT WORKAROUND

Despite their different applications, roundabout workarounds can shift power dynamics. I first noticed this trait through engaging with social entrepreneurs such as Elango Rangaswamy, a local leader of the village of Kuthambakkam in India, who pursued a clever workaround to challenge caste discrimination.

The Shift in the Caste System

Casteism in India splits the population into hierarchical groups. For more than three thousand years it has dictated almost every aspect of social life. There are four main groups (Brahmins, Kshatriyas, Vaishyas, and Shudras), which are further divided into about three thousand castes and twenty-five thousand sub-castes.

Dalits, otherwise known as untouchables, are fated to a life of ex-
clusion and expected to perform the least desired jobs, like clean-
ing toilets or raising pigs.

Intrigued by the self-reinforcing nature of casteism, I asked
Indian citizens of various castes about the best approaches to
fighting casteism, but they answered with great skepticism. Everyone emphasized that mainstream anti-caste efforts are based on
law enforcement, and they said that through strict punishment
things might gradually change, but institutional change is unlikely any time soon. Some academics think that education can
change people's behaviors, too, but the process of implementing it would take centuries to radically transform the country.
A more revolutionary expert told me that "nothing is going to
work except the destruction of Hinduism because if you remove
caste in Hinduism, there is nothing left." Despite different views
on how to deal with the problem, everyone agrees that because
it's so ingrained in the social fabric, caste discrimination has become normalized and self-reinforced.

Though castes seem inevitable, Rangaswamy, who grew up as
a Dalit in Kuthambakkam and experienced the caste clashes and
discrimination firsthand, employed a clever workaround in his
village. His roundabout hasn't solved the problem, but it has in-
terrupted the discriminatory practices that he all too often faced.

The story begins when Rangaswamy, an engineer, was elected
the first Panchayat Raj president of his village—a local leader
who enables bottom-up, participatory governance in Indian villages. The village had funding to build houses for the poor provided primarily by the state. Rangaswamy contemplated where to
build the houses and identified an available plot in an area Dalits

inhabited, segregated from the non-Dalits. When he announced he was building houses on land where Dalits lived, non-Dalits, many of whom were also very poor and lived in precarious rental houses, expressed their concern to Rangaswamy. As he recounted to me, they said: "Sir, you're giving housing only for Dalits. We're also landless and homeless. Who will give house for us?" He responded, "No problem, we can give you a house if you're prepared to live with the Dalits because the land is available there."

This response came as a shock to the non-Dalits. But by then Rangaswamy's workaround had already taken shape. Instead of addressing the housing issue on its own, he used it as an opportunity to address casteism in his village. "I took that as a chance to mix as much as possible," he told me. Then he continued, "I wanted to construct twin houses, one side a Dalit family, the other side a non-Dalit family." It took a lot to convince the non-Dalits, but Rangaswamy cleverly helped them look at the matter more pragmatically, rather than trying to change their opinions on caste: "I called all the people and said, 'I am not deliberately making you mix with Dalits . . . but the space is available only with the Dalit community. If you're interested, instead of fifty houses, we will make one hundred houses; fifty houses you people can come and occupy, fifty houses let the Dalit people occupy.' " The non-Dalits soon realized that they could either take the free, high-quality houses and live among Dalits or remain in their precarious rental houses.

What happened here? Neither law enforcement nor education was solving the issue on acceptable timescales. Yet the problem was too urgent and self-reinforcing for people to sit back and do nothing: with each generation, behaviors that discriminated against, isolated, and oppressed Dalits were reproduced. Rangaswamy's roundabout workaround shows us that you can use one problem (limited and low-quality housing) to approach another (casteism)—and this is particularly advantageous when we're dealing with tangled and hard-to-solve issues.

Rangaswamy's housing intervention in 2000 put stress on this self-reinforced cycle, reducing the distance—physical and emotional—that different castes took for granted. As families of Dalits and different castes lived with one another in similar conditions, the kids who grew up in those houses started to play together and stopped discriminating on the basis of caste. These caste barriers haven't completely broken down, of course, but at least animosity has diminished, and new generations are gradually challenging casteism. In 2018, when I walked around the village with Rangaswamy, he pointed out two young friends, one non-Dalit and the other a Dalit, walking side by side—something that would have been unthinkable before his workaround.

His roundabout intervention also led to other indirect impacts. Dalits and non-Dalits started to mobilize together to advocate for better public services, such as the creation of sanitation systems, housing for all, and the supply of water and electricity. The program created a benchmark for other villages. In fact, a few years after Rangaswamy completed the twin houses project, the government decided to replicate his model in more than 250 villages around the state of Tamil Nadu.

Rangaswamy taught me that the core of roundabout workarounds is to dance with inevitability. Rather than trying to change deeply ingrained behaviors and beliefs associated with the caste system head-on, Rangaswamy addressed casteism indirectly through unconventional housing projects that made people mingle.

THE "FIGHT THE POWER" ROUNDABOUT WORKAROUND

The rest of this chapter will look specifically at activists, social movements, and social entrepreneurs. I think we have much to learn from scrappy organizations and mavericks: they are driven by the need for immediate action on intractable issues, and they have to be resourceful, flexible, and quick. Let's defy the conventional wisdom that says that all organization types—such as nonprofits, social movements, and government agencies—should model themselves on businesses, and instead let's learn from activists' attempts to create small reprieves from oppressive systems.

Learning to Bounce Back

First, we will think about how the architects Swati Janu and Nidhi Sohane helped vulnerable communities resist evictions in Delhi. According to Janu, evictions of urban settlements in India are very common. Due to the lack of developed land at affordable prices, as well as the continuous flow of migrants to cities like Delhi, various types of unplanned settlements have arisen over time. Some of those, referred to as squatter settlements or encroachments, are located on land owned by a public agency, such as Indian Railways, or one of the municipal corporations of Delhi. These people build or occupy houses on the land illegally, without permission, and often for decades. Their settlements are generally in undesirable zones, next to a sewage drain or a railway track. But as cities expand, developers begin to want to build in these undesirable areas, too. Or, in her words, "the market forces make that land good real estate opportunities, and then they evict these settlers."

Settlers are informed of the eviction with a few days' notice. Authorities present evictions as inevitable: after all, the settlers are illegally occupying public land. Every time a vulnerable population is evicted, its members suffer considerable material losses. The government bulldozes their houses and crops, but evicted individuals often return a few days later. Talking to Janu, I naively asked if the actions of the government were futile because settlers were resilient and returned to the land. She politely corrected me: "It is not really resilience because that is romanticizing their situation. Not everyone comes back, and every time they come back, they have a bit less, and they are a bit weaker. Many of the settlers are on the streets because they are victims of multiple evictions. When someone suffers from many evictions, they lose their assets and the will [to live]."

Janu and Sohane were informed of the impending eviction of a settlement of small-scale farmers on the banks of the Yamuna River near New Delhi. In the past the area had been owned by a few individuals who rented the land to settlers, but it had been sold to the government a few decades prior. Nevertheless, the old landlords continued to charge the settlers rent. Even though the settlers knew the land was public, the landlords held local power and continued to profit. Then, when market prices in the area rose, evictions started, so the settlers were forced to pay rent for land they were being kicked off of. With nowhere else to go, the settlers were trapped in a vicious cycle of double oppression.

In a legal eviction in 2011 the government destroyed an informally operated local school that taught about two hundred students. The demolition was a clear violation of the country's right to education: even if the settlement where the school was built was illegal, the Delhi Development Authority did not have clearance to demolish the school. The community then appealed to the high court and received permission to rebuild the school on the land, provided that the school be classified as temporary. The court's decision inspired a roundabout workaround, which, in Janu's words, "emerged out of this need to provide for a community that survives with tenacity in a place they are not allowed to, and to assert the rights of a community to sustain and grow."

Janu and Sohane knew that the ideal solution (stopping evictions and granting the settlers the right to benefit from the land) was beyond their reach, and they first needed to interrupt the vicious cycles trapping the settlers in poverty. That is why, in Janu's words, "we were finding solutions around constraints, instead of having a clean solution." With this flexible mindset, in 2017 they designed and constructed a temporary modular school building, named ModSkool. The construction could be both assembled and dismantled in a day in order to protect it from demolitions and to ensure that it could continue to be used on the fringes of legality.

The two architects mobilized volunteers and community members and raised funds to implement the workaround. When the

school is in use, the metal frame can be filled in with locally available materials, such as bamboo, dried grass, and reused wood;
when an eviction notice arrives, settlers can quickly dismantle
the school and store the parts in a compact three-square-meter
compartment. Since this design leaves nothing to bulldoze, the
school avoids material losses and can quickly return to operation after eviction. This workaround enables the community to
resist better and for longer. "This transience, this sort of tem-
porariness, is really a coping mechanism by the communities to
survive," said Janu.

The collapsible school doesn't solve the problem of evictions,
and it doesn't necessarily improve the community's situation, but
at least it prevents further damage. This type of flexible perse-
verance can make their habitation on the land just as inevitable as the government's evictions. Bouncing back can be more
effective than throwing another punch if your most immediate
concern is to put off a fight so you have a place to sleep at night.

Learning to Buy Time

Let's look at a different case of resistance against evictions. When
I worked as a sustainability consultant in Brazil, I had read about
the repeated evictions of the indigenous Guarani-Kaiowá people
from the lands they historically inhabited. Years later, as I conducted my research at the University of Cambridge and learned
about workarounds from several scrappy organizations worldwide, I realized that the Guarani-Kaiowá had used workarounds
when they presented the Brazilian government with an ultima-
tum that bought them time and raised awareness of their plight.

I then traveled back to my home country and spoke to activists, experts, indigenous leaders, and government representatives to learn more about how they resisted oppression.

The Guarani-Kaiowá have a long history of facing forced eviction. Because their lands weren't officially demarcated, farmers purchased their territory, and the result was many legal and physical battles. Interested in the case, I reached out to a friend who works as a lawyer for the Brazilian government in the state of Mato Grosso do Sul. She started the conversation by telling me, "As a lawyer, I sometimes have to defend causes I don't particularly agree with." Negotiating the eviction of a Guarani-Kaiowá community from the land they inhabited was one such case. When she went to inform the tribe's leader that the court had upheld the eviction, she tried to soften the blow by telling him that the government had offered to compensate the tribe with another large swath of more fertile land. The tribe leader thoughtfully replied, "If I offered you a better mom, would you trade yours?"

The lawyer soon learned that the relationship of the Guarani-Kaiowá to their land is indeed maternal. In their cosmological view, they have to live and be buried on the same land of their ancestors. In their language, *tekoha*, the word for "land," also means "the place where I can exist." There's no plausible, conceivable life for them outside their land.

In 2012, the Tekoha Pyelito Kue/Mbrakay, a Guarani-Kaiowá community, learned that the local court had sided with farmers who claimed ownership of the land, and the community was to be evicted. Instead of their usual approaches—engaging in an open confrontation or leaving the land with hopes of returning—the

Guarani-Kaiowá people made a shocking request to the Brazilian authorities.

In an open letter, written in Portuguese and posted on Facebook, the community requested: "We want to die and be buried in this land with our ancestors, where we are today. We ask the Government and the Federal Justice not to decree the order of eviction, but rather to decree our collective death and bury us all here. We ask, once and for all, to decree our total extinction, besides sending tractors to dig a big hole to throw and bury our bodies . . . We have decided that we won't leave here, alive or dead."

The letter turned the eviction into ethnocide. With this twist, the indigenous people grabbed the attention of people who were previously unaware of the tribe's existence or their suffering. The letter was published in mainstream media, thousands of people protested in the streets and on social media, and hundreds of letters and petitions poured in to the government. The eviction was temporarily suspended, and in 2021 the community was still inhabiting their land, though their future remains uncertain.

Since 2012, other indigenous communities facing eviction cases have used similar tactics. Because the public has become aware of the human rights violations and agrarian tensions in the region, there is now more pressure to demarcate the lands of the Guarani-Kaiowá. Whether this workaround will have a more permanent impact in decades to come is yet unknown. To date, the appeals court has not made a ruling, but by taking the case to the court of public opinion the Guarani-Kaiowá staved off immediate eviction.

From Vicious to Virtuous

Just like the Guarani-Kaiowá, activists and social movements often use shocking, disruptive methods to bring attention to ignored subjects. Unfortunately, the effects of these kinds of workarounds often fizzle. An example of this occurred on the twentieth anniversary of the Bhopal disaster—one of the world's worst industrial disasters, during which over five hundred thousand people were harmed and over three thousand were killed by a toxic substance that leaked in 1984 from an industrial plant owned by Union Carbide, an Indian company whose shares were wholly acquired by Dow in 2001 and kept as a subsidiary company. That's when activist Jacques Servin appeared on a live program on BBC World News as "Jude Finisterra," a Dow Chemical Company spokesman. He claimed that the company took responsibility for the disaster and planned to disburse $12 billion in compensation for victims and in remediation of the Bhopal site. The gimmick's impact was immediate: in Frankfurt, Dow's share price fell about 4 percent in twenty-three minutes, reducing the company's market value by about $2 billion. But when the BBC issued an on-air correction and apology shortly thereafter, Dow's share price rebounded, and the company emerged relatively unscathed. Servin and other activists failed to leverage their moment in the spotlight, so the workaround had no enduring tangible consequence for the company or the impacted population.

Although these stunts may garner awareness and immediate support, they generally don't lead to permanent change unless activists pivot in a different direction. Here, we can learn from Scheherazade, the legendary Persian queen who used a series of workarounds to change the course of a seemingly inevitable fate bestowed upon her by her husband, King Shahryar.

The story goes that Shahryar discovered that his first wife had cheated on him, and he came to believe that all women would betray him. After having that wife executed, the king decided to marry a new virgin every day and have her beheaded in the morning, before she had the chance to dishonor him. The people in the kingdom grew angry with their monarch for killing their daughters, but they couldn't change his mind.

Then the king married Scheherazade. She had a gift for telling stories that left the listener enthralled and able to forget reality, if only for a moment. Once in the king's chambers, Scheherazade asked if she could bid one last farewell to her beloved sister, who had secretly been instructed to ask Scheherazade to tell her a story. The king lay awake, listening with awe to Scheherazade's story until dawn, when she broke off at an exciting moment.

Riddled with curiosity, the king delayed her execution: he insisted on hearing the rest of that story! She used her captivating storytelling method to work around the inescapable authority of the king on that night. The following night, Scheherazade finished that story and began another, again timing it so that with the break of dawn she left a dramatic cliffhanger. She repeated the same workaround for 1,001 nights, thus successfully delaying her beheading one day at a time. By the time Scheherazade finished her thousandth story and said she had no more to tell, the king had fallen in love and decided to spare the life of the woman who had by that time borne him three children.

With her indirect resistance, Scheherazade flipped the power equation. The workaround reconfigured the situation precisely because she wasn't tackling the king's authority head-on. Instead of acting with outright defiance, she prolonged her life day by day, gaining time to charm the king and slowly but surely reshaping her fate.

The lesson from Scheherazade is to use roundabout workarounds to buy time for pivotal change, but to be sure to pivot to those bigger changes. Having a temporary impact or briefly disrupting a self-reinforcing behavior is good, but these gains will likely fade if nothing else happens afterward. Scheherazade would have had her head chopped off if she hadn't parlayed her small wins into something more: her stories not only bought her time; they also taught the king valuable lessons and, of course, eventually captured his heart.

WHEN DO WE USE A ROUNDABOUT WORKAROUND?

Roundabouts don't so much tackle systemic challenges as interrupt self-reinforcing behaviors and buy time to mobilize, negotiate, and develop alternatives, alleviating an urgent problem while building momentum to pivot in a different direction.

Self-reinforcing behaviors, like public urination in India, are notoriously difficult to disrupt, unresponsive to situational interventions (providing more toilets) and confrontational approaches (fines and public shaming) alike. Wall owners diverted the stream (so to speak) by appealing to would-be urinators' piety with carefully placed depictions of gods. Did these knee-high icons entirely halt public urination? No, the dedicated will likely be able to find a god-free wall somewhere else. Yet this type of religiously inflected intervention was so helpful that innovators in other realms took note and implemented similar reminders to promote hygiene in restaurants and discourage littering.

Likewise, social distancing alone doesn't end a pandemic, but it does save lives and buy time for vaccine and treatment development. By delaying the inevitable, roundabout workarounds can also enable you to address challenges on your terms. Putting off assessment or unveiling an idea only when the time is ripe can be vital to an innovation's success. Without this type of workaround, we might never have gotten smash hits like aspirin.

Another roundabout approach is to use one problem to approach another, as Rangaswamy did when he indirectly challenged casteism by building housing units where Dalits and non-Dalits had to live together. Dealing with these tangled and contentious real-life issues requires adaptability and a willingness to accept temporary stopgap measures, which alleviate but don't entirely solve the problem.

The collapsible school on the banks of the Yamuna River and the Guarani-Kaiowá's reframing of an eviction notice represent two opposite but equally clever methods of applying this logic: the former embraced flexibility and the latter eschewed it, but both worked within their respective contexts to make the situation a little more bearable for a little longer.

The fictional Scheherazade, the godmother of roundabout workarounds, exemplifies all of these qualities: she teaches us that pivotal change stems from effectively accumulating and leveraging small, temporary interventions. Like Scheherazade, you too can stack workaround on top of workaround, night after night, imperceptibly but definitively changing the course of what at first appears inevitable. But pay attention to the key lesson of her stories: delaying an assessment or a decision won't be enough if you don't use that time wisely. By challenging the status quo a little at a time, roundabout workarounds don't necessarily make earth-shattering changes, but they can help to create conditions that unleash new possibilities.

4

The Next Best

I have lost track of how many overpriced travel adapters I have purchased in airports. I'm not a checklist person, and I tend to take for granted things we encounter every day, like the format of electrical sockets. So I often forget to pack a power adapter. And without it I'm literally and figuratively powerless when I travel.

According to the International Trade Administration, part of the US Department of Commerce, fifteen different electrical outlet plugs are in use worldwide. They all do the job, right? Why can't we have a single global standard?

In the twentieth century, the rise of electrical devices led manufacturers to develop their own plugs and sockets. In the absence of governmental direction, a few manufacturers won market allegiance, and as their designs became dominant, their plugs and sockets eventually turned into de facto defaults. This diversity of plug types across countries wasn't a big problem at first, but as society globalized, people began to travel more internationally, and electronic devices became more portable. The lack of a universal standard became an issue.

The International Electrotechnical Commission (IEC) began to advocate for a global standard in the early 1930s. Some governments formally adopted a single—or a few—standardized design. World War II and the subsequent economic recession halted the IEC's work until the 1950s. According to the IEC, "At that point, countries had most of their infrastructure in place and vested interests were built right into our walls."

A universal plug may be desirable for many who, like me, regularly forget to pack international adapters. But should this be a public priority—and, if so, who should bear the costs of switching the required infrastructure? To adopt a global standard, countries would have to agree on a single design, irrespective of geopolitical tensions, political ideologies, and differences in budget sizes and priorities. Imagine how politically unpopular replacing infrastructure would be—especially in low- and middle-income countries, where switching household plugs, sockets, and connectors could be particularly burdensome.

Even if it is imperfect, a travel adapter provides an immediate, workable alternative to the ideal but unrealistic solution of negotiating and implementing an international standard. Next best workarounds, like travel adapters, can act as patches. Instead of pursuing unlikely mass structural change, which involves the coordination of many different players with different agendas and capabilities, these workarounds enable us to get what we want using the resources that are available to us.

WHAT IS A NEXT BEST WORKAROUND?

When we can't do much to change our situational constraints, a next best workaround might get the job done with minimal fuss. Such solutions are particularly beneficial when stakes are high, structural changes are too intractable, and a frugal and imperfect approach seems to be the most viable alternative. A next best workaround focuses on repurposing or recombining resources, which can range from the most high-tech to the most basic. The key is to focus on alternatives that are available but largely ignored, as well as the different and unconventional affordances or assemblages of resources at your disposal.

Sometimes these workarounds appear to be stand-alone patches that enable us to achieve our goals more quickly. In other circumstances, next best workarounds either enable exploration of alternatives at the fringes of the mainstream or create precedents that facilitate long-lasting change. This chapter walks you through what I've learned by exploring the stories of entrepreneurs, lawyers, companies, nonprofits, social movements, and groups of anarchic geeks, all of whom pursued next best workarounds in different settings, for different reasons, using different resources and approaches.

FIND A NEXT BEST—AND FAST

Don't undervalue the power of a patch, especially in cases where time is short, information is limited, and the need to make a decision is urgent—such as in the event of an outbreak of a global pandemic. When the world realized that COVID-19 was going to hit us hard, I read a Twitter thread of unknown authorship that said, "The invisible hands of the market don't use hand sanitizer." It soon became evident that suppliers weren't ready to respond to the rapidly increasing demand for products like hand sanitizer, hospital ventilators, and face masks. This shortage had the potential to put us all at risk.

We couldn't expect the companies that manufactured these necessary items to meet the sudden growth in demand. Even the American giant 3M, with a yearly revenue of over $32 billion, could only commit to doubling its production of N95 face masks in March 2020. Expanding the capacity of production isn't trivial, and it takes time: it involves new or bigger facilities, extra machinery, additional raw materials coming from different parts of the world, and more skilled staff.

The crisis created a "new normal," and we weren't prepared for it. Situations in which stakes are high, resources are scarce, and time is short can become laboratories for next best workarounds. In highly complex circumstances we have to aim for a patchwork of multiple decentralized, fragmented responses rather than a single solution.

Governments and international organizations, like the WHO, started to ask manufacturers of products outside the healthcare sector, as well as licensed pharmacists and even physicians, to help produce much-needed hand sanitizer with the resources they had available. Engineering firms were asked to shift production to build ventilators, and we all saw everyone from social media influencers to friends and family making masks from old clothes and face shields from plastic bottles.

Even one of the most renowned businesses in the luxury goods sector turned to next best workarounds when needed. In March 2020, France entered a shutdown, and President Emmanuel Macron declared the country "at war" with COVID-19. About seventy-two hours after the French government issued a call to the country's industries to help fill gaps in medical supplies, the billionaire Bernard Arnault, chairman and chief executive at LVMH—a conglomerate of over seventy companies that owns various luxury brands, ranging from Dior perfumes to Louis Vuitton handbags and Moët champagnes—marshaled resources, drew on his network of influence, and initiated the production of hand sanitizer. Within a week, LVMH had produced and supplied 12 metric tons (approximately 26,450 pounds) of hand sanitizer to thirty-nine hospitals in Paris, subsequently ramping up production to supply other hospitals across the country.

This workaround was possible because the factory equipment could be repurposed. The cosmetics industry is a cousin to the pharmaceutical industry, and sometimes they use similar materials and machinery. LVMH is such a large conglomerate that, in contrast to other luxury companies, it has more control of its supply chain and has a larger stock of raw materials. Hand sanitizer contains three main ingredients—purified water, ethanol, and glycerin—all of which LVMH had on hand for producing its fragrances, liquid soaps, and moisturizing creams. The last two are similar in viscosity to hand-sanitizing gels, so LVMH could use its standard machinery and even its own plastic bottles. The metal tank at the Dior factory used to distill scents was repurposed to mix the ingredients, and the machine for filling soap bottles packaged the gel.

At any other time, LVMH manufacturing hand sanitizer would make no sense: it was the most unluxurious, inelegant, and cheap product the conglomerate had ever produced. In undertaking this workaround, however, the company wasn't interested in profit; LVMH distributed the product for free. This move positioned the company as conscientious and interested in the public good, and it challenged the image of companies targeting high-end consumer segments as elitist and superfluous.

EXTRAORDINARY USES FOR MUNDANE RESOURCES

Next best workarounds can be clumsy: they do the job, but imperfectly or temporarily. From LVMH, one of largest and most luxury-oriented companies in the world, we note the value of these workarounds in high-stakes situations. But it was through my engagement with mavericks and scrappy organizations all over the world that often repurpose and reassemble available resources with creativity and ingenuity in everyday activities that I learned that this process often entails the search for the extraordinary in the mundane.

It Takes a Next Best Workaround to Raise a Child

Tião Rocha is a Brazilian anthropologist and social entrepreneur who proudly told me that he's an educator, not a teacher: "Our schools are schooling, not educating . . . they remain white, Christian, selective, and conformist!" Rocha isn't against schools, but he thinks they are too rigid, discipline heavy, and clueless about teaching creatively with context. He adds that because of their one-size-fits-all approach, schools aren't meeting 10 percent of their educational potential: "If the school's size is M but the boy wears L, they ask him to chop off an arm."

But can you imagine the structural constraints he would face in changing the entire schooling system of a country like Brazil, which has more than forty million children of school age?

Rocha founded CPCD, a nonprofit that has worked around the school system for the past thirty years. Its approach challenges the basic assumptions of schools: there's no classroom, no predetermined topic or material, and no teacher. It builds on everyday activities and taps into popular culture to develop educational methods. "Whereas in schools there's a disciplinarian, in a samba school, there's a director of harmony," says Rocha, pointing out that education can be congenial and happen anywhere. He started off by gathering kids in unexpected places, like under a mango tree. The basic premise was that everyone teaches and learns— that's why they only sit in circles, so no one takes a leading position. In these spaces, children are no longer passive: they propose topics and creatively develop methods for their own learning experiences.

With an unconventional approach that works around state-provided schooling, the nonprofit goes to towns with some of the poorest education indicators in the country. Rocha's approach is based on an idea that he learned in Mozambique: "It takes a village to raise a child." When he reaches a town, he searches for the potentialities, for the extraordinary in the mundane.

He went to an impoverished town called Araçuaí, where 96.7

percent of the children who had completed the eighth grade had not sufficiently met the standards established by the Brazilian government, and 60 percent of those were in a "critical state." He created an "educational intensive care unit" in the town and asked a grandmother how she could help to address the high illiteracy rate in her town. She replied, "Oh, son, I'm just a dumb old woman, I have nothing to teach. The government is the one who should be responsible to do something." He reframed his question: "What do you do best?"

To his surprise, she told him that her "written biscuits"—biscuits that she baked into different shapes and letters—were delicious. With her help, Rocha created the "Biscuit Pedagogy": CPCD teaches kids how to read and do basic math operations by reading recipes instead of books and how to write using piping bags instead of pencils. With these kinds of next best workarounds, the nonprofit hasn't produced "excellence," but it quickly elevated the educational standards of the students in a "critical state."

Workarounds like Rocha's may not solve structural constraints, but they may create patches that both alleviate problems and stretch the boundaries of what is possible with available resources.

One Man's Trash Is Another Man's Treasure

The extraordinary can be found in what is unexpectedly valuable—like biscuits—and in what we throw away. This is what engineer Topher White did. He repurposed discarded cell phones to address one of the world's greatest environmental challenges: illegal logging.

According to Interpol, between 50 and 90 percent of logging in tropical rain forests is illegal, and it is a gateway activity to clearing rain forests, which is one of the primary causes of climate change and biodiversity loss and leads to the violation of the human rights of populations that inhabit the land. Unfortunately, most rain forests are located in low- and middle-income countries that do not have enough human and technological resources to monitor these massive areas in real time. Take the Amazon, the home of the world's largest rain forest, as an example: its area is about 2.1 million square miles (the equivalent of approximately 770 million soccer fields), and it spans nine countries. Can you imagine the difficulty of monitoring such a vast, cross-jurisdictional, and hard-to-reach space in order to guard against illegal loggers?

White decided to work around these constraints. In his words, his workaround "didn't come because of any sort of high-tech solution, it just came from using what was already there." He first had the idea when he went as a tourist to Borneo. There he realized how loud the rain forest is: from the chirps of birds to the banter of monkeys and the gurgle of water, the rain forest contains a lot of sounds. It is difficult for guards and rangers to hear and pinpoint where logging is occurring. But what if he could turn down the sound of nature and distinguish the sound of chain saws?

He realized that cell phone service was available even in some of the most remote areas of the rain forest, hundreds of miles from the nearest road, and he knew that old phones are being discarded by hundreds of millions of people every year globally. So here's the idea: he repurposes old cell phones to "listen" to the sounds of the forest in a three-kilometer radius. The phones are charged with solar energy and put in protective boxes hidden up in tree canopies, distributed across the rain forest to maximize coverage. Then artificial intelligence analyzes the sounds and distinguishes between chain saw noises and the sounds of the forest (such as birds chirping, the falling rain, and trees swaying in the wind). Because the phones are connected to a network, when they "hear" chain saws they send a real-time alert with the location of the logging to rangers and community patrols, who can catch the loggers in the act.

Using his next best workaround, White co-founded Rainforest Connection, a nonprofit that quickly expanded to ten countries on five continents. Besides directly impeding illegal logging, White's next best workaround also provided data for advocating for increased protection of these areas, expanding the boundaries of the possible in the fight against deforestation and showing us how repurposing some of the world's ubiquitous resources can lead to scalable opportunities to address complex problems.

MUNDANE USES FOR EXTRAORDINARY RESOURCES

Finding the extraordinary in the mundane—in biscuits and discarded phones—is one way of creating next best workarounds, but doing the opposite, searching for the mundane in the extraordinary, can also yield great opportunities to repurpose resources for workarounds.

I first thought of this approach when talking to a University of Cambridge researcher who was an excellent computer hacker. I worked in a nearby department and sometimes sneaked into his building to take advantage of a fancy coffee machine. Whereas my department afforded me instant coffee, his had a coffee machine that allowed me to choose a flat white using an iPad. He told me of a time when he wanted to boil an egg for lunch, but he didn't have a kettle or a stove at his disposal—only the sophisticated coffee machine. Although we tend to look at technologies in terms of the "fullness" of the functions for which they were designed, the coffee machine combined multiple functions: it was simultaneously a boiler, a grinder, and a milk frother. But he looked past the "full" technology and tapped into the part he needed, the water boiler, to make his lunch.

This was a very rough solution that worked around his office's limitations. Yet it signaled the potential of finding mundane applications in sophisticated technologies. I then started to investigate how mavericks at the fringes of the mainstream fiddle with technologies to find alternative uses.

Drones to the Rescue

There's been buzz around the possibility of using drones for delivery services. Many assume that Amazon will be the first mover—that when you order a product from Amazon Prime, you'll get a drone-delivered package within an hour. Only a few realize that although this extraordinary technology isn't yet viable in most settings where Amazon operates, it is already in use in Rwanda for delivering something that people in high-income countries take for granted.

About a third of the world's population lacks access to essential medical supplies, from blood for transfusions to vaccines. A major bottleneck is the poor or nonexistent transportation infrastructure, which impedes access to much-needed provisions in rural regions of low-income countries. Despite the efforts by the Rwandan government to improve the country's transportation infrastructure, only about 9 percent of classified roads were paved in 2015. The rest are treacherous, uneven dirt roads that are particularly challenging for the delivery of on-demand medical supplies. If someone is bleeding out, they can't afford to wait hours for the blood to arrive. These medical supplies have to be on hand quickly.

Addressing these infrastructure bottlenecks is incredibly challenging, time-consuming, and costly. It requires building better roads; creating decentralized facilities, such as distribution centers for medical supplies; and improving governance and logistics. Even if these low-income countries had the financial resources to better stock their healthcare facilities, keeping a surplus to avoid the risk of shortages, valuable resources that have short shelf lives would often go to waste.

Instead of contending with these structural challenges, the Silicon Valley company Zipline works around them: it partnered with the government of Rwanda to launch the world's first commercial drone delivery service. The service consists of a fleet of autonomous drones that promptly bring vital medical supplies across the country from a central facility. Zipline takes an average of five minutes to launch a self-driving drone from its distribution center after receiving an order. The delivery drone cruises in the Rwandan airspace guided by GPS and sensors at a speed of about 62 miles per hour. To avoid the risks imposed by landing at a destination, the drone drops a package with supplies with a simple parachute at a predetermined point near the hospital or clinic that placed the order where healthcare workers can retrieve it. The package consists of an insulated cardboard box that is suitable for supplies that need to be kept cold (like blood and vaccines). The package and the parachute can be discarded. With this system, healthcare workers don't have to rely on any sort of local infrastructure to receive much-needed medical supplies.

By leveraging an extraordinary technology to work around a lack of infrastructure, Zipline has not only served a noble cause in Rwanda; it has also created a test bed for integrating a network of autonomous drones into air traffic control—one of the most challenging constraints for the diffusion of drone delivery. Working in Rwanda, Zipline may be helping to stretch what is possible for other countries, too. The company communicates directly with the central air traffic control in Kigali's airport, and it has gradually developed designs and concepts that may support the deployment of drone delivery in countries with busier airspaces, like the United States, where the use of drones is currently unfeasible.

The Future Is Already Here

When we find mundane uses for extraordinary technologies, we unpack new opportunities for collective action. This is what happened when a group of computer geeks engaged civil society through a decentralized online social movement, which they called Operação Serenata de Amor, to develop and deploy artificial intelligence to investigate suspicious public spending in Brazil.

The expectation in representative democracies is that civic participation happens through elections. Citizens are expected to delegate public affairs to elected officials and the institutions responsible for running the public machine. These computer geeks shared a deep mistrust of centralized authorities. They also knew that investigative efforts in Brazil—a country where the cost of corruption may reach up to 2.3 percent of GDP, per the Federation of Industries of the State of São Paulo—lacked the human and technological capacity to identify most corruption cases.

This group worked around the country's investigative agencies. They realized that they could develop artificial intelligence to tap into open data to identify suspicious public spending. In 2016 they created an open-source artificial intelligence robot named Rosie that uses algorithms to automatically read congresspeople's reimbursement receipts. In the process, they created a sort of open engagement between citizens and public officials.

The robot's name reflects how this group wanted to make the extraordinary potential of artificial intelligence more accessible. They borrowed the name of their robot from the robotic maid that handles the household chores in the animated cartoon *The Jetsons*. As William Gibson—the Canadian American science fiction writer credited with pioneering the subgenre known as cyberpunk—said, "The future is already here—it's just not very evenly distributed." The Brazilian activists knew artificial intelligence was the future, that it was already here, and they wanted to make its use more mundane, more evenly distributed.

The moment was ripe to stretch the boundaries of the possible. Coding had become more accessible through open libraries and open-source technologies. Furthermore, as part of a multilateral initiative for transparency in public disclosure, the Brazilian government has required open data from all public bodies since 2011. Public information was freely available to access, use, and share. The group had engaged more than five hundred volunteers through the social coding platform GitHub to develop and improve Rosie's algorithms. Others without technical knowledge also joined the movement through social networks and spread the word.

The activists started with the investigation of the Quota for Parliamentary Activity, a reimbursable monthly allowance for a congressperson's routine business expenses. The government doesn't have the capacity to verify all the receipts because of their sheer volume: a small team receives about twenty thousand expense reports per month, and the process of checking them is labor-intensive. With artificial intelligence, the group automated the process and worked around the resource constraints in public administration. Their algorithms calculated the probability of irregularity of each expense and the team justified its conclusions, which were subsequently reported to the governmental agencies responsible for taking legal action.

Approximately six months after deploying Rosie, the algorithms identified more than 8,000 potentially irregular expenses, and 629 of them—relating to 216 of the 513 Congress members at the time—were reported to the responsible authorities. Rosie identified many sources of corruption, such as padded invoices, reimbursements requested by bogus companies, and expenses for products or services that were not specified (or allowed) by the law, including some absurd ones, like buying popcorn at a movie theater with public money.

A civil servant responsible for auditing governmental expenses said that the movement "in a week revealed more suspicious claims than what the responsible governmental agency did in a year." Besides the immediate impact of the project, the group also extended the boundaries of the possible. Since the algorithms are fully open-source, anyone can build on them for other purposes, like investigating corruption in other countries or even companies.

THE POWER OF STACKING NEXT BEST WORKAROUNDS

Next best workarounds often emerge and gain traction as alternatives to mainstream ways of doing things. We tend to think of disruptions as heavy blows that quickly change everything, but the reality is they often result from a series of workarounds that gradually challenge the status quo, making new possibilities more visible and accessible. Let's look at what happened in cryptography, a field replete with next best workarounds. In the following pages you will see how a series of workarounds stacked one on top of another led to radical changes on- and off-line in how we communicate and in the currencies we use.

The Birth of Bitcoin

You may remember from high school history class British mathematician and computer scientist Alan Turing's singular contribution to ending World War II, cracking the Enigma, a type of enciphering machine used by the German forces to send encrypted messages. Being able to decipher the codes from the Nazi military forces was a turning point in the war, allowing the Allies to intercept communications and act preventively.

With that in mind, can you imagine the technology—and the battles for secrecy—that ensued in the United States and the Soviet Union during the Cold War?

Beginning in the early 1950s, the US National Security Agency (NSA) kept the country's codes secret and worked to break the codes of their enemies. The nation, mostly through the NSA, held a sort of cryptographic monopoly. But this monopoly evaporated when random computer geeks started performing some serious cipher work outside the government. In their efforts to defy an emerging surveillance state, they expanded the boundaries of what was possible with cryptography and who could engage in cryptography.

These individuals weren't breaking the rules; there was no formal rule barring them from engaging in cryptography. Yet the government and the general public regarded them with suspicion.

By the 1970s, cryptographers were flourishing and working around the NSA's monopoly, operating either autonomously or at universities like MIT and Stanford. A turning point came when Whitfield Diffie and Martin Hellman (a research programmer and a young electrical engineering professor at Stanford, respectively) described "public key" cryptography in a 1976 article titled "New Directions in Cryptography." Their work was very controversial at the time—an NSA employee even warned the publishers that Diffie and Hellman could be subject to prison time. But, since the authors weren't breaking rules, just working around them, they weren't charged with any misdeeds. Almost forty years later, Diffie and Hellman received the Association for Computing Machinery (ACM) A. M. Turing Award, often referred to as the "Nobel Prize of Computing," for taking cryptography beyond the realm of classified espionage and making possible many subsequent developments. In the words of Dan Boneh, a professor of computer science and electrical engineering at Stanford, "without their work, the Internet could not have become what it is today."

Previously, a user's privacy depended on administrators who could easily sell information for money or be subpoenaed by the government. Diffie and Hellman wanted the content of communications to be accessible to recipients but protected from unauthorized access or use, and a public key does just that: a message can be decrypted only if the sender has the receiver's public key and the receiver inputs their own private key.

This development hit the geek communities hard. The workaround granted privacy in messaging and opened up a wide range of subsequent workarounds. The stakes were high, though: on one side, privacy; on the other, national security. Still the government only implicitly threatened independent cryptographers because these workarounds weren't violating any kind of law; the cryptographers gracefully worked around what was permissible.

Also, during the Cold War, the NSA was mostly concerned with international threats.

By the time the NSA started to look at the internal threats that arose from public-key cryptography, such as private communication among child molesters and gangsters, the genie was already out of the bottle.

As cryptography developed, those pushing the boundaries of privacy sought total anonymity online. They wanted online interactions to leave no trace of conversations, credit histories, or phone bills—and these objectives slowly came to fruition with next best workaround after next best workaround. This was particularly important at the time because, with the growth of online transactions, people were leaving more online traces. By following the trails, interested parties could piece together identities, problems, preferences, beliefs, and behaviors. Cryptographic workarounds presented new ways to limit the degree of traceability of online transactions.

With this vision of privacy and anonymity gaining traction in the early 1990s, and with the rapid development of information and communication technologies, geeks mobilized in unprecedented and novel ways, through scrappy webs of collaborators, where they assembled resources in many novel ways to work around obstacles that hindered the diffusion of cryptography. You may have realized where I'm going with this story. Most of the indirect moves that unleashed the power of cryptography in the past fifty to seventy years weren't confrontational; that is, they didn't clash with the dominant sources of power. Most of them didn't infringe upon laws. Working around the government in a constant pursuit of the "next best" workaround for privacy and anonymity, they gradually stretched the boundaries of the possible. And with that they also paved the way for one of the most famous workarounds ever pursued by computer geeks, which emerged in 2008: bitcoin.

This cryptocurrency—and the blockchain technology upon which it relies—was created in the aftermath of the 2008 financial crash, when distrust of and dislike for financial institutions were at a high. Experiencing the worst crisis of their lifetimes, geeks saw people in debt while governments bailed out big financial corporations they believed to be responsible for the crash. The corporations that received all sorts of public support were exactly the ones in control of a centralized system that manages all our financial transactions: the money you have, your credit scores, the flows of money. The geeks knew that in the past many had unsuccessfully tried to confront these big financial corporations, yet these corporations seemed as resilient as ever, bouncing back even when they messed up.

By inventing cryptocurrency they found a way to bypass the centralized structures of the financial system, providing an alternative for anonymizing members and making possible transactions that left no detectable traces.

Satoshi Nakamoto—a pseudonym that disguises the (still unknown) identity of a person or group of people—registered the domain bitcoin.org and subsequently authored a paper on a peer-to-peer electronic cash system, explaining what it consists of and what it entails. In early 2009 the network came into existence, allowing everyone to "mine" the digital coin through a lottery-based system and to transact bitcoin digitally and untraceably. Nakamoto also mined the Genesis Block of the digital currency, named Block 0, and simultaneously shared an article about governments bailing out banks, presumably urging followers to think of bitcoin as a way to defy the financial system.

The idea was so promising—and the timing was so good—that bitcoin quickly took off. Early supporters engaged in its development. Hal Finney, a member of the Cypherpunk movement who found out about Nakamoto's bitcoin proposal early on, offered to mine the first block of coins. About a year later, a few retailers started accepting bitcoin, and many others joined later on. The growth of the cryptocurrency was tremendous: in May 2010, in the first transaction for a tangible item using bitcoin, a man from Florida paid 10,000 bitcoins for two Papa John's pizzas. The last time I checked, in 2021, that same amount was worth over $470 million.

Nakamoto bypassed the centralized rules of the financial sector instead of clashing with them. This strategy was particularly powerful after the financial crisis: if you can't change the "rules of the game" in the financial system, this workaround showed that a lot can be done at the edges. Cryptocurrency—and blockchains more broadly—stretched the boundaries of what was possible at the fringes of mainstream systems of power.

For better or worse, cryptocurrency systems opened up room for many others to creatively work around problems. Whether you're a drug dealer who needs to stash cash where it can't be traced, a wealthy individual who wants to dodge the tax system, or an expatriate wanting to transfer money home without paying exorbitant fees, you can work around law enforcement and mainstream financial organizations with cryptocurrency.

FROM THE EDGES TO THE MAINSTREAM

Next best workarounds often run in parallel to mainstream rules and practices. In some cases, as with the use of cryptography, distinctions between workarounds and the mainstream gradually become more blurred. But not all workarounds run in parallel to the mainstream. Some dramatically disrupt the status quo, setting precedents that trickle down and change entire systems. This is what Justice Ruth Bader Ginsburg did in one of her first and most prominent cases as a lawyer.

The Notorious RBG

Ruth Bader Ginsburg became a pop culture icon in the United States and beyond for her titanic influence on the law, her defense of civil rights, and her powerful dissenting opinions when the top court leaned in a conservative direction. But before becoming a judge, she was a preeminent scholar and litigator for women's rights.

Her path to women's rights law was circuitous. Despite her impeccable academic credentials (she was the first woman to be on the *Harvard Law Review* and *Columbia Law Review* and was tied for first in her law school class at Columbia University in 1959), no law firm in New York would hire her. In her words, "I was Jewish, a woman, and a mother. The first raised one eyebrow; the second, two; the third made me indubitably inadmissible."

Somewhat reluctantly, she got a job at Rutgers Law School,

where she gradually built her expertise in gender equity and, more specifically, women's rights law. In her talks she often cited Sarah Grimké, noted abolitionist and advocate of equal rights, who said in 1837, "I ask no favors for my sex . . . All I ask of our brethren is, that they will take their feet from off our necks." This quotation not only reflected her academic stance; it also illustrated her own experiences as a woman in a male-dominated profession.

In the 1960s she dove into feminist literature. She read foundational feminist contributions, and her view became progressively shaped by Swedish feminism, which argued that both men and women had to share parental responsibilities and both the burdens and compensation of work. When her students at Rutgers requested a class on women and the law, she read every federal decision on women's rights and many state court decisions in a month. According to her, "That was no great feat, for there were precious few of them."

She was very aware that the legal system was unfair, but she also knew that battling sex discrimination would be tough: gender inequality was deeply ingrained in the laws and belief systems of the powerful—who, needless to say, were men. How can you topple sex discrimination in the law when those who benefited from it decided how the law was to be interpreted? The US Supreme Court was composed only of men, and the dominant narrative in the justice system was patronizing to women.

RBG knew that those in power weren't only afraid of losing their privileges; they genuinely believed that they were protecting women. In other words, they thought women were the privileged ones, receiving benefits without sharing responsibilities.

Thus from their perspective discrimination against women was justifiable and legitimized.

The time was ripe for change. At Rutgers, RBG started to take on cases of discrimination against women. For example, she assisted a former student in the case of Nora Simon, a woman who was unable to re-enlist in the military after having a child, even though she had put the child up for adoption. These small cases helped women like Simon, who rejoined the armed forces, but RBG knew they weren't shifting the bulk of the law.

Things changed in the United States with her first well-known case: an ingenious next best workaround. RBG says that her husband, Marty, a tax lawyer, stumbled on Charles Moritz's case and brought it to her. She promptly told him off, saying that she had no interest in tax cases. But when she realized it was a case of sex discrimination against a man, she knew that *Moritz* could topple the whole legal system of discrimination on the basis of sex. Why was this workaround so promising? If she could prove that institutional sexism disadvantaged a man— who wouldn't be patronized or seen as a fragile individual who gets "the best of both worlds"—then she could set a precedent for women, too.

Moritz was a bachelor whose job in publishing required frequent travel. He was denied a tax deduction for the money he had paid a caretaker for his dependent eighty-nine-year-old mother simply because he was a single man. This was a case of sexism because a single woman in the same situation would be entitled to the tax break. Columbia Law professor Suzanne Goldberg explains how this exemplifies the sexism in the US legal system at the time: "This tax law sought to give a benefit to people who had to care for dependents but could not imagine that a man would be doing so."

The Ginsburgs worked together on the case and split the argument in the Tenth Circuit Court of Appeals, and the case reached a verdict in November 1972. Marty was a specialist in tax law and Ruth in gender law. They convinced Moritz to appeal and commit to setting a precedent even if the government offered to settle, and RBG secured support from the American Civil Liberties Union (ACLU) after convincing its director that she had hit upon "as neat a craft as one could find to test sex-based discrimination against the Constitution."

In *Moritz v. Commissioner of Internal Revenue*, the Ginsburgs' entire strategy was circuitous. They worked around all sorts of constraints and avoided direct confrontation; otherwise they would have clashed with the assumptions and discriminatory mindsets of an all-male court. They focused on Moritz's specific case: a seemingly low-stakes case for the court (up to $600 tax deduction for a caregiver's expenses), rather than a case against the broader sexism in US laws that afflicted women the most.

On the opposing bench was the solicitor general—the Ginsburgs' former Harvard Law School dean Erwin Griswold—who adopted a combative strategy. His legal team made the case that the future of the "American family" was at stake in the Moritz case; that a pro-Mortiz decision could put hundreds of sex-based statutes on unsteady legal footing, compromising the country's social fabric. They aimed to elicit the fears and concealed prejudices of an all-male court, arguing, for example, that the case could lead to kids coming back from school and not finding their mothers at home, along with lower wages in the country because of women flooding the job market.

The workaround tactic works particularly well against a confrontational opponent. *On the Basis of Sex*, the biographical legal drama about RBG, portrays ACLU director Melvin Wulf instructing RBG to tone down her passion about women's rights in a mock trial: "Look, you either make this case about one man, or you lose. Because to the judges, you're not talking about women in the abstract. You're talking about their wives at home, baking briskets." Marty then underscores the circuitous tactic. Even if faced with a question that she felt strongly about, he tells RBG, "You should evade. Should women be firefighters? With all due respect, Your Honor, I haven't considered it because my client isn't a firefighter. Or you can redirect: With respect, Judge, this case is not about firefighters, it's about taxpayers and there's nothing inherently masculine about paying taxes. Or crack a joke: Your Honor, anyone who's raised a child couldn't possibly be intimidated by a burning building. And then bring it back to your case."

This is what they did in court. In Moritz's trial, says University of California, Santa Barbara, professor Jane Sherron De Hart, RBG "would try to educate, she would not be confrontational or emotional, but she would try to bring the judges along to see the injustice of *men* not being able to get a benefit that women in comparable situations could get." The Ginsburgs won the case. Denver's Tenth Circuit Court of Appeals unanimously reversed the Tax Court's decision. It determined that the tax code made an "invidious discrimination based solely on sex" and was, therefore, unconstitutional.

Toppling a System of Sex-Based Discrimination

By arguing from the position of a man's diminished rights, RBG and her husband, Martin Ginsburg, successfully set a historic precedent that unequal treatment on the basis of sex is unconstitutional. By engaging with this workaround, RBG also honed and shared her foundational argument. In the spring of 1971 she mailed a brief with the key arguments that she had developed a few months earlier for Moritz's case to the ACLU, whose lawyer Allen Derr was gearing up for the case *Reed v. Reed*, which was going to be argued at the Supreme Court. Sally Reed had not been appointed to administer her deceased son's estate because she was a woman. This case, which RBG referred to as "Moritz's fraternal twin," was the first major Supreme Court case that struck down a state law on the grounds that it discriminated against women.

In 1972 these two cases defending both men and women set precedents for many of RBG's subsequent accomplishments. Interestingly, in making the case that the future of the American family was at stake, the opponents in *Moritz v. Commissioner* made the lives of gender rights lawyers and activists much easier in the following years. Erwin Griswold appealed the Tenth Circuit's decision to the Supreme Court, claiming that the outcome of *Moritz v. Commissioner* could "cast a cloud of unconstitutionality" over a tremendous number of federal statutes. To back up his claims, he presented a list named Appendix E (allegedly obtained from a computer at the Department of Defense) that enumerated 876 sections in the United States legal code that contained sex-based references.

Griswold did precisely what opponents often do when losing

to a workaround tactic: they go ballistic, not realizing that their momentum and efforts can be used against them. Griswold's team suddenly gave RBG and like-minded lawyers, politicians, and activists a sort of blueprint for tumbling sex discrimination from the US legal system.

The approach no longer needed to be circuitous as it was before (involving educating judges and avoiding their concealed prejudices). An article RBG wrote a year after the trial has a section titled "Judges' Performance Poor to Abominable," which reflects a change in strategy. Gender rights lawyers, politicians, and activists could now be more direct. With precedents from the *Moritz* and *Reed* cases and the blueprint in hand, lawyers could go after each of the 876 codes listed in Appendix E, both pressing for changes in laws in Congress and contesting court decisions on the basis of sex discrimination. RBG showed that when sidestepping obstacles, we work first with the possible, and that next best workarounds may in turn change more permanently what society deems viable, acceptable, and desirable.

WHEN DO WE USE A NEXT BEST WORKAROUND?

Next best workarounds can be stand-alone fixes that address problems quickly, but sometimes they pave the path for structural changes. They require using what's available rather than what's ideal, such as a travel adapter or LVMH-produced hand sanitizer. "Biscuit Pedagogy" and Rainforest Connection are examples of how what's on hand—biscuits or old cell phones bound for the bin—can take on new purposes if you're willing to look at the mundane with new eyes.

Sometimes next best workarounds mean parsing a system into its components to boil an egg in a fancy coffee maker; other times they involve using a high-tech intervention, like drone delivery, to work in an unexpected location. In all cases, using next best workarounds means sidestepping complexity in pursuit of an immediate goal. Rosie, the robot that spots suspicious public expenditures in Brazil, and the development of cypher technologies demonstrate how these seemingly small interventions running in parallel with the mainstream can have major impacts. RBG's approach to sex discrimination litigation shows how a next best workaround can open precedents that can cascade down and lead to more durable change.

Next-best approaches showcase a special aspect of all workarounds: they shine when the most obvious solutions have failed or are impossible to execute. Using limited resources, scrappy organizations and mavericks teach us that often the best step forward is not focusing on what the ideal ought to be but instead drawing attention to available opportunities that tend to be ignored. Resources are almost always at our disposal, even if they're present in ways we tend to disregard or that challenge our way of thinking. Scrappy organizations repurpose and reimagine resources and benefit from unconventional uses. Anyone who's ever given a new toy to a baby and watched them play with the wrapping paper more than the gift can see that the outcome may not be what was intended, but it still makes for a happy baby.

Next best workarounds aren't necessarily about providing

a one-to-one replacement for the "perfect" solution—which would be a more direct approach; rather they're about sidestepping obstacles and working with the possible. And sometimes these small flickers from creative, intermediate patches wind up illuminating entirely new possibilities and paths in the midst of seemingly insurmountable challenges.

Part II

Using Workarounds

Workarounds are clever, unexpected, economical, and effective. In Part II, we'll start putting Part I's stories—and you—to work. Winding our way from the more conceptual to some nitty-gritty, practical elements, we'll reflect on how you can adopt the workaround attitude, how you can develop the right mindset to find and explore workarounds, how you can ideate workarounds in different settings, and, finally, how your organization can be more workaround friendly.

First, we'll critically reflect on the value of deviance, zooming out to think about how workarounds can enable us to deviate effectively and gracefully from all sorts of conventions, from explicit rules to implicit norms. Since a new outlook on nonconformity isn't in itself going to help us address our challenges, we'll also dig into how this appreciation for deviance can help us reframe how we think about our information, our resources, our opportunities, and ourselves. We'll explore how a workaround mindset necessitates a willingness to experiment quickly, fail productively, and repeat the process rather than conduct methodical assessments and define contingency plans.

Then we'll think about building blocks to generate ideas

for workarounds, using the four workaround approaches that you've learned in Part I, and we'll discuss how you can put the new ideas that you brainstorm into practice. Finally, we'll reflect on the challenges and opportunities that come with developing workarounds while reviewing recommendations for strategy, culture, leadership, and work relationships.

5

The Workaround Attitude

My mom is a psychoanalyst. In my adolescence, most of my friends broke their parents' rules through direct confrontation. I tried that too, obviously, but it seemed pointless: she only had to raise her eyebrows to remind me who was the boss. Then I discovered that the best way to act out was to use jargon from psychoanalysis, terms and phrases that were often underlined in her many books. I attributed my wrongdoings to, for example, "manifestations of my unconscious" or my "death instincts." Caught off guard, she either laughed and joked around or engaged in a detailed explanation of how I had misused the term. Either way, this tactic successfully distracted her from disciplining me.

The world is full of deviants. Whereas some of them get grounded or land in jail, others get away with their deeds. In Part I, I walked you through stories of the latter. I described how deviants successfully work around the obstacles that hold them back. Though their actions may be morally ambiguous in some cases, they promptly and pragmatically address all sorts of complex problems.

Yet while reading Part I you may have felt morally conflicted about some of the workaround examples. What happens when we suggest that everyone intentionally bypass the rules? What happens when bypassing the rules becomes the rule of thumb?

Because it's human nature to play by the book and place judgment on those who break rules, many of us believe that the world needs to enforce more order and more discipline upon those who deviate. I think we don't deviate enough.

In this chapter, we'll go over five thought-provoking incentives that will drive you to become more deviant. You'll learn that conformity isn't always preferable, that we often fail to notice which rules hold us back, that rules are a means of exerting power, that blaming deviants often does more harm than good, and that deviance is different and more transformative than disobedience. I'll conclude by sorting out different approaches to deviance and explaining how workarounds can enable you to deviate gracefully and effectively.

CONFORMITY ISN'T ALWAYS PREFERABLE

We are raised to think that conformity is always preferable and that society needs at least some authoritative rules to restrain our tendencies to harm others. But why do we think that conformity is the best way to prevent harm?

The Social Contract

Let's start with the father of psychoanalysis, Sigmund Freud. In *Civilization and Its Discontents* Freud details our innate tendencies to harm others: "Men are not gentle creatures who want to be loved . . . their neighbor is for them not only a potential helper or sexual object but also someone who tempts them to satisfy their aggressiveness on him, to exploit his capacity for work without compensation, to use him sexually without his consent, to seize his possessions, to humiliate him, to cause him pain, to torture and to kill him." He then rhetorically asks, "Who, in the face of all his experience of life and of history, will have the courage to dispute this assertion?"

According to Freud, we have an unquestionable predisposition to act on our harmful instincts, and he's not the first or only person to think so. "A man is a wolf to another man," says the old Latin proverb. This widespread assumption justifies what moral and political philosophers like Thomas Hobbes and Jean-Jacques Rousseau call the social contract: to live in society and ensure social well-being, we need to sacrifice individual freedoms to the state, granting it the authority to make and enforce rules.

Seems reasonable, right? We are all familiar with the idea that we have to conform to the law, and if we don't we shall be punished. We assume that without discipline we would live in brutal anarchy. The problem is that the social contract makes us believe that conformity is always preferable: that our unconditional compliance is part of a humanization process that stifles our savagery and frees us from our harmful natural instincts.

We may indeed sometimes act on animalistic instincts, but why do we assume that savagery supersedes all our other natural instincts and undesirable behaviors?

What If Rules Are Unfair?

Comparing only our harmful instincts to those of savage animals conceals more than it reveals. We may indeed sometimes act on animalistic instincts, but like sheep we humans also like the comfort of being part of the flock. Like lions, females carry twice the burden of their male counterparts, hunting and caring for cubs. Like bees, thousands of workers support the queen's egg-laying activities.

A better way of looking at conformity and deviance is by contrasting ourselves with machines. Conformity means doing as we're told, or as we've been programmed to do; it means we haven't critically evaluated our options or acted based on reasoning. Simply changing the analogy makes us realize that deviance is what humanizes us, what makes us stand out.

The worst harm to humankind was perpetrated and validated by people who followed a system of rules—and that is why we have to challenge the social contract. We are prone to thoughtlessly following orders, including the most harmful ones. Just think of slavery, the once lawful right to own people, depriving them of their most basic rights. It shouldn't be difficult to recollect other stories from the past about behaviors that we now find appalling—and, if you think critically, in our times, too. The plot repeats itself more often than we think. Protagonists and contexts may change, but a central theme is that incontestable conformity to unfair rules causes harm.

The Dangers of Conformity

Hannah Arendt, a Holocaust survivor, was one of the most influential political theorists of the twentieth century. In 1961 she covered Adolf Eichmann's trial in Jerusalem for *The New Yorker*. She later published a book on it called *Eichmann in Jerusalem: A Report on the Banality of Evil*, which is an eye-opening account of the dangers of conformity.

Captured in Argentina, Eichmann was charged with organizing and facilitating the mass incarceration and extermination of Jews in concentration camps. Covering the trial, Arendt argued that rather than a pathological monster, Eichmann was a bland bureaucrat who blindly conformed to the rules. In her words, he was "terribly and terrifyingly normal": his crimes were fueled by conformity, not a murderous appetite. Arendt coined the famous term "banality of evil" to describe how even the most horrendous crimes can be routinized and implemented without moral indignation by rule followers.

We fault Eichmann precisely for his inability to think critically and defy the Nazis' rules. But if we, like Eichmann, also tend to conform to the rules, would we have acted similarly in the same circumstances?

A Shocking Result

Inspired by Arendt's coverage of Eichmann's trial, Stanley Milgram, an American social psychologist, conducted a famous study during the 1960s known as the Milgram experiments while serving as a faculty member at Yale University. He found that people have a tendency to conform to rules, even if doing so means hurting other people. He designed a role-playing experiment that tested the extent to which volunteers would follow orders that they were led to believe involved administering shocks to others. Participants gradually increased the voltage of the shocks as an authority figure demanded. The shocking result: 65 percent of the volunteers fully conformed and administered the highest 450-volt shock, one that could kill a person; 35 percent of participants conformed partially, continuing up to 300 volts.

This and many other studies have shown that we are basically conformists, even in cases where with hindsight we can see that the moral thing to do—not shocking people—is quite undisputable. Milgram's experiments showed how far we are willing to go to obey authority; that "monsters" aren't too different from the rest of us.

Similarly, how many times have you heard or said, "I'm just doing my job," or "I'm just following the rules," to justify actions you knew were unfair? The problem is that when we blindly accept the order and discipline that authorities impose, we ignore that rules aren't necessarily fair. In other words, there's nothing inherently positive in following rules, and there's nothing inherently negative in deviating from them.

WE FAIL TO NOTICE THAT RULES HOLD US BACK

We are conformists not necessarily because we choose to be but because rules make us numb. Rules serve a purpose. Rules save us from the cognitive burden of reasoning and deliberating in every situation of our lives. They help us know how to respond without having to think much. They create predictability and familiarity, and for that exact reason we usually don't pay attention to how they shape the ways we think and behave.

Explicit Versus Implicit Rules

Rules range from authoritative edicts to traditions that mold how we customarily think and act. As with speed limits, we are often reminded of formal, authoritative rules enforced by the state. But authoritative rules aren't always codified, and they extend beyond the state. A set of parents might not let their teenage child pierce her ear, the Church demands the unmarried abstain from sexual relations, and the editors of academic journals won't let me publish my research if I use a very unorthodox method to collect and analyze data. Some of these rules may be publicly acknowledged, and some may go unspoken. Whether they are formalized or not, we are very aware of these kinds of rules because authorities constantly remind us of their existence and consistently enforce them.

In contrast to authoritative rules, our traditions conceal the most imperceptible social norms. Many are experientially invisible to us because, as French philosopher Pierre Bourdieu puts it, "what is essential goes without saying because it comes without saying." Rules silently guide us through our relational interactions. Many times it is good to go along and conform to them. But these rules aren't always desirable, and the more we are exposed and follow them, the more we fail to think of alternatives.

Think of how differently you behave with friends in a bar,

your colleagues in the workplace, your family at home, or strangers in a club. There are no explicit rules that say you have to be cheerful in a bar, clearheaded in the workplace, caring at home, and enthusiastic in a club. But you still kind of have to; after all, you don't want to appear too different from the crowd.

Context Clues

Social rules are rarely universal. Context matters. We can think of how they impact our lives through a sports analogy, as devised by Douglass North, an American economist and Nobel laureate renowned for this work on institutional change. There are "rules of the game," the ones that mold how the players think and act in each circumstance. In the NBA, for example, there are some formal, codified rules, like how long the game lasts, the number of players on each side, and what constitutes a foul—all of which are enforced by an authority, the referee. But there are other customary norms that exist both on and off the court, even though they aren't strictly imposed on the players or enforced by a referee. For example, in the 1991 Eastern Conference Finals, the Detroit Pistons players walked off the court with a few seconds left so they would not have to congratulate the winners, the Chicago Bulls. Decades later, basketball fans still remember this disrespect of the norms of sportsmanship.

Just like in sports, we are players in different kinds of games, depending on our respective contexts. Although most rules can be categorized as formal or informal and as authoritative or customary, they often come in bundles, shaping what we see, how we act, and what is expected from each of us. We very rarely make an active effort to parse the rules that shape our behaviors because bundles of rules allow us to quickly make sense of our surroundings. But even when we don't notice them, these rules silently shape what we find adequate, acceptable, feasible, or desirable. In other words, rules often become so normalized that we don't question their morality, and we fail to consider deviance as an option.

Rules give us cognitive shortcuts, which are mental rule-of-thumb tactics that help us to make decisions quickly without stopping to think much about our course of action. They reduce the cognitive load of decision-making, whether we want them to or not. That is why most of the time we don't intentionally choose to conform to them. It is also the reason deviance can be freeing. It allows you to think critically. Will you do what's expected, or will you carve out your own path?

RULES EXERT POWER

Conformity can be very harmful, and deviation is cognitively emancipating. But there's yet another reason to deviate from rules, one that I learned from French philosopher Michel Foucault. According to him, each period of history has its own "epistemes": dominant and often implicit knowledge assumptions that determine what is possible or acceptable as they influence how we make sense of the world, our values, our preferred methods, and our sense of order. These assumptions don't distinguish between true or false, but rather between what may or may not be considered scientific. This is important because these assumptions become scientifically justifiable ways of imposing social order and exerting power.

In his book *Madness and Civilization,* Foucault exposes how the scientific category of "mad" accommodated, stigmatized, and ostracized the poor, the sick, the unhoused, and many other marginalized members of French society in the eighteenth century. The "mad"—those who didn't fit the moral, ideological, or productive interests of the dominant classes—increasingly became the "other," the "incorrigible." This category included, for example, unruly students, workers who slacked off or revolted against their bosses, repeat offenders, prostitutes, and gamblers. The usual disciplinary apparatuses (schools, factories, churches, and the like) didn't successfully get them into line. By claiming "scientific neutrality," Foucault says, modern medical treatments for insanity concealed powerful instruments of social control to get rid of the undesirables. Scientific knowledge therefore justifies rules that exert power and impose discipline upon others.

Foucault's contributions may sound abstract, so let's look at a historical example. In 1958, Clennon King Jr., a professor at Alcorn State University in Jackson, Mississippi, was forcibly committed to a mental asylum in the United States after applying to graduate school at the University of Mississippi: the judge ruled that a Black person must be "insane" to believe he could be admitted to the university. King's ongoing fight for civil rights, including his candidacy for the US presidency, earned him the nickname "the Black Don Quixote." Not only was King othered by a knowledge assumption that was imposed on him, but his attempt to deviate from it, to challenge the rules that excluded him, was ridiculed.

These aren't isolated cases; the "maddening of others" is much more pervasive than many of us think. Consider, for example, how calling women "crazy" or "hysterical" minimizes their frustrations and disagreements, silencing or shaming them. Marginalizing others based on socially accepted knowledge assumptions is a common and subtle way to impose order and control. "Othering" elevates the standing of the ones in power in any social context, enabling them to reap benefits and to take the moral high ground in justifying power imbalances with "scientific neutrality."

This doesn't mean that "mad" people don't exist. The problem Foucault raises isn't about whether a scientific observation is true or false, but rather that these types of knowledge assumptions both come from and become sources of power. While they help us by classifying and imposing order on the world, they also create and reinforce social hierarchies that reflect existing privileged status and inequity. This pattern enables people with credibility and authority to turn assumptions into rules that benefit themselves more than they benefit other groups, and sometimes to benefit themselves by taking away from other groups.

"Madness" isn't the only label used to delegitimize attempts to challenge power structures. You may have heard of neoliberal economists who give primacy to free-market capitalism and are often associated with policies of economic liberalization, including deregulation and austerity in government spending. They defend the "rules of the market" as the only way to grow and prosper: the "invisible hand" regulates the market to our benefit. State interference can only harm social well-being, they say. But when assumptions like the "rules of the market" are treated as unquestionable truisms, we may forget to ask ourselves: Why do these rules exist? Who benefits from them?

Because, according to these economists and the dominant social tropes, the market is all knowing and self-calibrating, interference is seen as illegitimate or even harmful. If we take what they say at face value, however, we fail to notice how power is exerted through this scientific rule. Think for a second: Who, in fact, benefits from treating laissez-faire economic policies as inevitable in a world where the richest twenty-six individuals hold wealth equivalent to that of the poorest 3.8 billion?

Even when we want to challenge scientific rules, we struggle to find opportunities for deviation. Because the values and interests of dominant groups come disguised as scientifically neutral facts, we are often patronized when we diverge. For example, if you want to dispute economic policies of austerity on the basis of evidence of rising income inequality, prepare yourself for admonitions about the "rules of the market" that govern "how the economy works."

When assumptions become rules, power is exercised subtly but effectively. The "othered" are left with a feeling of powerlessness and resignation. That's why it is important to deconstruct knowledge assumptions and reveal the values and interests that they obscure. Only then can we fight against disenfranchisement and actively engage in defiance against injustice.

BLAMING DEVIANTS OFTEN DOES MORE HARM THAN GOOD

Now that we have gone over how rules are systems that benefit those in power and not necessarily truths that keep us safe, should we blame the deviants who decide not to conform?

Discipline and Punish

Before talking about what we *should* do, let's first look at what we *already* do—again, with help from Foucault. In *Discipline and Punish*, he examines how prisons became the most conventional mechanism of social control. The prison system gained traction after the Enlightenment (the same period that gave us the social contract), when imprisonment was considered a reformist alternative to public torture and execution. Prisons supposedly represented a more humanitarian way of maintaining order and guaranteeing social well-being.

Foucault claims that imprisonment is not only a gentler way to impose order and discipline but also more effective. In the Middle Ages, the aim of punishment was to promote fear among potential wrongdoers and to express the supreme authority of rulers. The problem was that rulers sometimes faced pushback, and convicts could become heroes or martyrs, just as rulers and executioners could come to be seen as the bad guys. Rulers can avoid that risk by substituting public execution with incarceration because prison isn't seen as purposefully cruel. Instead of seeing convicts crying, bleeding, and begging for mercy in an open square, we lock them up where we can't see them. They are subjected to a gradual process of dehumanization.

According to Foucault, the carceral disciplinary method is so effective that it has expanded to other social arenas, like hospitals, schools, and factories. In the present day, reproducible skills, movements, timing, speed, and surveillance discipline us much more than brute force: students must learn to behave in a classroom, workers must obey their managers, and the sick must follow their doctors' orders. In other words, we are told where we need to be, are always monitored, and are relentlessly subjugated to the commandments of professional authority.

Furthermore, no one can be named and blamed if things go wrong. That's how prisons became a very effective means of exerting disciplinary power: we blame individuals for crimes, but we can't blame individuals for punishment. Who's responsible and who's held accountable in the case of a wrongful conviction? We may try to accuse the judge, the police, the witness, the lawyer, the victim, the forensic methods, or even the president. But in contrast to when an execution is ordered by a ruler, we can't point at one person who is responsible for wrongfully putting a person in jail.

But here's where our incoherence lies. Most of us would morally agree that we can't simply blame judges for wrongful convictions. So why do we think there should be a straightforward explanation or approach that blames criminality solely on individuals? If we understand criminality as a complex problem, we should also understand that it can't be explained exclusively by individuals' wrongdoings.

Marginalized

In the same way that we can no longer think of conformity as the only option, I don't believe that individuals are always the cause of society's ills. We often blame individuals when they violate the law, without noticing that they may have been following a different set of rules that are not codified in legal documents but nevertheless dictate what is acceptable, desirable, and viable in their respective contexts.

We tend to think of criminals as deviants who threaten social life, who violate the social contract. After all, we have all seen blockbusters about psychopaths: "I ate his liver with some fava beans and a nice Chianti," said Dr. Hannibal Lecter in *The Silence of the Lambs*. These types of movies are so memorable and fascinating that we fail to see how statistically insignificant psychopaths really are. These aren't the kinds of people we actually punish for deviance, says prison scholar and activist Professor Ruth Wilson Gilmore. With statistics on carceral demographics, her book *Golden Gulag* shows that jails aren't packed with those who stand out, who couldn't contain their animal instincts, but rather with the ones who were left behind.

In environments where criminal activity is the norm, breaking the law doesn't necessarily make you deviant. Counterintuitively, many people in prison actually conformed to some "rules of the game," just not the ones enforced by the criminal justice system. Mafiosi, gangsters, and drug dealers all have codes of conduct. Disloyalty, for example, can be ranked as worse than committing murder. Members of criminal groups abide by a set of rules on which they organize themselves to intentionally deviate from state laws. They conform and deviate simultaneously to different sets of rules. This is why conformity, deviance, and morality have to be put into context.

Blaming individuals for complex problems isn't only inaccurate; it diverts our attention and efforts to individuals instead of to the causes that brought about the problems in the first place. This is counterproductive and often creates a self-reinforcing practice that does more harm than good. The more we blame individual deviants, the more we ignore the root causes of our problems. When we move away from individual blame, we observe that the root causes of our problems reside in all sorts of rules—formal or informal, authoritative or customary—that shape how we think and act and what society expects of us. That is why we are better off examining and defying the "rules of the game" instead of blaming the players. It isn't only fairer; it is also much more effective.

DISOBEDIENCE ≠ DEVIANCE

Humans are conformists, but that doesn't mean we are naïve or blindly rule abiding. In order to recognize the contours of deviance, we have to understand that disobedience isn't the opposite of conformity. Disobedience blatantly antagonizes the establishment, and the establishment almost always retaliates. Deviance, on the other hand, is trickier. Like many of the workarounds we discussed in Part I, deviance entails unconventional approaches that use parts of the status quo that work (as intended or not) in order to change the parts that don't.

Once I heard a story about a well-liked high school chemistry teacher who allowed his students to bring a piece of standard printer paper to an open-book test. "Whatever you can fit on an 8.5-by-11-inch page you can use to help you during the exam," he told his students. Some forgot and showed up to the exam empty-handed. Most took advantage of the situation and filled a page with as many formulas as they could. A few thought they wouldn't be caught if they used slightly larger sheets. Whose naked eye could discern the difference of a few millimeters? But the teacher anticipated this type of disobedience and measured each student's page, ripping up and throwing away any pages that were too large. One student stood out when she arrived to take the exam with an entirely blank 8.5-by-11-inch page. She then placed the paper on the floor and asked her teacher to stand on it for the duration of the test. Impressed by her ingenuity, the teacher acquiesced and quietly answered her questions. I don't know if the story is true (I suspect it isn't), but it perfectly encapsulates the attentive, inquisitive, and slightly cheeky disposition that characterizes deviant—as opposed to disobedient—approaches.

Now we will take a closer look at the differences between disobedience and deviance through examples of cheating, so I can persuade you to look more sympathetically at the deviant attitude.

The Cost of Deception

You may recollect how Lance Armstrong fell from grace. With his reputation tarnished and stripped of his seven Tour de France titles, he was named a "serial cheat" by the US Anti-Doping Agency and held accountable for what has become known as one of the most sophisticated doping programs that any sport has ever seen. Although many see him as an outlier, cheating isn't that rare. The first large-scale survey on cheating, published in 1964, reported data from students at ninety-nine US colleges and revealed that three-fourths of students had engaged in one or more incidents of academic dishonesty.

Cheating, however, doesn't just happen at the front of the race or in the back of the classroom. A study published in *Nature* in 2005 found that a third of scientists engaged in questionable research practices, including misconduct like falsifying data and changing the results to please funding agencies. Many disobey the rules on methodological rigor and transparency, but only a few get caught. The most tragicomical case I know of is that of Harvard professor Marc Hauser, an American evolutionary biologist. The tragic part of his story is that he was found guilty of fabricating data, manipulating experimental results, and incorrectly describing how studies were conducted. The comedy is that over a decade before getting caught, he published an article with this title: "Cost of Deception: Cheaters Are Punished in Rhesus Monkeys."

Why is disobedience so common? And, more important, under what circumstances does it occur? I will answer these questions, but not just yet. First, let's try a thought experiment.

Are You a Cheater?

Suppose you're taking an important final exam in college, competing against thousands of other students for a prestigious fellowship. Would you cheat?

No? Wait. What if you heard from a colleague that the faculty overlooks cheating? Apparently, professors can't stand the long bureaucratic university procedures required to punish cheating, so they avoid "catching it" at all costs. Would you cheat now that you know the rules are the same but so loosely enforced?

Still no? Now you take a quick scan of the room and see your competitors cheating because they also know it will go unpunished. If you don't cheat, you would be at a disadvantage. Does that trigger the cheater in you?

Suddenly, cheating has become more morally justifiable, right? As nicely put by an influential study in behavioral economics, "People behave dishonestly enough to profit but honestly enough to delude themselves of their own integrity." We are all a bit disobedient as long as we don't stand out too much from the crowd.

Deviance > Disobedience

That's why it's so important to distinguish deviance, the opposite of conformity, from disobedience, the opposite of obedience. We are conformers to the de facto "rules of the game": disobeying rules feels morally acceptable when it levels the playing field. That explains why when we are confronted with our mischief, our responses resemble those of defensive children: "But, Mom, *everybody* else does it!" We justify our disobedience by mentioning our conformity with the crowd.

Try to reflect on your everyday acts of mischief—it can't be too difficult to pinpoint some situations where you think it's reasonable to disobey. Personally, I don't wait for the green pedestrian figure every time I cross the street in Brazil. But when I lived in Germany, I felt pressured to wait with the crowd because no one else crossed. Both cases show how I conform, but in Brazil I simultaneously conform and disobey. With this nuanced view we realize that disobedience is deviant only if it stands out from what is seen as ordinary or the standard practice in our respective contexts.

So here are two big reasons why you should look at deviance more sympathetically. First, as opposed to disobedience, deviance is transformative. It involves critical thinking and challenges the status quo. Second, while disobedience makes you liable for breaking rules, deviance doesn't have to be hostile—just think of how the many workarounds in Part I showed that it is possible to stand out from the crowd without breaking rules.

Now that I have convinced you of the value of a deviant attitude, let's look at different approaches to deviance and how workarounds enable us to deviate more effectively and gracefully than is possible with the other approaches.

APPROACHES TO DEVIANCE

Rules are so insidious that they become part of our thoughts and identities. We conform because we become numb to them. But if conformity isn't the great panacea we expected, what do we do? How can we escape from a system of rules that benefits those in power, leads us to misdiagnose our problems, and punishes us when we disobey?

When we find ourselves trapped in an unfair system of rules, deviance provides a way out. It enables us to address our needs and to attempt to change the status quo. Because deviants stand out from the crowd, the common belief is that being deviant depends only on personal traits. Fortunately, deviance isn't a case of "either you have it or you don't." It's a learned attitude much more than an innate talent.

I generally think there are three key approaches to deviance: confrontation, negotiation, and workarounds. Each strategy has its own strengths and weaknesses, but only one—the workaround—is accessible, yields quick returns, and minimizes the consequences of failure.

The Three Approaches to Deviance

To unleash our deviance potential, we have to understand the three different approaches to standing out from the crowd; some we may be prone to employ, and others may scare us off.

CONFRONTATION

A confrontational approach often entails breaking rules and always means clashes with dominant power structures.

NEGOTIATION

We can deviate by engaging in long-term negotiation, during which actors slowly organize themselves and put constant pressure on authority figures to legitimize changes in the system of rules.

WORKAROUND

Through workarounds, we can promptly get things done and defy the status quo without directly antagonizing rule enforcers.

There's no best method: there's the most adequate depending on your goals, resources, and circumstances. The first two are much trickier to pursue than workarounds. So let's compare each of them with the workaround.

Confrontation Versus the Workaround

Fear of punishment often holds us back from openly breaking rules. Think of how Dr. Martin Luther King Jr. confronted the dominant rules through civil disobedience: he was charged for violating many criminal code provisions, like disturbing the peace, marching without a permit, trespassing, engaging in criminal libel, and conspiracy. These rule-breaking activities were stepping-stones along the way to changing discriminatory laws in the United States, but they came at a cost. In his "Letter from Birmingham Jail," he noted, "One who breaks an unjust law must do so openly, lovingly, and with a willingness to accept the penalty . . . I submit that an individual who breaks a law that conscience tells him is unjust, and who willingly accepts the penalty of imprisonment in order to arouse the conscience of the community over its injustice, is in reality expressing the highest respect for law." By being punished for breaking an unjust rule, the transgressor becomes living evidence of the injustice, possibly motivating others to join the cause and pursue change.

Not everyone has Dr. King's serenity and willpower to "accept the penalty" of imprisonment. We all know that if we break rules we risk punishment and even other forms of reprisal—like what happened to Dr. King, who not only landed in jail but was later assassinated. The stakes of overt rule breaking are too high for most of us.

As opposed to rule breaking, workarounds provide a low-stakes alternative for deviance. This is particularly powerful because, as Rebecca Gomperts—one of the mavericks whose story you read in Part I—told me, "When people move beyond the fear of backlash, they can do actually much more than they were made to believe." She was openly defiant of restrictive abortion laws and the interests of powerful conservative groups. But because she worked around rules instead of breaking them, she wasn't legally liable for her deviance. From her I learned that workarounds can be opportunities to deviate without exposing ourselves to the kinds of risks that could paralyze us.

Negotiation Versus the Workaround

The second approach, anchored in negotiation and mobilization, is fairly low-risk. Its main limitation is that in order to be successful, it almost always eventually needs support from within power structures. Think of how social movements, despite exerting pressure for much-needed change, rarely have a big impact if they are not endorsed by people who occupy positions of power, like legislators, judges, and businesspeople. Gaining support, mobilizing, and coordinating players to change rules takes time, resources, and access to dominant power structures.

As American jurist and Harvard law professor Paul Freund put it: "The Court should never be influenced by the weather of the day, but inevitably they will be influenced by the climate of the era." Though changes in rules (and their interpretation) may reflect the climate of an era, if you're concerned about today's rain and don't want to get drenched, you may want to work around these rules instead.

The Workaround Advantage

Workarounds are attainable, lower-risk options for deviance and can produce potentially outsized payoffs. Just because workarounds require less effort than negotiation and confrontation doesn't make them less valuable. After all, there's no shame in enjoying low-hanging fruit. It may be just as nourishing as fruit from higher up in the tree, and you don't risk harming yourself in your quest for higher fruit.

But it's not only about getting good enough results with minimal fuss. As we've learned from scrappy organizations deviating from rules in many contexts, we don't always have to play by the rules to change them.

Workarounds often expand the realm of possibilities as they increase the range of what can happen next. This is because workarounds change how we interpret, judge, and respond to the status quo, thus offering new opportunities that can be pursued by other like-minded would-be deviants. Think of how RBG employed a workaround to create the precedent of a ruling based on sex discrimination, later leveraged by many lawyers and activists, or how Gomperts built momentum for changes to Portuguese legislation on abortion, which benefited pro-choice grassroots movements and policymakers. These workarounds not only promptly addressed time-sensitive issues; they also planted seeds for longer-term structural change.

6

The Workaround Mindset

Growing up in Brazil, I was exposed to my fair share of Catholic and Yoruba spiritual practices. Because of the transatlantic slave trade, descendants of the Yoruba—one of the largest ethnic groups in West Africa, inhabiting countries like Nigeria, Benin, and Togo—have an important presence in Brazil, Cuba, and the United States, and some members of the Catholic Church remain less than pleased with the persistence of their traditions and beliefs. In fact, some Catholic leaders have gone so far as to misrepresent Eshu, a sort of divine trickster who both blurs and illuminates reality in Yoruba theology, as the devil.

As a teenager I went to a Catholic school and had fun undermining authority figures in the Church just for the sake of rebelling. It wasn't until I started thinking more seriously about the ambiguity and flexibility of workarounds that I considered the lessons Eshu offers. Eshu definitely isn't the devil, but he isn't unequivocally benevolent either. He can both confuse and instruct us because he occupies a special place in Yoruba theology. In this belief system, 401 powers of the right, called *orisha*, act as protectors and enablers of humankind; 201 powers of the left, the *ajogun*, present humans with challenges and obstacles.

As humans, we often face this apparent duality between what constrains and what enables us. But Eshu, in contrast to all other deities, is both an *orisha* and the leader of the *ajogun*: he's the only one who muddles through this seeming opposition. Through his apparent trickery Eshu challenges what we take for granted and helps us discover new perspectives and possibilities.

This instructive bafflement is why the Yoruba consider him the god of change, chance, and uncertainty. He confuses us in order to demonstrate that our problems are often difficult to parse, and we can't always trust what seems natural or obvious. If we see too much, we may feel paralyzed or numb; if we see too little, we may become disoriented and even make things worse.

The workaround approach takes Eshu's lessons to heart. I first connected computer hackers to the mischievous deity because they are often described as tricksters, illuminating secret depths while keeping themselves out of sight. After engaging more closely with dozens of workarounds I realized that the resemblance goes beyond that. The protagonists of the cases profiled in Part I didn't aim to see too much: they embraced complexity. Their approaches may seem confusing or even clumsy at first, but they made possible new approaches that were previously imperceptible.

In this chapter I challenge the conventional wisdom that the best course of action is always to understand the full picture and remove visible obstacles. The three principles I explore here—recognizing the limits of your knowledge, adjusting lenses, and thinking like an outsider—will help you embrace complexity and find opportunities for workarounds. We'll conclude by exploring how the workaround mindset is well suited for complex situations.

THE KNOWN, THE KNOWN UNKNOWN, AND THE UNKNOWN

Our knowledge can curse us: it shapes our reasoning, personal development, the avenues we identify and pursue, and how we communicate with others. Once we know something, we can't unknow it—and it becomes hard to imagine what it is like not to know it. But we can at least appreciate that we don't know everything and make an active effort to deconstruct what we think we do know.

The Benefit of the Doubt

An old Yoruba tale teaches us a lesson about the dangers of relying too much on what we think we know. It illustrates how Eshu confuses us and challenges our knowledge of and ideas about reality. In this story, two best friends are tilling their respective fields, which lie across a road from each other. Eshu, dressed on his right side in black and on his left side in red, briskly walks down the road separating the properties. When Eshu disappears beyond the fields, one of the buddies asks, "Did you see the stranger dressed in red?" and the other replies that he saw the stranger in black, not red. The discussion escalates and becomes heated, each man calling the other a liar. Only when Eshu reappears do the friends realize that they were both right.

This story illustrates how incomplete information is only part of the challenge—we also need to take into account how we process different and partial stories as if they were complete. Neither of the two friends knows the whole story, but each thinks he does, and that is what creates tension. Overconfidence is misleading, and, to teach us this lesson, Eshu only has to shed light on the "contradictory certitudes": the different (and often incompatible) diagnoses of reality.

There are many fragments of a story—some people may use a fragment to jump to a conclusion; others may try to assemble the fragments in different ways. The workarounds you've read about in Part I were implemented by people who weren't obsessed with what they knew. Instead of stubbornly rushing into conclusive answers, they benefited from doubt: they tried to look at things from different angles, to experiment with unconventional approaches, and to learn from people who had other points of view.

Decision-Making in an Unsettled World

Unfortunately, even when we make an active effort to learn more, we often tend to reinforce the same well-worn assumptions. Management models that influence decision-making in organizations of all sizes and sectors are habitually built on the conjecture that formal analysis helps organizations make better decisions. The problem is not necessarily the accuracy of the conclusions of analysis, but the assumptions that pass unquestioned and silently channel how analysts diagnose the situation.

Working as a consultant for large companies, for example, I realized how studies frequently become ammunition in battles that managers have already designed: higher-ups predetermine the battlefield and the target, so the expert assessments just help them justify and execute the fight. Armed with reports from external consultants, top managers then try to persuade others in the company, imposing a dominant story on the interested parties and assigning roles for implementing the recommendations. The problem is that many consultants don't challenge clients' assumptions. Instead they validate and expand on what is known, based on information provided by the managers who hired them. Were these consultants to embrace complexity, they would investigate with less depth and more breadth. They would question what the top managers assume to be facts, values, and objectives, possibly identifying conflicting views or pointing out other battlegrounds that may pass unnoticed.

Consulting for intergovernmental organizations is a bit different. Analysts who do this work often use data to accommodate everything: conflicting assumptions, goals, and views on who is meant to take the lead. But if the scope grows too broad, the story becomes clunky and unhelpful. Here we are better off embracing what the poet John Keats called "negative capability," or what the Heath brothers called "forced prioritization": appreciate the nuances of multiple perspectives, but don't linger there too long. Think of how Shakespeare introduces characters without revealing their background and presents issues with no clear answer or solution. Because he recognizes that the world is unsettled and that a story will never be "complete," the playwright allows readers to explore different angles and imagine how a story could come to any number of different conclusions. That's why Portia is such a compelling character: through her inventive solution she defies expectations and slyly encourages the audience to do the same.

Making the Strange Familiar and the
Familiar Strange

So how can we challenge what we know and thereby develop a workaround mindset? My answer is a crude one: we have to embrace ambiguity. We must recognize that we make decisions without having the full picture and that we are better off pondering (and defying) our assumptions than thoughtlessly building on them. The challenges are both to turn our "unknown unknowns" into "known unknowns" that we can explore and to deconstruct our assumptions about what we know so we can then recombine fragments that we might never otherwise see as belonging together.

To practice deconstructing and reconstructing our knowledge, we can take inspiration from anthropologists who say that their aim is to "make the strange familiar and the familiar strange." Think of how the ColaLife workaround stemmed from asking, "Why does Coca-Cola seem to get everywhere in developing countries, yet lifesaving medicines don't?" People in remote regions of low-income countries know they can find Coca-Cola everywhere, but Jane and Simon Berry made this familiar fact strange when they connected the presence of something as superfluous as soda with something as seemingly unrelated but as important as medicine. Conversely, consider how Ruth Bader Ginsburg made the strange familiar when she focused on a man as the victim of sex-based discrimination. Some people didn't believe that sex-based discrimination existed, but by showing how a man could suffer from this type of discrimination she made a pivotal case for it.

By making both the strange familiar and the familiar strange, we are better equipped to navigate between the two extremes of management strategies: the arbitrary and ill-conceived approaches that move forward in the absence of sufficient fact-finding and analysis ("extinction by instinct") and those that focus on too much ("paralysis by analysis"). If you can identify knowledge gaps without falling into them, you'll be better prepared to think creatively and laterally.

THE LIMITS OF YOUR PERCEPTION

You're visiting the Louvre Museum in Paris. First you stop to see Leonardo da Vinci's *Mona Lisa*—so cliché! At first glance you are surprised to think that the painting is small and a bit underwhelming, but then you focus on her eyes: there's something spine-tingling about how she looks at you. Your impulse is to stare at her and move sideways, noting that her eyes follow you.

It's too crowded, though, so you walk to an adjacent room and stop to admire Delacroix's *Liberty Leading the People*. There's so much in it! First you look at the flag: it seems to be moving; it was probably windy that day. The bare-chested woman holding it seems so powerful. Does she represent liberty? What does her half nudity mean? Then you look at the others around her: the bodies, the man on his knees—is he begging for mercy or showing his devotion to the woman? You observe that the people holding guns are odd, too. Some are dressed like noblemen, others like peasants. Does it mean liberty is worth fighting for regardless of social class? You feel overwhelmed by the painting's many nuances.

You leave the Louvre and head to the Musée de l'Orangerie. Your first stop: Monet's water lilies. When you walk up close to the painting you see only blurry daubs of color. You step back and you can then understand the patterns and shapes; now the painting makes sense. The composition inspires a sense of serenity, and you reflect on how proximity changes what you see in Monet's painting, but not in Escher's famous lithograph *Relativity*. You recall studying it in mathematics in high school and finding it both disturbing and intriguing. Two people use the same stairway in the same direction on the same side, but one seems to be descending and the other ascending. You remember how you tried looking at the image from different angles and how turning it led to different interpretations.

When we analyze a problem, our instinct is usually to get a fuller, more detailed picture, but *what* we see depends on *how* we see it. Similar to how we look at and interact with art, playing with our proximity and angle can help us revisit and reinterpret our surroundings. It's a little like taking a good photograph in that you can experiment with what will be in your frame by adjusting the settings on your camera.

The Focus

In photography your subject provides different opportunities and constraints for the more technical aspects of making the picture look good: taking a picture of a flower is very different from taking a picture of the whole landscape. Both subjects can make for good photos, but they'll convey different information. Of course, you don't have to take only one or the other—you can play with both and see what suits your preference.

If you start by focusing on the individual flower, you may find details and nuances you missed before. Maybe you notice a labyrinth of deep-scarlet veins on the petals; maybe the powdery flecks of pollen catch your eye. You begin to visually break the flower down into its components, finding intriguing facets that someone looking at the flower as a whole—let alone the entire landscape—would miss. Taking this type of narrow focus when conceiving a workaround might help you to find possibilities that would be invisible if you approached an entire system head-on. That's the tactic that Women on Waves used: rather than directly combating abortion bans in one country, the group focused on legislation in another and used the minutiae of maritime law to circumvent restrictions.

On the other hand, sometimes looking at the entire land-scape is beneficial. If you spend all your time looking at a single flower you might miss how the slopes of the hills have a surpris-ing rhythm or how the colors of the meadow contrast with the slowly darkening sky. Sometimes understanding the bigger pic-ture enables you to use it to your advantage; that's the beauty of piggybacking. If healthcare experts focused only on providing a single micronutrient in a targeted way, they might get bogged down in figuring out how to get a specific population to take, for example, an iron supplement. How would they identify the target population? How would they distribute the supplements? How could they ensure that the right people were actually taking the supplement at the right time? Examining the entire breadth of consumption patterns and adding the micronutrient to critical foodstuffs has achieved a breathtakingly successful outcome at a fraction of the cost and hassle.

Exposure

Taking a good photo is as much about what's in the frame as how the camera captures it. Let too little light in through the lens and your image will be dark and indiscernible, but let in too much light and it will be overexposed and equally useless. The exposure of your photograph is determined by the interaction of three components—ISO, aperture, and shutter speed—and using each of them, we can see and interpret problems in different ways. Just remember that there's no single correct way to take a photograph (even leaving the camera on the "auto" setting isn't wrong!), and experimentation is key. But knowing a little more about what each of the three controls does can help you play around and take different photos of the same subject.

ISO, which deals with light sensitivity and how saturated or grainy an image will be, can help us to think about our resources. We often assume that a more detailed picture is better, just as we assume that more—and more specialized—resources will always help us deal with our problems. What if instead we thought a little more like a hacker, working only with the materials we have immediately at hand? If we embrace working with what we have rather than what we want, we can still start addressing pressing challenges with next-best approaches. That's how biscuit making came to be crucial to teaching kids reading and basic arithmetic.

The second component, aperture, measures how wide the opening of a camera lens is and one of its effects is that it dictates the depth of the field: letting in less light means the image should be in focus throughout, whereas letting in more will lead to a blurrier background. Again, conventional wisdom would have us believe that the more we have in focus, the better we can understand a problem, but that's not always the case. In photography, having too much to focus on can lead to an overwhelming and unpleasant image; in addressing complex challenges, it can lead to "paralysis by analysis." As we've seen with public urination in India, sometimes a small stopgap measure (like individual wall owners installing plaques depicting gods) is a viable way to deter a behavior that full state-led interventions have failed to eliminate.

Shutter speed is how long your film is exposed to light. If you set a fast shutter speed and don't let a lot of light in, you'll be able to distill motion into a clear image; if you use a slower shutter speed and let in lots of light, motion will show up as blurry. We tend to think that the more directly we can control and confront a problem, the better we can solve it, but sometimes the "blur" can convey more information. Shutter speed reminds us that our interventions can be quick and snappy (like transferring money between a network of individuals to circumvent bank fees) or help us see beyond conventional boundaries (like building twin housing that enables Dalits and non-Dalits to interact).

Play with the Settings

Just as ISO, aperture, and shutter speed are components of capturing an image, rethinking our resources, focus, and scope is a way to emphasize different aspects of a phenomenon. To para-phrase French philosopher Gilles Deleuze and French psychoanalyst Félix Guattari, a brick can build a courthouse or be thrown through the window—the circumstances matter! By playing with our subjects and "settings," we can highlight different aspects of a given situation, allowing us to reinterpret and re-engage with it.

I encourage you to use these strategies as you would fiddle with the settings on a digital camera: curiously, playfully, and frequently. Two benefits of a digital camera are the memory space and the immediate feedback. Don't feel confined to the couple dozen shots you'd get on a roll of film—take hundreds of pictures. You don't have to wait to find out if you're happy with the camera settings until you develop the photos—glance at the digital preview and adjust accordingly. We are better off appreciating and exploring "known unknowns" than fixating on the little that we do know.

THE POWER OF THE OUTSIDER

Every six months Anil Gupta, social entrepreneur and professor at the Indian Institute of Management Ahmedabad, leads a one-week walk that covers approximately 155 miles, passing through rural districts in India that are deprived of regular transport connectivity. Gupta, tall, bearded, and always dressed in white, has an engaging smile and a genuine interest in what the villagers have to say. He shows a special appreciation for the villages' oddballs. This walk is called *Shodhyatra*, which is Sanskrit for "a walk to find knowledge." In these explorations Anil and his team have uncovered and documented over 160,000 inventive products and practices created by the minds of people at the margins—and these, Anil asserts, "aren't marginal minds."

There is something special, intriguing, and powerful about outsiders like Anil who challenge political, economic, and social conventions. Their vantage point enables them to see things differently than insiders who are too accustomed to a certain way of doing things. As one hacker put it, "Hacks don't come from people who have been faced with the problem every day because they are sort of numb to it." Most experts' cognitive thermostat is set to a low simmer of anticipation: they live in the near-future tense, always expecting what comes next. On the one hand, this keeps them focused. On the other hand, it limits their ability to see beyond conventional approaches.

Insider Versus Outsider

The expert's problem is that they rely too much on what they know—in other words, they become numb to different ways of interpreting and acting in situations that are all too familiar to them. The upside is that insiders are rarely surprised, but the downside is that they are rarely surprised. Alternatively, an outsider who is just learning something new can approach old problems from new angles. For example, when children naively spout funny and unexpected observations—like "Why can't it be Monday, Tuesday, Saturday, Sunday, Wednesday, Thursday, Saturday, and Sunday?"—they challenge adults' ingrained and undisputed conventions, thus catching us off guard.

When outsiders—or people lacking expertise—begin making sense of something new, they often tinker with the novel tools and concepts, sometimes combining and reconfiguring them in ways that experts find surprising, unintuitive, or even counterproductive. Though their ideas may sometimes seem absurd, outsiders have the freedom to think and act in ways that insiders can't. Outsiders' fresh perspectives can prove revolutionary. Remember how Portia outwitted Shylock? She was far from a professional lawyer or accountant, but she didn't need to be an expert to beat the system.

Also, as opposed to insiders, outsiders tend to have weaker feelings of ownership toward the new challenges and concepts they encounter. Ownership is more than a title. In the words of novelist John Steinbeck, "That's what makes it ours—being born on it, working it, dying on it. That makes ownership, not a paper with numbers on it." Behavioral economists have shown that our feelings of ownership apply to assets, tools, jobs, and organizations, in addition to everything else we engage with closely, like our points of view. Once we take ownership of an idea or even a problem, we become protective of it, and we have trouble letting it go. Being an outsider means harboring fewer or weaker protective instincts, which promotes flexibility. The founders of TransferWise succeeded *because* they weren't working within a formal banking institution. Their outsider status afforded them creativity, flexibility, and the ability to challenge the status quo.

The Inner Outsider

We can use different tactics to nurture our "inner outsider," both personally and organizationally. If we learn to value generalist knowledge, we can bring a wide breadth of experience to our hyperspecialized world by employing lateral thinking. Rather than unduly prizing the expertise of those who automatically address problems with pre-existing strategies, we can benefit from applying knowledge from one domain to a different context. Of course, not every approach or piece of information is transferable, but when this strategy succeeds the impact can be transformative. In his best-selling book *Range*, investigative reporter David Epstein tells persuasive stories about people like Roger Federer, J. K. Rowling, Vincent van Gogh, and Tu Youyou (the first Chinese national to win a Nobel Prize in Physiology or Medicine and the first female from the People's Republic of China to receive a Nobel Prize) who challenged the mantra that success requires early and narrow specialization. They all were generalists who flourished in complex environments where patterns were hard to discern and there were many known unknowns.

Another approach is to be nosy. In our stratified society, fairly clear boundaries demarcate where we do and do not belong. Challenging these laws or conventions can generate fresh perspectives, especially when we gain access to "restricted" areas. Organizations including Google, Facebook, Goldman Sachs, Mastercard, Tesla, and even the US Department of Defense actually pay computer hackers to try to break into their systems to find and report whatever vulnerabilities they come across; these are often referred to as "bug bounty programs." Hackers discover what insiders (companies' programmers and cybersecurity experts) are numb to or overlook. Craigslist may not have appreciated Airbnb's early marketing strategy, but the tale demonstrates how underdogs can effectively exploit vulnerabilities by sniffing around where polite society would tell them not to.

Outsiders on the Inside

Companies often try to find a balance between exploiting existing expertise and exploring new opportunities that require fresh eyes. Organizations—especially larger and more regimented ones—have adopted different approaches to encourage fresh perspectives without fully giving up on insiders' expertise. In Japan, "job rotation" schemes have become very common. In these programs, employees move between different fields within the same company. Once an employee gets too comfortable in their first position in, say, sales, they go to marketing, then to operations, then to finance, and then back to sales. These rotating employees become sort of nonradical outsiders, knowledgeable about the business but able to promote cross-fertilization between its silos. Companies sometimes hire consultants for similar reasons: in some circumstances, consultants are meant to explore what full-time employees overlook.

Likewise, companies put in effort to hire historically marginalized groups not only to create an equitable work environment but also because a diverse workforce makes possible perspectives that are not always considered by white cisgender heterosexual men. If you've watched the TV show *Mad Men*, you may have gotten an idea of how the advertising industry changed as more women and Black people were hired. The white male advertising executives didn't know that they didn't know about the consumption aspirations of some market segments. The show reminds us that lived experiences that all too often are ignored—and the privileged experiences that all too often go unquestioned—profoundly impact what we see and how we think.

Outsiders—or those who can adopt outsider perspectives—tend to be good at coming up with workarounds because they know that they don't know and aren't afraid to make unconventional suggestions. Think of the many scrappy organizations in Part I that worked from the fringes of power structures: they didn't start from the assumptions that come with familiarity. The citizens of Troy expected to defend their city from behind their wall, a strategy that had been serving them well. That, presumably, is why the Greeks—literally outsiders—had to conduct such an unusual operation to gain entry to the city. The gambit paid off, and the concept of a Trojan horse remains a vivid testament to creativity and deviousness millennia later.

COMPLEX, NOT COMPLICATED

The only way to adopt the workaround mindset is through challenging your past convictions and embracing ambivalence and doubt. In hazy situations, the best option is to search for piecemeal improvements that may illuminate new possibilities—and for that we have to question what we know and what and how we see so we can explore unconventional approaches to our problems.

Computer hackers excel in these situations because they focus on what they call "essential complexity," or the key properties of the beast they're trying to beat. They try to strip away the "accidental complexity," or the unintentional challenges that we often take for granted but that can distract us from the task at hand. Hackers circumnavigate those inessential or "accidental" obstacles, often as simply as possible, and this is why workarounds are at the core of the hacker approach.

Simple is good, and workarounds rely on that. Yet when I talk about my research to managers and students I am frequently met with skepticism when I explain why simplicity often excels in complex situations. What the skeptics fail to notice at first glance is that complicated is different from complex! Complex situations have no clear cause-and-effect relationships; they may rely on self-reinforcing behaviors, be contentious or disputed, and the myriad interpretations they spawn might mean that they have no single solution at all. Complicated approaches rely on knowing too much and trying to contend with every aspect of an issue. Unfortunately, the more components you add to your intervention, the higher the chances that something will go wrong. In the words of computer hackers, complicated solutions add a lot of accidental complexity.

If we believe that every complex problem requires a complicated solution, we wind up trying to tackle our obstacles head-on and fail to parse essential complexity from the accidental. Some of the world's toughest challenges are complex because they are constantly evolving and intertwined, and would-be solvers who try to address every facet are bound to come up short.

Workarounds are well suited to complex situations because they embrace uncertainty and imperfection and address our most urgent needs while exploring otherwise invisible pathways toward more robust alternatives. I encourage you to follow Eshu's approach. When Shango, the god of thunder, asks the trickster why he doesn't speak straightforwardly, Eshu responds, "I never do; I like to make people think."

7

The Workaround
Building Blocks

So far I've presented many stories of workarounds that emerged thanks to extraordinary observations or out of sheer necessity in a high-stakes situation. As workarounds deviate from the standard problem-solving script, people often assume either that they are serendipitous or that they arise from the originality of a few special individuals. The reality is that anyone can create a workaround, and in this chapter you'll learn how. We'll explore the principles of a workaround ideation process, as well as the building blocks that will help you assemble piggyback, loophole, roundabout, and next best workarounds for your particular situations and problems.

THE PRINCIPLES OF A WORKAROUND

The default problem-solving approach walks us along a straight line from problem to solution, starting from identifying the problem. It relies on the idea that clearly pinpointing an issue will enable you to develop a logical, stepwise approach that involves identifying the problem, defining the problem, examining strategies, acting on those strategies, then learning from the results. This approach is not only intuitive; it is also continuously reinforced by managers and higher-ups who tend to overvalue familiar modes of operation. But it won't help you come up with workarounds.

The Problem with Problem-Solving

The default approach may seem comforting and broadly applicable, but in practice it is static, and people who follow this approach may fail to recognize that, sometimes, the way that we interpret the problem is *itself* a problem. Many of today's biggest challenges are messy. Problems are interconnected and constantly changing, and what looks like the beginning of one problem may be the solution of another. Often we're dealing with knotted bundles of problems, and that makes identification difficult if not impossible. Think of anything from climate change or food insecurity to inequality; these problems overlap in inconvenient—and sometimes contradictory—ways.

Our problems aren't neat puzzles that can be assembled only one way, so it doesn't make sense to approach them as if they were. Also, workarounds thrive in messes; after all, there are many possible workarounds to each problem and context. So don't expect that the creative process described in this chapter can yield only one possible configuration!

Be Messy

When you're dealing with messy circumstances, the process doesn't end with identifying the problem, and it doesn't even necessarily have to start there either. Happily, workarounds don't follow a stepwise process, so you don't need to complete one task to move on to the next. Instead I prefer to think of this approach as a kind of mindset that involves a continuous exchange between the "defaults" and the "problems" in our lives.

Coming up with workarounds is more like playing with Legos than completing a puzzle: you have building blocks, and your challenge is to build something. Remember: finding two-dimensional corner pieces won't help you if you want to build a Lego castle. Your creativity can flourish with the support of the building blocks, allowing you to explore different assemblages as you go. You can use as many or as few of the blocks as you'd like, and you can build anything you can imagine. Sometimes you don't even know what you want to build until you start fitting the pieces together.

Square One

After years of working on this research and using many students and fellow researchers as guinea pigs, I realized that you can start in two ways.

First, you can strike out from the recognition of a problem that you care about. But you don't need to fully understand or define it before you try to find an entry point for action. That's precisely the beauty of workarounds: you can apply them even to problems you don't understand very well. By experimenting and being willing to embrace ambivalence and doubt, you can gradually expand the horizon of the possible.

Second, you can also start by recognizing the "default" reaction to different circumstances and seeing how it falls short. We rely too much on our scripts in our lives, but as psychologist Abraham Maslow said in 1966, "I suppose it is tempting, if the only tool you have is a hammer, to treat everything as if it were a nail." When you challenge the default, you start from a different entry point, your standard actions, instead of from problems. This process then makes you consider multifaceted problems—including issues that you may have not been aware of beforehand.

Fortunately, the start is just a start. A better approach is to systematically and simultaneously tinker with both—the problem and the default reaction—by looking more closely at the foundation of your knowledge. Once you assemble a foundation, you may even forget where you started.

SETTING UP THE FOUNDATION

The foundation of the workaround creative process is the recognition of what you know and what you know that you don't know. Remember, this is the foundation of a Lego construction, not a real house. This means that you don't have to worry much if you don't have a building plan and all the pieces up front. This step is just to get you started.

If you have a challenge in mind that you want to tackle,

identifying and writing down what you know about it is only half the battle. So if you start by identifying a problem, I suggest thinking through the general problem, the obstacles, and explanations of why the problem exists in the first place. If you begin by thinking about your default reactions in a circumstance, you can then identify the traditional solutions and responsible parties.

Ultimately, the order doesn't matter, and you don't have to take much time in this exercise. Get started and, later, when you start brainstorming with the four kinds of workarounds, you will likely revisit the foundation of your knowledge to add or change some building blocks.

The Problem

A problem can be simple and well specified (e.g., I can't boil an egg for lunch) or complex and multifaceted (e.g., high rates of diarrheal deaths of children under the age of five in Sub-Saharan Africa). If your problem is simple, great—just write it down and move on. If it's complex, it may be best to scribble what you know and what you know you don't know about the problem. Then move on to obstacles and to the explanations of why the problem exists in the first place.

Your observation of the problem may result from a lived experience or from something that has been reported. The hacker who boiled an egg in a coffee machine experienced the problem as part of his routine. Simon and Jane Berry hadn't worked with prevention of diarrheal deaths; they learned about the problem from reports from others. Naturally, if you've experienced the problem you'll very likely know the problem best—but your experience may also blind you to alternative ways of addressing it. If you haven't experienced the problem, you start with a cleaner slate, which means less firsthand knowledge of the problem, but also less bias because you have no default way of addressing it.

Obstacles

Obstacles are often visible when we are dealing with simple problems. When the hacker wanted to boil an egg for lunch, the obstacle was obvious: he didn't have a stove in his office. When problems are more complex, you may learn more about them as you read, or as you try the default and fail. When Jane and Simon Berry investigated the challenge of making diarrhea medicine more widely available in remote regions of Sub-Saharan Africa, they read reports and spoke with a bunch of people who told them that the obstacles included poor infrastructure, logistics, and funding.

Another possibility for studying obstacles when problems are complex is that you'll try the default and fail. When I was a baby and my parents tried to save my life from life-threatening diarrhea, they tried the default multiple times and noticed the obstacles only when they banged their heads against them—first with the problem of importing medicine, then again when they found out that the breast milk banks were on a strike.

Note that you don't need to know the obstacles up front—in fact, having no notes here can be as telling as having many, as it will make you realize the importance of learning more. And as you scribble down obstacles, your list doesn't have to be exhaustive; as you learn more about the problem and the default solutions you may also revisit the obstacles.

Default Solutions

We almost always know the default. The default way to boil an egg is to use a stove and a pan and, depending on how you like your yolk, you'll decide how long you'll boil it. Defaults feel so natural that we don't think much about them—they silently shape what we deem adequate in every circumstance.

When you start from a problem, your attention automatically turns to the default—so in the case of the coffee maker hacker, he thought about the default and defied it only because he had a problem: he couldn't boil an egg in his office.

Even in more complex situations we may get a hint about the default without knowing much about the problem; after all, the default is naturally intuitive. For example, as Simon and Jane Berry learned about lack of access to diarrhea treatment in impoverished regions, they didn't need to sweat much to realize that the default solution in the international development context is to freely provide treatment through the public sector. As they learned more about the problem, they quickly found out that some projects were centered on private-sector distribution instead, especially when targeting the so-called last mile—the remote regions far from public healthcare facilities.

The default changes, though, when the problem is framed differently. If instead of looking at the "lack of access to diarrhea treatment," you center your attention on "diarrheal deaths," you may end up thinking more about preventative solutions—such as rotavirus vaccination, clean water, sanitation—rather than access to treatment. Looking from different angles is normal and healthy when we're thinking about how to approach multifaceted problems.

Responsible Parties

In our siloed world, default solutions often come with assigned responsibilities—with a definition of who takes a leading role. Who boils your eggs? Who is responsible for delivering diarrhea treatment to remote regions?

This path not only prevents others from taking an active role; it also limits our ability to address our problems differently. When people encounter the same kinds of problems multiple times and use the same default solutions to address these problems, they become numb to alternatives. Coming from the margins gives you a different angle to finding alternative solutions. Concentrating on the responsible parties sometimes helps us to think of what *not to do* in a workaround.

Explaining Why the Problem Exists

Why does the problem still exist? This question helps us connect the nature of the problem with the default solutions and the responsible party, which are especially suitable things to explore when we are facing more complex problems. As you try to unpack this link, shy away from generic answers such as "the responsible party doesn't care enough." Even if it's true, this presumption won't make you think much, and it may also create a feeling of fatalism, as if we are all paralyzed and doomed to fail.

When Simon and Jane Berry looked at lack of access to diarrhea treatment for young children, one of the most persistent problems in the world, they didn't stop with generic and fatalistic observations that prevented them from acting. Yes, the problem is neglected and exposes rampant inequalities—for example, Zambia's diarrheal death rate was about 720 times higher than that of Finland. The disparity doesn't mean that people aren't trying to address the problem; neither does it mean that they are failing: between 1990 and 2017, according to the Institute for Health Metrics and Evaluation, the yearly rate of diarrheal deaths of children under five in the world dropped from about 1.7 million deaths to approximately 500,000 deaths.

The beauty of asking why a problem still exists is precisely that doing so permits you to refine the way you look at the systemic nature of some of your tough problems, making you realize the extent not only of your knowledge but also of your ignorance. In this process, you may note that there is an expectation that diarrheal deaths will be solved by international aid and the governments of low-income countries, and that is the perfect hook to ask some "what if" questions. For example, what if the medicine is dispensed through the private sector? What if we don't need to build better roads to improve the transportation of the medicine? What if public healthcare can be provided outside clinics or hospitals? These kinds of questions may take you to different places, and they will most definitely make you consider the problem and the default from different angles.

THE FOUR CONFIGURATIONS OF WORKAROUNDS

After assembling the foundational building blocks, it is a good time to start tinkering with workarounds. Again, while brainstorming workarounds you will likely revisit the foundation of your knowledge, and that's expected. Some people may even ignore the foundation and jump right into tinkering with workarounds—and that's okay, too.

It is difficult to break free from linear, stepwise problem-solving approaches, but the essence of a deviant approach, one that is favorable for a workaround attitude, is that you won't follow orders—and "orders" means both what is imposed on you and a presupposed sequence of how things are meant to be done. So chill out, look at the building blocks (or don't), and follow your instincts.

In Part I, you learned what each workaround is and how they have been used in scrappy organizations and by mavericks throughout the world. But how do you choose which of the four workarounds would yield the best outcome for your situation?

It helps to think of each of the workarounds as different sorts of Lego assemblages: a castle, a bridge, and so on. Consider how a castle can look like Rapunzel's or Dracula's, but despite the differences they both have ceilings, walls, and so forth. Likewise, there are some key features in each of the four workaround approaches, and knowing what these are will help you choose the most suitable way to assemble a workaround to fit your needs.

Each of the workarounds has a primary element at play. When you think about piggybacks, consider the existing relationships in your situation. Loopholes require paying close attention to different sets of rules. Roundabouts involve examining behaviors that lead to inertia. And if you're searching for next-best approaches, fiddle with the resources you have on hand. Not every situation is going to necessitate using each of these four workarounds, and that's okay. In the end, you really need only one workaround for most challenges. The following chart is not exhaustive; rather it is meant to provide some inspiration and guidance as you begin to identify workarounds.

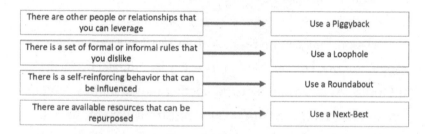

Now we'll explore how to brainstorm each type of workaround. Asking yourself a few simple questions can help you determine which workaround(s) will be relevant to your context, building on the foundation that you've assembled, even if only provisionally.

How to Brainstorm Piggybacks?

Piggyback workarounds rely on relationships, so you'll want to consider the relationships and networks involving and surrounding your challenges.

PROMPTS FOR A PIGGYBACK WORKAROUND

- What other actors are present?
- What other connections or networks are present?
- How can you use existing networks to deliver something new? What can be learned or used from a different system?
- How can you use existing networks to eliminate an actor or connection that already exists?
- What can be leveraged from "your system" to do something else?

Relationships can be broader than just interactions between people. Actors, connections, and networks can take many different forms. Actors can refer to competing movie studios or Vodafone executives, and networks can range from webs of Coca-Cola distributors to television advertising standards. Noticing how different relationships and systems inevitably crisscross can help you to think creatively about how to utilize interactions. Can you use existing systems to deliver something new, the way Cola-Life delivered lifesaving medicine, or to eliminate or replace an existing node, as Airbnb did when it diverted traffic away from Craigslist?

How to Brainstorm Loopholes?

Loophole workarounds are based on rules—and beginning to think about sidestepping the standard rules can be daunting, but these prompts are here to help.

PROMPTS FOR A LOOPHOLE

- What are the vulnerabilities of current systems?
- Where does or doesn't a limiting rule or obstacle apply?
- How can you follow the mandate but not the spirit of the rule?
- What are different sets of rules that could apply?
- What or who needs to get through the obstacle?
- How strictly enforced is your limiting rule, or how can you make the law or convention more difficult to enforce?
- How can rules be reinterpreted to your benefit?

Rules—and their limits—can be reinterpreted to your benefit. Like Portia in *The Merchant of Venice*, can you make a rule impossible to enforce? Like Women on Waves, can you find an instance where certain limiting laws don't apply? If there are formal and informal rules to circumvent, you're well on your way to thinking about a loophole workaround.

How to Brainstorm Roundabouts?

Perhaps you notice that your challenge persists because of self-reinforcing behaviors, and that we are surrounded by them, at both the individual and community levels. The more you drink coffee in the morning, the more you'll think you need coffee in the morning. So, if that's the case, you may be able to employ a roundabout workaround, and these prompts will help you understand what the self-reinforcing behavior is, why it happens, where it happens, and ways to delay or disrupt it.

PROMPTS FOR A ROUNDABOUT

- Is there any self-reinforcing behavior?
- Why is the behavior self-reinforcing, and how does that behavior interact with other needs?
- How can you create a distraction that disturbs the momentum of the self-reinforcing behavior?
- In what circumstances does the self-reinforcing behavior not exist?
- How can you delay the self-reinforcing behavior?
- Who behaves differently, or who is the outlier, and in what circumstances?

Now begin to think about how activities, habits, and needs interact. A roundabout may mean making use of a seemingly unrelated problem, like how addressing housing needs led to the building of physical infrastructure that disrupted casteism. Alternatively, you could follow Scheherazade's or pandemic-era public health officials' leads and come up with approaches that incrementally distract from or put off an undesirable but ostensibly inevitable outcome.

How to Brainstorm Next Bests?

Start by asking yourself if you have access to resources that can be used or repurposed. Think of resources as broadly as you want—from the high-tech to the basic—but focus on "things" and on "the ways to get things done."

PROMPTS FOR A NEXT BEST

- What resources are easily immediately available?
- How can resources be repurposed or reinterpreted to achieve different goals?
- How can resources be reassembled in unconventional ways?
- What's the lowest-tech solution for this problem?
- What's the highest-tech solution for this problem?
- What functions exist beyond your accessible technology's originally intended design?

The scope of resources today is vast, which can be a curse and a blessing. On the one hand, specialization and new technology can lure us toward the conventional approach that demands each problem be fixed by a specific, purpose-built tool. On the other, the sheer array of *stuff* means that we are bound to be able to use something designed to accomplish one task to complete another—you just have to be creative enough to recognize an object's secondary or alternative uses. Think back to how a fancy coffee machine can be used to boil an egg. This type of strategic use of a pre-existing resource is a great example of an observation leading to a workaround. Once you develop situational awareness of the resources at your disposal and the ways in which you (and others) interact with them, you'll get more comfortable thinking about how they can be used in different contexts.

LET'S GET TO WORK

My pet peeve is when people say that you must think outside the box, and then they follow a one-size-fits-all brainstorming approach. Not every creative activity needs Post-its and flip charts. Just play with what is in front of you. Sketch, draw, jot down bullet points, start a Google spreadsheet, find mind map software online, engage with others (or don't) . . . Just don't let lack of manpower or resources be a constraint.

Use the workaround prompts along with the building blocks in your foundation iteratively and creatively to conceive workarounds. Recognize the multiplicity and interconnectivity of your obstacles, that you don't and can't know everything, and get comfortable asking questions that you don't yet have the answers to. It's precisely this boundary-pushing self-interrogation that enables us to evaluate and upend our default approaches.

First, we'll start with a fable, one that may be familiar to you, before moving on to a more complex example. These brainstorming examples will show that multiple workarounds can exist in any given situation and highlight ways to use building blocks iteratively and creatively to identify workaround opportunities.

The Three Little Pigs

I hope you remember the story of the three little pigs. The first two built their houses of straw and sticks, respectively, but the Big Bad Wolf huffed and puffed and blew their houses down, forcing them to seek refuge with the third pig, who had built his house of brick. Huffing and puffing did no damage to this last house, and the pigs set a pot of water boiling in the fireplace that would scald the wolf if he tried to climb in through the chimney. How could the wolf work around these obstacles and finally enjoy a nice feast?

In general, we know the wolf's problem is that he wants to eat the three little pigs. But there's a lot we don't know about Mr. Wolf's predicament. For example, does he have a specific hankering for ham, or will any snack suffice? Some goats are grazing nearby—if the wolf is just feeling hungry and is not that picky, perhaps one of them would do as a nice treat? Or, if he was going after the pigs out of habit, perhaps this interlude could inspire the wolf to consider planting some soybeans and developing a vegetarian alternative. Or it may be just the reverse: maybe the wolf really is something of a bacon fanatic.

If that's the case, then Mr. Wolf really does need to get to those pigs. He can't huff and puff and demolish the brick house, so he needs to come up with another way to get the pigs. Unfortunately, the pigs already anticipated his first backup plan and laid a trap of boiling water in the fireplace. But if time is on his side, the wolf has more options. If the wolf could be patient enough, maybe he'd wait for Christmas to come. Surely the pigs would put aside their trap to let Santa down the chimney, giving Mr. Wolf an opportunity to sneak in, too. Or perhaps the wolf could dig (or hire some friendly moles to dig) a tunnel right into the cellar of the brick house.

In fact, we know several stories about the wolf and his neighbors, not just moles. Did the wolf keep his sheep costume or Little Red Riding Hood's grandmother's dressing gown? Perhaps he could disguise himself and gain entry that way. What networks—legal, social, or commercial—exist in the fairy-tale world? Maybe the pigs have hired Three Bears Security (established in response to Goldilocks's escapades) to install alarms. Unfortunately for the homeowners, Papa Bear may be friends with Mr. Wolf and might agree to "forget" to install an alarm on one window in exchange for some tasty breakfast sausages.

But then again, maybe the pigs are too clever and are already suspicious of the gang of carnivores. Instead, they decide to hunker down and not let anybody—from Santa to security contractors—into their home. Under what circumstances might the pigs want or need to abandon their fortress? Maybe Mr. Wolf must just wait for pigs in heat (and ready to breed!) to come to town. Such company might lure the pigs out of hiding and keep them distracted, allowing the wolf to spring into action and hunt multiple pigs at once.

Coming up with a number of ideas, even including some that might not work out in the end, allows you to consider different aspects, making the possible interventions seem more or less feasible or preferable. You might first assess viability. Growing bacon from cell cultures might hypothetically sate the wolf's craving, but if the fairy-tale world is stuck with preindustrial technology, he'll need to get his fix another way. You might also consider how much time and effort you're willing and able to invest. For example, the wolf may be able to purchase the land where the pig's house is built, but does he really want to spend all the money and time tied up in court cases just to evict the pigs? It would be much faster to act in the dead of night, when the pigs are asleep. The wolf could take straw and sticks from the first two houses, throw them into the brick house via the chimney, set them on fire, and seal off the chimney to kill the pigs with smoke inhalation. When the pigs are dead, the wolf could let the smoke out, get into the house through the chimney, and eat smoked pork.

Likewise, the scale of the expected impact is important. We don't know if the wolf is looking to make a small, individual-scale impact (in which case snacking on something else might work just fine) or if he has an idea to alter the entire community's food supply (in which case growing soy for a vegan bacon alternative might be more suitable). Finally, you, like the wolf, might want to consider public perception. Sure, the wolf is a predator, but is he comfortable being known as the guy who introduced roundworms to the local water supply just to get those pesky pigs? That might make things awkward with his neighbors, assuming they survive.

Clearly, coming up with scrappy interventions for Mr. Wolf is intended to be a humorous low-stakes exercise. But it still illustrates how you can employ the workaround mindset to come up with different paths or endings for even the most familiar stories. Now that you're more comfortable creatively engaging with the prompts and brainstorming without judgment, let's move on to a trickier and more realistic example.

Hello, Hilda

Your name is Hilda Grunwald. You're a German woman, a computer programmer, who lives in Berlin and votes for the Green Party. You have a liberal stance toward immigration, and, moved by the situation of refugees, you want to do something to help. You recently met your Syrian neighbors, who struggled through your country's bureaucracy to sort out their paperwork and become legally entitled to make a living. But how can you help?

You know that you don't know much about the refugee crisis, but you're a data-savvy individual, so you start looking for information from the United Nations High Commissioner for Refugees (UNHCR). First, you realize you have a lot to learn. You had no idea that, as per 2020, of the roughly eighty-two million people forced to flee their home country, only about twenty-six million had been granted refugee status in other countries. Given all the media attention surrounding the issue, you'd hoped that high-income countries would have taken in more than 15 percent of displaced people.

You want to educate yourself on *why* displaced people are forced to leave their home country, but you struggle to see a clear reason. It seems that most people leave their country of origin— even if they aren't considered "forcibly displaced"—because of a ton of problems that, combined, make them vulnerable. Suddenly you're trying to wrap your head around pervasive and intertwined problems like global hunger, poverty, and water scarcity, which impact the lives of vulnerable immigrants.

Armed with some answers that yield even more questions than you started with, you know you must support displaced people, regardless of whether they were granted "refugee" status. Focusing on trying to specify the problem completely and accurately will divert too much energy from achieving your goal. It's time to get creative.

The next day, on your walk to work, you pass a tourist information center. As you're reminiscing about your gap year travels, you think about how different that time would've been if you'd had access to all the Apple technology you now carry in your pocket. Those tourist centers seem to get less and less busy with every passing year. Unless . . .

What if there were a way to tap into these disused centers' potential? After all, they're still functioning facilities with employees. Could they pivot to providing information and guidance to recent arrivals and connecting them to local employment opportunities or job training? You'd have to work with government officials or bypass them and go straight to the employees, but it just might work.

By noticing how existing resources can be repurposed, you've come up with a potential workaround! But you're not done yet. You decide to continue brainstorming and see what other ideas you can come up with.

It's a slow day at work, and as you're checking your email you notice a message asking you to volunteer to teach at a coding bootcamp. Teaching immigrants to code could be an interesting first step, but they'd also need to be given a fair chance to transform coding skills into employment.

As you mull over the volunteer request you realize something else. Recent immigrants may not be legally allowed to work, but no one's stopping them from volunteering, and no one's stopping you from donating to them. What if you set up a web development company under your name, and you worked with "volunteers" instead of "employees" who received "donations" instead of "salaries"? It would be a daring loophole to execute, but the idea is certainly worth exploring.

Over the weekend you get a coffee with your good friend,

a political scientist named Arthur Lebkuchen. You're chatting about the alarming growth of the far-right populist party, Alternative für Deutschland, and how they seem to capitalize on sensationalist headlines and often inaccurate reporting that is overshared on social media. The more people read and share these comments, the more normalized xenophobic, anti-immigrant ideas become.

Arthur points out that it's almost impossible to stem the creation of fake news in our highly connected world, but that it is probably possible to make it less easily accessible. As a skilled programmer, you know that the links that appear in a Google search aren't random; they are ranked according to certain measures. The algorithms tend to rank links shared by reputable sources (like university or government websites) more highly. What if you created a partnership with a network of university professors who would repost verifiable, fact-checked news? Then those credible sources might have a better chance of appearing first in people's searches.

It's an interesting idea, but after talking it through with Arthur, you realize it might not be very effective because news—especially "fake news"—is more often disseminated via social media and direct messaging apps than through Google searches. Besides, you're more excited about helping your new friends and neighbors than getting tied up in disrupting far-right trolls. Maybe the self-reinforcing patterns of fake news dissemination just aren't something you're up for working on right now.

As you bike home after meeting with Arthur, you keep thinking about how you might be able to make life a little easier for people who are newly arrived in Germany. You realize you've thought about repurposing resources, exploiting rules, and disrupting self-reinforcing patterns, but you haven't yet considered other relationships—maybe the most obvious intervention of all. Other immigrants and refugees have passed through the same bureaucracy, and there might possibly be some who would be willing to help. It's time for dinner, and all the excellent Syrian restaurants scattered around the city are on your mind. Maybe you could connect restaurant owners and employees to new arrivals looking for guidance.

As you consider what type of assistance recent immigrants might prioritize, you circle back to your first idea, which involved using resources devoted to tourism. What if, instead of repurposing tangible resources, you piggybacked on an existing tourism *network*, like CouchSurfing? The online community connects travelers to hosts willing to share their homes, but maybe this social networking website—or something similar— could help immigrants find temporary housing. In addition to addressing a pressing need, this idea would have the benefit of not requiring that you interact with government officials.

Hilda, you've come up with a few interesting ideas for doable interventions to address a set of problems in a highly complex system. How do you choose which path to pursue first? It's up to you. You can decide to start with whatever you think will make the biggest impact or where your skills would best apply—the important thing is to start. Once you begin to execute a workaround, you'll have the freedom to revise your approach, start over with another idea, or gain inspiration and respecify your goals along the way.

FROM INSPIRATION TO IMPLEMENTATION

Attempting to fabricate workarounds requires flexibility, and flexibility can particularly help you approach complex, poorly specified problems that tend to stump traditional management strategies. Scrappy organizations excel in these flexible pursuits precisely because they can't rely too much on traditional ways of solving problems. If you allow yourself to embark on a free-flowing and iterative exercise, you will also be able to assemble many different workarounds with the support of some simple building blocks, which adapt not only to your contexts but also to your motivations.

When I run these ideation exercises with students, there's always a group who tries to map out all possibilities, using all the building blocks. This perfectionism leads to failure. Don't assume you'll find your final destination up front. Good ideas take you somewhere unfamiliar. Remember, when building with Legos, you can explore different configurations and use as many or as few pieces as you like. Just as when we tried to help Mr. Wolf, not every prompt was fruitful or feasible, and some ideas were more appealing or appropriate than others. What is "appropriate" is up to you to judge, depending on your resources, power, the amount of time you want to dedicate to the work, and the kind of impact you expect. As when we role-played with Hilda, once you've found a workaround possibility that excites you, and that seems feasible, then you're ready to implement.

Ultimately, it is in practice that these ideas matter the most. As much as I wish I could guarantee your success by encouraging you to simply follow a recipe, I cannot. The beauty—and challenge—of workarounds is that you must try them out. Because they are well suited to messy situations, you have to get your hands dirty.

That does not mean you must dig with your hands. Although every challenge comes with its own unique context, desired outcomes, and nightmare scenarios, my research has helped me to identify a number of tips for implementing workarounds, and these are built on the stories of these scrappy organizations. So if you keep the lessons that you've learned about the *four workaround approaches* from Part I in mind, and if you embrace the *workaround mindset* and *attitude* that I have described in Part II, you'll be best equipped to make judgment calls and muddle through your situation when working around your obstacles. In other words, you will be better prepared to think and act like a scrappy organization!

As you may remember from the examples in Part I, the more you try to work around problems, the more you'll develop a knack for it, and one workaround may lead to another. When Women on Waves began using a loophole to provide safe abortions aboard a ship, its engagement in one area grew into other opportunities. Before long the organization was providing country-specific recommendations to women who needed to access reproductive healthcare. This is because as you explore you'll naturally ask new questions, and your early attempts will cascade into a bunch of other unforeseen ideas—even more so if you use the ideation exercises here again and again as you bump into new problems and challenges on your way.

Some of those ideas and attempts to work around obstacles

will be useful, and some will be absurd—it's part of the journey that branches out to unexpected places. And, as we adventure into new lands, we must all be a bit like Alice asking the Cheshire Cat which way she ought to go. The Cat answers, "That depends a good deal on where you want to get to." Alice, however, doesn't seem to have a specific destination in mind: "I don't much care where . . . so long as I get SOMEWHERE." If you start going, you'll get somewhere.

And don't worry too much. After all, the whole idea of the workaround is that it is doable, it aims for the good enough, and it doesn't require a lot of time, resources, or power.

8

The Workaround in Your Organization

*I always have people come to me who have professions—
bankers, lawyers—and they want to go right away and get a
paid job working in the field with refugees. And I say to them,
would you hire someone who had no other qualification than
working with refugees to be a banker in your bank or to argue
a case in court?*

This quotation summed up a frequent frustration of mine from
my years working in business schools, where it's not uncommon
to come across McKinsey or Goldman Sachs employees (or recent ex-employees) eager to impart their wisdom to the third
sector and tackle poverty, inequality, or healthcare. I have nothing against anyone who wants to pivot their career trajectory or
make a more direct and positive impact on other people's lives.
What I take issue with is the assumption that businesses are inherently superior, better run, and better equipped than nonprofits, and that any organization wishing to make an impact would

be best served to mimic those organizations that exist to maximize their profits.

And it's not just a few Deloitte alums parachuting into organizations, proposing to save social ventures from themselves. Academic articles, popular books, politicians, and think tanks often repeat the conventional wisdom that all organizations can improve themselves by becoming more like businesses, ignoring the fact that different organizations have different goals and affordances. I'll take my claim one step further: not only should we fight the assumption that all organizations benefit from emulating businesses, but businesses can *learn* from scrappy organizations that aren't motivated by profit making.

Yes, this chapter's opening quote clicked—and in more ways than one. Not only did it articulate a view that I had been developing as I learned from scrappy organizations, but those words were spoken by Mary Anne Schwalbe, founding director of the Women's Refugee Commission, whose son happens to be the editor of the book you're currently reading.

The research behind *The Four Workarounds* builds on the knowledge and experiences of scrappy organizations, intrepid social entrepreneurs, and computer hackers from all over the world—not from big businesses or global powerhouses, but from the little guys with limited resources, often scraping by on the periphery. This chapter explores how organizations can take these teachings to heart and become more workaround friendly. More specifically, we'll reflect on recommendations for strategy, culture, leadership, and teamwork that can help workarounds flourish in organizations of all sizes and sectors.

STRATEGY

Different business strategies can promote or hinder workarounds. To embrace and facilitate workarounds in your organization you need to stir the ashes of some worn-out management tenets of efficiency, long-term planning, hierarchical decision-making, and obtaining full information about a situation to make decisions to adopt more adaptable strategies. This involves planning less, engaging in more horizontal decision-making, changing course to respond to opportunities as they arise, pivoting and stacking to make the best of unforeseen opportunities, and deciding how to scale your impact.

Plan Less

An obsession with planning hinders the implementation of workarounds. Individuals and organizations—global funders, corporations, governments, and community groups—who believe they can solve every problem with a long-term plan think rational design, comprehensive evaluation, and logical implementation supersede adaptation. Despite these organizations' best intentions, we've seen time and time again that it's often impossible for them to plan their way out of complex problems.

Overplanning explains why stand-alone projects often overpromise, overspend, or drag on interminably. It is also a reason why so many of us fail to take advantage of opportunities around us: we spend so much time and energy focusing on following the plan we (or our cultures, families, or organizations) set for ourselves that we neglect to assess and reassess what we can and want to be doing. Despite our obsession with planning, studies in psychology suggest that in the long run we seem to regret inaction more than action. Common regrets include, for example, failing to chase profitable business opportunities or not going to college. In other words, we regret our failures to act more than we regret our failures themselves.

Not only do we overcommit to our plans at the expense of new or evolving opportunities, but we pay a price for the act of planning itself. When we confront decisions—especially difficult ones, like what career to pursue or how to invest—we tend to get bogged down in internal deliberations. In the words of English novelist Ian McEwan, "At moments of important decision-making, the mind could be considered as a parliament," not a unified voice of reason. We hesitate, we try to peer too far into the future and account for the unaccountable, and sometimes we mask insecurity with overcommitment.

Instead of attempting to anticipate and decide upon every detail at the outset, encourage yourself and those around you to take small, exploratory steps. Because, as Canadian educator Laurence J. Peter says, "Some problems are so complex that you have to be highly intelligent and well informed just to be undecided about them," stop aiming for intelligence and perfect information and start acting. Since workarounds require less time and resources than standard, well-planned approaches, you don't have much to lose. It's then easier to build on what works and pivot away from what doesn't without having to rethink the entire operation.

Furthermore, we can even, or especially, apply workarounds to problems we don't understand very well. Systems change practitioners advise that we "seek health, not mission accomplished." If your goal is to lead a healthy life, you may plan to lose ten pounds, but losing weight won't necessarily solve all your health problems. As your body changes, you need to continue adapting and re-evaluating what it means to be healthy. For example, an intense workout regimen could lead to an exercise addiction or a knee injury. If you go on a long-haul protein-heavy diet, you could develop a liver problem years later or encounter other problems that you can't now predict. Does this mean you should abandon your weight-loss goal? Of course not. But you need to acknowledge that a limited criterion of good health (like losing some weight) doesn't, can't, and shouldn't account for what is complex and, too often, unpredictable. Instead of fixating on and planning for one be-all and end-all target, find and explore different pathways that embrace complexity and seek health instead of pretending that good planning will lead to a perfect solution that will make the problem disappear.

Who Makes the Decisions?

You may remember that I first started exploring workarounds after studying hacker communities, whom I found to be almost the opposite of many corporate settings. Rather than requiring prestigious degrees or specialized training, novice hackers just teach themselves. Whereas most businesses rely on strict hierarchies and carefully delineated domains, anonymous hackers can work on whatever they want whenever they want, teaching and learning along the way. Unlike organizations that assign responsibility for certain projects (and their successes or failures) to specific individuals or teams, hackers develop out of collaborations that praise contributions without ascribing ownership.

Needless to say, there's much that organizations can learn from hackers. Many of the most effective workarounds we explored in Part I benefited from hacker-like cooperation and collaboration between seemingly disconnected actors and resources—surprising complementarities that are often discouraged in hierarchical, compartmentalized organizations.

To take inspiration from hackers, an organization could articulate a central unifying vision while also allowing ideas to be shared and modified more freely. Motivated by creativity and curiosity rather than name recognition or status, hackers are also quite entrepreneurial and run into some of the same challenges that more traditional organizations face. Many open-source, self-run projects balance the need for accountability and adjudication with collaboration and flexibility through a so-called benevolent dictator for life (BDFL) model (originally a reference to Guido van Rossum, who created the Python programming language). In this model, anyone can implement improvements and make changes, but the founder retains final say in the case of large disputes or decisions about future strategy.

Like the work of hackers and communities of open-source developers, workarounds benefit from open, collaborative environments precisely because novelty doesn't start in a vacuum. Innovation results from an amalgam of contributions, knowledge, and experiences that combine to expand what is possible. Overemphasizing ownership of a specific task or domain hinders these organic explorations and creates a barrier to recombining contributions, contexts, adaptations, and individuals.

Changing Course

Adopting a workaround-friendly strategy means embracing flexibility, and that means getting comfortable with the rough starts, shortcomings, and failures of different workarounds.

Workarounds often originate as organic responses to hard problems, so it can be difficult to predict if any given intervention will become a onetime experiment or a scalable venture. Encouraging workarounds entails being open to either of these outcomes and anything in between. Some, like the ceramic tiles depicting Hindu gods wedged into walls in India, have finite life spans. Once a tile comes loose, the wall gets drenched in urine again. Others may be test beds for larger-scale operations; Zipline's operations in Rwanda may help the company to develop designs and concepts for drone delivery in countries with busier airspaces. Still others may fail—or initially appear to fail—entirely. When Women on Waves made its maiden voyage in 2001, it failed in its goal of providing abortions to women in Ireland because the ship had not yet obtained the proper Dutch licenses that would permit the doctors to perform abortions. Nevertheless, this apparent "failure" galvanized the team to both mobilize other supporters and identify necessary next steps.

Implementing and facilitating workarounds necessitates a willingness to play by ear. Developing this kind of awareness will help you identify both opportunities for workarounds and warning signs that a workaround isn't actually working. Since many workarounds require relatively little investment, it can be less painful to take stock, adjust course, or even wind down an unsuccessful attempt. Ideally, this type of ongoing reflection and reformulation can foster an environment that encourages lots of trial by accommodating low-stakes errors. This type of creative momentum is key—and it requires acting your way through your challenges and changing course when needed.

Psychological research tells us that accomplishing small, immediate tasks allows us to build momentum; we can use that momentum as motivation to continue exploring and experimenting. In 1996 researchers Roy Baumeister, Ellen Bratslavsky, Mark Muraven, and Dianne Tice baked lots of chocolate chip cookies, filling a lab with their undeniably tasty aroma. Then they welcomed two sets of study participants and asked them to wait in a room before undertaking a task that, unbeknownst to the participants, was designed to be impossible to finish. In the waiting room, one set of subjects was encouraged to indulge in the readily available freshly baked cookies, while the other was told to eat from a bowl of radishes. The radish eaters gave up on the tricky puzzle more quickly than those who ate the chocolaty goodness. In addition to teaching us never to turn down a chocolate chip cookie, this famous experiment illustrates the importance of maintaining momentum and avoiding burnout. Allowing yourself or your organization to take advantage of the short-term impacts of workarounds while also assessing their viability and your next moves can better prepare you to take advantage of future opportunities.

Pivoting and Stacking

Unsurprisingly, this type of engaged, curious, dynamic flow of ideas has benefits beyond determining if a workaround is viable or not. By staying attuned to the changing resources that a situation presents or demands, you'll be better equipped to pivot and stack your workarounds.

Pivoting means redirecting your attention to address needs or contingencies that you hadn't anticipated. When Nick Hughes started putting M-Pesa into motion in Kenya, the idea was to provide microloans that piggybacked on Safaricom's existing infrastructure networks. But during the trial Hughes's team realized that the core challenge for Kenyans wasn't a shortage of funds, as they initially thought, but rather moving money. In order to pivot, the M-Pesa team needed to respond to the evidence they had collected—a task that's often easier said than done. The decision to pivot may be tough because it can feel as if you're abandoning your earlier efforts and all the time or resources you poured into them. However, failing to pivot can be far more damaging, causing you to waste precious resources on subpar "solutions" and miss other more promising routes.

Stacking necessitates a similar openness to new ideas but entails combining an assemblage of workarounds to achieve your goal. Scheherazade stacked the same workaround, night after night, just as Governor Dino combined a series of different workarounds to import ventilators to his state or many different defiant people and communities gradually pushed the barriers of cryptography, eventually giving rise to bitcoin. These complementary approaches demonstrate how stacking workarounds can multiply their effectiveness and open up completely new possibilities.

Developing the skills necessary for pivoting and stacking can also help amplify impact. Rebecca Gomperts, for example, became a mastermind at spotting loopholes in legal systems that outlawed abortions. Along with her colleagues she has used many other loopholes, looking beyond providing abortions in international waters. Even masters, however, have their limits: I've found that once an individual or organization starts to use one type of workaround, they begin to specialize and use more and more of that same type of workaround. I encourage you to challenge yourself to combine different types of workarounds and practice them all. Each has its own strengths and weaknesses, and they facilitate different types of approaches.

Scaling Impact

While workarounds can provide useful, one-off quick fixes, they can also be developed to address longer-term goals. Sometimes one quick fix grows into something larger. As workarounds—and your goals—evolve, you'll likely face tricky questions about whether and how to scale impact.

As you practice active experimentation (instead of overplanning each step along your path), you'll still want to consider how to align your actions with your goals. Thinking through different directions of scale (up, deep, or out) can help you to calibrate your workaround with your context and expectations. Do you want to expand your reach or "scale up"? Will you "scale deep," aiming to establish longer and more durable ties? Or do you hope to "scale out" and increase your workaround's self-sufficiency and make your own involvement obsolete?

Scaling up means replicating your workaround in different contexts and expanding your reach. At Women on Waves, the organization's goal is to provide accessible abortion services to women residing in countries where abortion is illegal. Gomperts's first workaround (providing safe abortions on a Dutch ship in international waters) could in principle be replicated near any country that has a coastline; it doesn't matter much if the ship sails to Poland, Brazil, or Morocco. The organization's second workaround (mailing off-label abortion pills with a prescription from a Dutch doctor) is even more flexible and has greater growth potential because it requires less time and resources to mail pills than to sail to various countries.

Scaling deep means establishing stronger ties and making yourself (or your organization) more deeply embedded in the context where your workaround operates. "Deep" and "up" aren't mutually exclusive—consider how M-Pesa pursued both strategies simultaneously. While Vodafone and Safaricom eagerly scaled M-Pesa's services "up" to reach different countries, they also ensured that the new banking platform became more "deeply" connected to local governments, businesses, and even traditional banks in Kenya. By focusing on these local and contextual factors, M-Pesa gradually influenced more of the country's policies and its citizens' daily lives than it would have had it not looked beyond its originally intended purpose.

Scaling out has to do with ensuring that your workaround

will outlast you. If your workaround relies on your knowledge, effort, or resources, what happens when you are gone (e.g., when you take up a new position or retire, when your funding runs out, when your company changes priorities, etc.)? This consideration is particularly relevant in the international development context: low-income countries have seen so many aid organizations and self-styled "hero"-like entrepreneurs, who often portray themselves as white messiahs. Instead of solving problems, their interventions frequently create more dependence and sometimes make things worse. Once a funding cycle ends or the entrepreneur gets distracted, the patches fall apart and cause hemorrhages: infrastructures collapse, money is divested, and people lose hope that things can change. When I went to Zambia to study ColaLife, locals reported that when they saw a USAID sign they assumed that the project would collapse basically upon its completion.

ColaLife's founders shared this frustration. From the outset, Jane and Simon Berry knew the organization's impact had to outlast their presence. In Simon's words, "We knew from the beginning we wanted to leave Zambia in a self-sustaining way, we've built in our own demise." They used piggyback workaround after piggyback workaround and made use of existing structures, gradually making themselves redundant so that they could leave the country, in Jane's words, "without being noticed." Although they set out to implement one workaround, they wound up using many in order to empower others, build autonomy, and better connect local actors to each other, so local actors can scale the approach "up" to more districts across the country. When the Berrys left the country, access to diarrhea treatment scaled up more organically, led by local players.

CORPORATE CULTURE

Workarounds happen in all kinds of organizations of different sizes and sectors. From hierarchical mining conglomerates to hyped start-ups, three key attributes in corporate culture can shape how people create, pursue, and value workarounds: dynamism, pragmatism, and accountability. The three best practices to implement them are to act first, then think; get to good enough; and ask forgiveness, not permission. We will now dive deeper into each of them.

Act First, Then Think

The essence of a workaround strategy is that it should be quick, malleable, and well suited to changing circumstances, including networks, resources, and knowledge. Yet we often fail to recognize that new experiences not only change how we think; they also change who we become—or, as organizational theorist Karl Weick puts it, "How can I know who I am until I see what I do?"

London Business School professor Herminia Ibarra says that we have to reverse the conventional wisdom that demands we "first think, then act" if we want to make change. Only after we try something unfamiliar can we observe the results, note how it feels, watch how others react, and reflect upon what the experience taught us.

Taking such an active, dynamic approach doesn't mean that you should think less. Rather it means that our sense-making processes—the ways we interpret our surroundings, develop our identities, and identify our possibilities—happen in situations of ambivalence and doubt, because the world around us is complex and constantly changing. I encourage you to embrace that uncertainty and explore the opportunities it produces—*then* reflect on your reactions.

When ColaLife started implementing its idea of piggybacking on Coca-Cola distribution to deliver lifesaving diarrhea medicines, the organization first developed the medication packaging and explored its piggyback idea through a quasi-experimental trial. By jumping in and acting first, Simon, Jane, and their local partners engaged with many stakeholders and then collected data and observations about what worked and what didn't. After running and assessing the trial, they realized that the space in the Coca-Cola crates wasn't what mattered most; in fact, they learned that transporters—riding bikes or motorcycles to deliver consumer goods to remote regions—often strapped the medicine around soda crates and other products, like sugar, coffee, and cooking oil. Their award-winning design for the packaging was nice, but it was actually the interplay between all members of the value chain that made it possible for ColaLife to build a self-sustaining model. Jane and Simon needed to act in order to react to the information they gained; they then pivoted from literally piggybacking on Coca-Cola crates to more abstractly piggybacking on the pre-existing value chains of consumer goods. That dynamism enabled the workaround to scale quickly across the country.

Get to Good Enough

Even the world's largest companies don't have complete knowledge and information about their problems, and their resources and skills are limited. And even if it were possible to take a perfect snapshot of the reality, their knowledge would be outdated almost immediately because the world changes in quick and unpredictable ways. The reality of our imperfect information is precisely why we need to value incomplete and partial approaches: they may be clumsy, but in the words of Steve Rayner, who was a professor at Oxford University, they "damn well work."

So what is the best way to create a nurturing environment for personal development in an organization while recognizing and actually valuing imperfection? We can start by learning from child development studies. British psychoanalyst Donald Winnicott was the first to conceptualize the idea of a "holding environment." He observed how parents who were available and reassuring but not demanding and intrusive provided a holding environment that facilitated their children's healthy growth. Not too lax and not too protective, "good enough" parents are the best equipped to lead their children into adulthood. They make children comfortable and curious while supporting but not stifling them as they gradually develop a robust and more independent sense of self. These adults-to-be will even be able to identify their parents' missteps—and that's excellent: children need to learn to cope with an imperfect and complex world.

A holding environment is exactly the kind of culture where workarounds flourish. Think of the many young scrappy organizations profiled in Part I: because they don't have much in the way of resources or power, they embraced a "good enough" ethos, and that allowed for partial, imperfect, and unconventional attempts at solutions.

Yet, like very rigid parents, leaders at large organizations often have a view of the "right" approach, and this stifles the personal development of their staff. The culture of "perfection" encourages staff to think about goals, tools, and opportunities traditionally rather than creatively, and it makes them feel too confident about a certain direction, in ways that lead them to miss out on other pathways that could be revealed through experimentation with the unknown.

The scrappy organizations featured in Part I have shaken things up and inspired new change-making opportunities by stretching the boundaries of the possible. For example, when Gomperts started providing abortions in international waters, most thought that "nothing was possible" for women in countries where abortions were illegal, except for the arduous process of changing the countries' legislation. Thanks to Gomperts's practical approach, others joined her cause, mobilized, and were inspired to try out new, good enough ways to push for change.

This culture of practicality can be nurtured in companies of all sizes and sectors, but most especially in the ones developing cutting-edge technologies. It can even be promoted by a series of workarounds coming from the company's basements. Consider how the early defiance of bootleggers at 3M and Hewlett-Packard changed those companies' corporate cultures and led to policies that support autonomy and flexibility for innovation. A culture of pragmatism doesn't need to be initiated from the top down; employees can trigger these changes by working around norms and challenging others to see the value of an imperfect and more experimental approach.

In some ways pragmatism and workarounds form a self-reinforced behavior: the more staff work around their obstacles, the more this behavior tends to instigate a culture of pragmatism in the organization, and the more the culture of pragmatism is shared by others, the more workarounds are likely to be conceived and implemented.

Ask for Forgiveness, Not Permission

Because workarounds bypass all sorts of visible obstacles, don't expect them to thrive in cultures that demand that members ask for permission for everything. Workaround-friendly cultures do benefit from some rules (otherwise what would there be to work around?), but workarounds flourish in rule-flouting cultures.

Centuries-old universities like Oxford and Cambridge have many, many rules stemming from long-standing traditions. At Cambridge, rules range from not stepping on certain colleges' grass to not singing "Happy Birthday to You" in the presence of fellows to being required to stay within a three-mile radius of Great St. Mary's Church for at least fifty-nine nights each term. People don't take these traditions too seriously. In fact, many students take pride in disregarding and bypassing them, and I often saw people pondering (or actively trying) to work around these rules. Sometimes this resulted in pranks (would ever-watchful doormen allow you to crawl instead of walk on the grass?), but more often it resulted in productivity. Staff and students often leveraged the ambiguity of rules to work around them.

This book, for example, was born out of an exploration enabled by a workaround. When I applied for my PhD at Cambridge, I wanted to study how to hack all sorts of complex systems to address pressing sustainability issues. This was uncharted territory for me: I knew very little about it, there was modest evidence on hacking at the time, no one had studied "hacking" as a means to expedite much-needed socio-environmental change, and I knew it would be seen as very risky by the university, since I'd have to engage with hackers, who often get a bad rap from the media. I also knew that the selection process at Cambridge is competitive, and having studied in Brazil most of my life I would compete against other PhD candidates who held degrees from Ivy League universities. I needed an amazing research proposal to get in, and the time wasn't ripe for "hacking." I then worked around my obstacles: I wrote a research proposal on a different topic that I knew well and that was clearly attractive for the university and funding bodies. Luckily, when I joined the Institute for Manufacturing at Cambridge, the shared ethos was "ask for forgiveness, not permission." So I didn't ask for permission—if my hacking idea worked, and if I could convince the university and my funders that it was worth pursuing, excellent; if it didn't, I could continue with my other research.

Though this shared ethos wasn't a formal rule, the oft-repeated instruction created an environment that nurtured deviant ideas, sometimes meant to push the boundaries of science and education one workaround at a time.

LEADERSHIP

In an article for *The New Yorker*, Malcolm Gladwell wrote, "The great accomplishment of [Steve] Jobs's life is how effectively he put his idiosyncrasies—his petulance, his narcissism, and his rudeness—in the service of perfection." Two problems with the idea of "perfect outliers" are immediately apparent. First, the portrayal and idolization of rich white men like Steve Jobs is inaccurate and intrinsically connected to pervasive racial, gender, and income inequalities. Their portrayal leads us to believe that they had rare hero-like abilities, when in reality the achievements attributed to them aren't only theirs, and it also excuses poor behavior—like petulance, narcissism, and rudeness—that is much more connected to privilege than to aptitude. Second, perfection is overrated; it's an unreachable abstraction, a speculation. The world changes because people are constantly attempting to explore *better* paths and manage messes, not because some visionaries have found and stubbornly pursued the *right* path.

Instead of idolizing these so-called change makers, I suggest focusing on two key aspects that the management community undervalues in leadership: the importance of a safety net and the ability to manage messes.

Taking Risks

University of Pennsylvania professor and best-selling author Adam Grant recognizes he missed a great investment opportunity because he assumed that all successful entrepreneurs are bold risk-takers. In his book *Originals*, Grant reports that an MBA student pitched Warby Parker's idea to him in 2009, offering Grant the chance to invest in the eyewear company, which is now worth billions of dollars. Grant declined the offer because Warby Parker's co-founders didn't behave like stereotypical successful entrepreneurs: they were unwilling to drop out of school, and none worked at the company full-time—they had job options lined up in case the company's launch flopped.

Business books often perpetuate the myth of the school dropout who with great determination and willpower pursues bold ideas from his (and these books do tend to focus on men, specifically) parents' garage. These leaders and risk-takers delay gratification and resist short-term temptations in pursuit of the right vision. While these incomplete and often inaccurate stories might make for nice television dramas, it is time to debunk the myth of the fearless hero-visionary. Many media darlings portrayed as great visionary risk-takers actually had a safety net and hedged their bets. For example, Bill Gates—whom his biographers often portray as the garage-based, solitary genius par excellence—waited an entire year after selling a new software program to leave school and concentrate on Microsoft full-time. And he didn't even drop out at first: he applied for a leave of absence and counted on his parents to bankroll him, keeping his options open in case Microsoft failed.

Leadership is not an innate ability of a few special individuals; it results from a series of decisions in situations of uncertainty, made by humans who experience fear and make mistakes while exploring new opportunities. In the midst of uncertainty a safety net helps us hedge our bets. Many people have been disenfranchised from turning into leaders because they didn't have a safety net. In contrast to testing out a business idea, devising workarounds doesn't require an initial great safety net; in fact, workarounds tend to flourish in frugal and scrappy contexts. Our future leaders can explore alternatives from the fringes without relying too much on privilege to protect them while they put a workaround to the test.

Things get more complicated when workarounds grow and new opportunities sprout from them. As workarounds develop they often require more implementation efforts—and that's the time when a safety net becomes critical. Consider how some of the most impactful workarounds profiled in Part I emerged from people who had full-time jobs or other safety nets, which gave them the stability they needed for their lives while they pursued workarounds that addressed the problems they actually cared about. For example, many of the cypherpunks who pushed the boundaries of cryptography had jobs in universities (such as MIT and Stanford) or in IT companies (such as IBM). Ruth Bader Ginsburg had a job at Rutgers Law School while she worked on the side on her first cases on sex-based discrimination with the American Civil Liberties Union. Hedging their bets allowed them to develop their workarounds further to amplify their impact without compromising their lives too much.

Managing Messes

The myth of the right path comes with the expectation that leaders have a nonnegotiable vision that they passionately pursue, even against all odds. The underlying assumption is that the future is predetermined, but it only reveals itself to a few privileged beings who negotiate the present to guide us all into the inevitable. Gianpiero Petriglieri, a professor at INSEAD, recounts that when he asks students what makes a good leader, someone promptly says "vision," and everyone nods in agreement. The students tend to think that visionary individuals direct and motivate the masses who follow. Petriglieri shows that effective leaders actually interpret times of uncertainty, soothing distress and helping to make sense of confusing predicaments. These leaders selectively illuminate challenges, providing just enough light or insight for orientation, reassurance, and cohesion, but not so much as to overwhelm or disturb.

Workarounds are only good enough, and leadership that encourages workarounds can, at best, be good enough, too. Leaders, in the words of organizational theorist Russell Ackoff, "manage messes well" rather than trying to paint a tidy version of a world that doesn't exist. Consider how different leaders responded during the height of the COVID-19 pandemic. New Zealand's Prime Minister Jacinda Ardern allowed citizens to understand the nature and severity of the challenge, gave them reassurance, and nurtured social cohesion while simultaneously pursuing the social distancing workaround. On the other hand, Brazilian president Jair Bolsonaro attempted to pretend the problem away, refusing to acknowledge the mess, let alone manage it. His self-aggrandizing leadership style didn't just take a toll on creativity and workaround friendliness—it cost thousands of lives.

TEAMWORK, OR THE LACK THEREOF

An organization's workaround friendliness isn't just up to leaders and higher-ups; it still often relies on workplace interactions. Yet the ones who aren't at the top often find themselves in a straitjacket: their bosses don't accept their bold ideas, their companies are too focused on the bread and butter, their colleagues are obsessed with punching the clock from nine to five . . . The good news is that workarounds don't *necessarily* require the engagement of others. If you do involve others your impact can be even greater, but you won't want would-be collaborators standing in the way of you reaching a goal. Here I'll give you some entry points to reflect on whether and how you would like to collaborate with others.

Working Around with Others

Methods of engaging with potential workaround partners are probably as diverse as workarounds themselves. Nevertheless I've benefited from using what management scholars call "robust action" to generate ideas with people from all walks of life in many different organizational contexts. The central tenets of robust action echo themes that run through this book: we don't really know much about our problems, and short-term interventions facilitate later growth and exploration.

Robust action suggests three forms of engagement. There is no specific order, and you can combine them. The first is to engage with multiple viewpoints and learn as much as possible from many different interpretations and observations. Since inspiration for workarounds often comes from exposure to different perspectives, you can particularly explore beyond the confines of your organization. Seek out different voices, including those you may be unaccustomed to hearing. The second is to design architectures of participation that provide platforms (from social media to in-person meetings) for heterogeneous actors to interact, share, and learn together. The third is to allow for experimentation with others. Invest in incomplete ideas and in finding complementarities, which will allow you to identify new opportunities.

This approach can still be used one-on-one and benefit from the prompts from chapter 7. For example, you can simply reach out to some people via email to ask for input. You may list the problem you're thinking about, outline the visible obstacle, run through the conventional solution, and then ask them for a workaround idea. Start a conversation.

If you're at an organization, you might host a workshop. From my experience running these sorts of gatherings, I can happily report that they need minimal instruction. You'd need to explain the four kinds of workarounds and present a prompt or two to get participants to think about specific challenges, whether they are personal or organizational problems. Then encourage creativity, nurture "good enough" responses, and allow people to discuss, share, and think differently. Finally, ask participants to prioritize ideas based on their (or your organization's) interests, feasibility, and potential impact.

Working Around Despite Others

Collaboration may be very fruitful, but it doesn't always make sense to solicit advice from everyone you can squeeze in a conference room. In fact, workarounds may help the ones who want to get more (or different) things done despite others in their workplace, or even to procrastinate without grave repercussions.

If you think creatively enough, you'll find opportunities to work around your time constraints despite others, if you, for example, parasitically piggyback on other people's efforts; through next best workarounds that will be good enough to deliver on your tasks partially and with minimal effort; if you identify roundabout workarounds that buy you extra time to hand in that boring report; or if you spot loopholes that are "technically right" so that you can extend your deadlines.

I once had a boss who answered emails erratically, causing me constant stress as I wondered if he'd get around to sending me information in time, and bringing on countless hours of ruminating about how to elicit quicker responses. In what order did he answer emails? How did he prioritize them? Did he start from the top or from the bottom? As a lowly intern and generally conflict-avoidant person, I felt powerless to demand prompt responses. I asked other colleagues who worked with him and slowly gathered information about his email-answering habits. I finally figured out that he frantically wrote responses early in the morning, around five-thirty a.m., beginning with, and paying more attention to, the most recent emails at the top of his inbox.

Thanks to this information, I realized that the emails I sent him during the workday were basically going to the bottom of his inbox. Then I tried something new: instead of sending an email as soon as I wrote it, I programmed the message to be sent at pre-scheduled times in the wee hours of the morning. I'd vary the times, sending a message one day at 1:47 a.m. and at 2:03 a.m. on another, to avoid suspicion. In the first month, the response rate grew by 63 percent (I know, I'm such a nerd that I did the math). My ex-boss still thinks I was a night owl, whereas in fact I'm an early bird who was enjoying my best REM sleep as my emails arrived in his inbox.

Sometimes we want or need to work around others rather than with them. It's up to you to decide what's necessary or appropriate in a situation. All things considered, my email anxiety was pretty trivial. We often find ourselves facing worse daily hurdles in our workplace, from colleagues' annoying habits to codified rules imposed by higher-ups to unwritten expectations. With workarounds, you can mitigate those challenges as quietly and subtly as you see fit.

With or Without Others?

Much like fashion, different business strategies fall in and out of favor. In the not too distant past, businesses focused on keeping their innovation projects secret, in-house, limiting collaboration. More recently businesses have embraced open innovation strategies, increasingly valuing input from diverse sources, sometimes even collaborating with their rivals. They not only consult others; they also actively engage with a wider array of stakeholders in the process of co-creation.

Collaboration has advantages and disadvantages. The advantages are pretty obvious: working with others means access to more resources, knowledge, and experiences upon which you can build. On the other hand, collaborating is challenging and time-consuming. Identifying and engaging partners; actively listening; harmonizing different goals, schedules, and work styles; and forging agreement are all big undertakings.

Furthermore, group decisions aren't necessarily best. In fact, psychologists and behavioral economists have long indicated that groups' preferences for conflict aversion lead to overconfidence in popular but poor decisions, a phenomenon psychologists call "groupthink."

Pursuing workarounds doesn't mean putting together elaborate collaborations just for the sake of collaboration. Instead, you may want to begin by focusing on consulting with a select few people you think can contribute with skills or resources (including enthusiasm) rather than building a large, heavily invested team that would require management and consensus building. As your workaround gains traction and your needs change, you'll organically find and work with other collaborators in different capacities.

The workaround is immediate, resourceful, and good enough, and its core benefit is that it allows you to get things done unconventionally. Collaboration may facilitate workarounds, but flexibility trumps collaboration. If you are hyper-fixated on teamwork or ruminating without putting new ideas to the test, you may yet come up with a great, people-pleasing solution, but you aren't approaching it with a workaround attitude, and you won't ultimately help your organization become more workaround-friendly.

Coda

Workarounds Outside of Work

You're ready to put that new cake recipe to the test. As you start prepping your ingredients you realize that you're out of milk—and hell no, there's no way you're driving all the way to Walmart for milk. There's cream in your fridge, though. What if you dilute it with water and use it as a substitute? You bake and devour your cake while binge-watching Netflix, piggybacking on your parents' account. The next morning you feel like an old sloth, so you won't have time to go to the gym to burn some of those cake calories. Instead, you get off your bus one stop early to get your steps in . . .

Even if you don't notice them, workarounds shape your routine. While clumsily helping you cope with your messy life, they allow you to try alternatives to the commonplace way of doing things and to organically use what works and forget about what doesn't. Once a workaround succeeds, it may seem quite obvious that it was always the right path forward.

Workarounds are so silently effective that we don't give them the praise they deserve. During a lecture, after briefly introducing my research in a classroom, a skeptical student dismissively said that workarounds were like "ordering a Big Mac with a Diet Coke," as if they were futile efforts that merely provide the emotional comfort of feeling like you're "doing something" but leaving the real problem unsolved.

I must give the student some credit: A "Big Mac with a Diet Coke" is at best a marginally healthier choice, and workarounds are imperfect, too. Yet this student's analogy is misleading. It doesn't take into consideration that too often we assume that problems are clearly specified and that there's a single way to solve each of them. Would a slightly less caloric fast-food order alone solve health problems? Probably not, but was she referring to the bad eating habits of an individual or to a complex system that feeds us highly processed but not very nutritious foods? What does it mean to be healthy in the first place? Can a paleo diet permanently solve an individual's health problems? A society's?

If you seek good health, you're aiming at a moving target. We are better off if we stop fixating on ideal one-off solutions and focus instead on addressing our problems adaptively, continuously, and imaginatively—and workarounds may unlock the process of ongoing change that the world needs.

A better analogy is to think of workarounds as you would address a migraine. If you've had one you know the value of addressing a symptom even if you don't understand the underlying cause. These interventions may not be optimal solutions, but they damn well work, quickly addressing our urgent needs. As with migraines, repeatedly encountering and coping with the same challenges might help you to begin recognizing patterns and developing more long-lasting solutions, including some that were completely unexpected from the outset.

You may recall how Ruth Bader Ginsburg found a workaround that served as an entry point, which eventually enabled her and others to topple a whole system of sex-based discrimination. What you may not have considered when reading Part I is that her workaround helped to illuminate and re-evaluate different challenges, too. She may not have thought much about gender identity or sexual orientation when she was first arguing for women's legal rights, but her workaround enabled reinterpretations of gender expression and identity, which have later changed the understanding of discrimination in many other legal decisions.

Workarounds like RBG's allow us to gracefully and creatively deviate from the script that constrains us. It's by deviating from the script that we explore alternatives that gradually push for deeper changes to how we interpret, judge, and interact with the world.

Workarounds also allow us to shake things up, especially in situations where we feel paralyzed. This outlook applies to our mundane challenges, but it is even more pronounced when we look at large-scale social problems that are more complex and uncertain. Think about poverty, climate change, inequalities. They persist for a reason. Often decision-makers drown themselves in complex analysis and bureaucracy. Those of us who don't have an important seat at the table are left feeling powerless and trapped by hierarchy.

The scrappy organizations featured in this book saw a world of dynamism and possibility despite their minimal resources, power, and information. Thanks to them I understood how simple workarounds can help us muddle through uncertain situations, alleviate our urgent needs, and even explore previously uncharted roads that may take us to new and better places.

Acknowledgments

When I finished writing this book, I recollected a memory from my adolescence—a reminder of how much my parents have influenced my interests, values, and aspirations. They gave me a credit card and a warning: "You must ask before purchasing anything that isn't books or food." A couple of decades later, I find myself publishing a book and married to a pastry chef! Could Freud explain that, Mom?

My partner, Ju, supported me every step of the way. She read early drafts, gave advice, helped me find cases, and even tolerated me when I felt tired and grouchy. I am very thankful for her love and encouragement as we navigated new terrains.

This research wouldn't have started if not for Steve Evans. When I scheduled my first meeting with him, I assumed I would find a professor wearing a tweed suit, speaking in complicated jargon. He came to our meeting wearing cargo shorts and unmatching socks—one red, one green. Steve has since inspired and stimulated me to find unconventional pairings, too.

One of the greatest pleasures of writing this book was the opportunity to work with, and learn from, some incredible people. Max Brockman was very supportive from the outset. He helped translate my Bracken Bower Prize essay into a book proposal. He also bridged me with Will Schwalbe, who I quickly realized was the perfect match for this work. Will helped sharpen my ideas, structure the book, and improve my writing. Since Sam Zukergood joined the editorial team, I could count on her fresh eyes, enthusiasm, and detail orientation. I am thankful to Maggie Carr for her careful copy editing and to Morgan Mitchell for her attention to detail as the production editor. And my ideas would have been indecipherable if I hadn't had the privilege to draft with, and learn from, Andrea Brody-Barre.

I have been very fortunate to receive funding and institutional support from multiple sources for the past seven years, which were critical for the completion of this research—primarily from the Gates Cambridge Trust, Brazil's CNPq, IBM Center for the Business of Government, Santander, the Ford Foundation, the Skoll Centre for Social Entrepreneurship, and the universities of Oxford, Durham, and Cambridge.

The advice and unwavering support from Marc Ventresca and Tyrone Pitsis in the last three years were more than I could have hoped for! In Oxford, I have also benefited from interactions with many colleagues, such as Ronald Roy, Jeroen Bergmann, Malcolm McCulloch, Marya Besharov, Daniel Armanios, Thomas Hellmann, Pinar Ozcan, Annabelle Gawer, Tom Lawrence, Richard Whittington, Peter Drobac, Zainab Kabba, Jessica Jacobson, Bronwyn Dugtig, and many others who have supported my work.

This research was sharpened through many discussions with people from all walks of life. Some were pivotal in identifying or connecting me with scrappy organizations, such as Arthur

Kux, Asiya Islam, Alice Musabende, Anil Gupta, Raghavendra Seshagiri, Arjun and Nikita Hari, Luis Claudio Caldas, Mariana Savaget, Ana Claudia Grossi, Eduardo Maciel, and Lucia Corsini. Others have either promoted my work, helped interpret data, or shared valuable feedback—such as Cassi Henderson, Tim Minshall, Frank Tietze, Mike Tennant, Thomas Roulet, Rob Phaal, Cansu Karabiyik, Courtney Froehlig, Susan Hart, Christos Tsinopoulos, Flavia Maximo, Curie Park, Catherine Tilley, Martin Geissdoerfer, Olamide Oguntoye, Kirsten Van Fossen, Thayla Zomer, Clara Aranda, Aline Khoury, Juliana Brito, Laura Waisbich, Flavia Carvalho, Tulio Chiarini, Ali Kharrazi, Gabriela Reis, Nisia Werneck, Ana Burcharth, and Carlos Arruda.

I am grateful for all colleagues in my institutional homes, the Department of Engineering Sciences, the Saïd Business School, and Worcester College (University of Oxford), and the many students who have helped me experiment with early ideas. Last but not least, this work would never be possible without the knowledge of Simon and Jane Berry and the many other interviewees around the world who opened their minds to me. I hope this book does justice to their generosity and wit.

Notes

Author's Note

ix *roughly 1.7 million children . . . worldwide* UNICEF, "Diarrhoea—UNICEF Data," UNICEF Data, July 29, 2021, https://data.unicef.org/topic/child-health /diarrhoeal-disease/.

Introduction

2 *computer hacker . . . ATM numbers* James Verini, "The Great Cyberheist," *The New York Times*, November 10, 2010, https://www.nytimes.com/2010/11/14 /magazine/14Hacker-t.html.

4 *"Wherever there are systems . . . everywhere"* Paul Buchheit, "Applied Philoso-phy, A.k.a. 'Hacking,'" Blogspot.com, November 5, 2021, http://paulbuchheit .blogspot.com/2009/10/applied-philosophy-aka-hacking.html.

1: The Piggyback

12 *low-income countries* For a definition of "low-income" economies, see the World Bank Atlas method. In the 2022 fiscal year, these were defined as those countries with a GNI per capita of $1,045 or less. Lower middle-income are those with a GNI per capita between $1,046 and $4,095; upper middle-income econ-omies are those with a GNI per capita between $4,096 and $12,695; and high-income economies are those with a GNI per capita of $12,696 or more. For more information, see the World Bank, "World Bank Country and Lending Groups," Data World Bank, 2022, https://datahelpdesk.worldbank.org/knowledgebase /articles/906519-world-bank-country-and-lending-groups.

12 *In biological terms . . . parasitic* Jan Sapp, *Evolution by Association: A History of Symbiosis* (New York: Oxford University Press, 1994).

13 *BBC article* Peter Day, "ColaLife: Turning Profits into Healthy Babies," *BBC News*, July 22, 2013, https://www.bbc.co.uk/news/magazine-23348408.

14 *according to the CDC . . . worldwide* "Global Diarrhea Burden," Centers for Disease Control and Prevention, 2021, https://www.cdc.gov/healthywater/global/diarrhea-burden.html#one.

14 *higher rate of mortality among children . . . combined* Li Liu, Hope L. Johnson, Simon Cousens, Jamie Perin, Susana Scott, Joy E. Lawn, Igor Rudan, et al., "Global, Regional, and National Causes of Child Mortality: An Updated Systematic Analysis for 2010 with Time Trends Since 2000," *The Lancet* 379, no. 9832 (June 2012): 2151–61, https://doi.org/10.1016/s0140-6736(12)60560-1.

15 *Public-sector responses. . . . fronts* World Health Organization and UNICEF, "Diarrhoea: Why Children Are Still Dying and What Can Be Done," 2009, http://apps.who.int/iris/bitstream/handle/10665/44174/9789241598415_eng.pdf;jsessionid=2DE9081A5630B2F287B434D374E9F218?sequence=1.

15 *Only 50 percent of rural households . . . shortages* Ministry of Health, Republic of Zambia, "National Health Strategic Plan 2011–2015," December 2011.

15 *Improving infrastructure . . . barriers* Rohit Ramchandani, "Emulating Commercial, Private-Sector Value-Chains to Improve Access to ORS and Zinc in Rural Zambia: Evaluation of the ColaLife Trial," PhD diss., Johns Hopkins Bloomberg School of Public Health, 2016, https://jscholarship.library.jhu.edu/bitstream/handle/1774.2/39229/RAMCHANDANI-DISSERTATION-2016.pdf.

16 *fifty-nine pharmacies . . . expansion* Dalberg Global Development Advisors and MIT-Zaragoza International Logistics Program, "The Private Sector's Role in Health Supply Chains: Review of the Role and Potential for Private Sector Engagement in Developing Country Health Supply Chains," October 2008, https://healthmarketinnovations.org/sites/default/files/Private%20Sector%20Role%20in%20Supply%20Chains.pdf.

17 *BBC feature* Simon Berry, "A Video of the Full Interview with iPM," Cola-Life, July 5, 2008, https://www.colalife.org/2008/07/05/a-video-of-the-full-interview-with-ipm/.

19 *the uptake . . . comparison* Ramchandani, "Emulating Commercial, Private-Sector Value-Chains."

22 *use . . . 53 percent* Simon Berry, Jane Berry, and Rohit Ramchandani, "We've Got Designs on Change: 1—Findings from Our Endline Household Survey (KYTS-ACE)," ColaLife, March 31, 2018, https://www.colalife.org/2018/03/31/weve-got-designs-on-change-1-findings-from-our-endline-household-survey-kyts-ace/.

23 *collected data . . . together* ColaLife, "The Case for Co-Packaging of ORS and Zinc," ColaLife, December 4, 2015, https://www.colalife.org/co-pack/.

23 *the WHO's Essential Medicines List* World Health Organization, "WHO Model Lists of Essential Medicines," accessed April 2020, https://www.who .int/groups/expert-committee-on-selection-and-use-of-essential-medicines /essential-medicines-lists.

24 *convince governments . . . decisions* Simon Berry, "The ColaLife Playbook Launches Today (28-Oct-20)," ColaLife, October 28, 2020, https://www .colalife.org/2020/10/28/the-colalife-playbook-launches-today-28-oct-20/.

25 *number of people who owned a television . . . younger* Christopher H. Sterling and John Michael Kittross, *Stay Tuned: A Concise History of American Broadcasting* (Belmont, Calif.: Wadsworth, 1990).

25 *They owned . . . TVs* Deborah L. Jaramillo, "The Rise and Fall of the Television Broadcasters Association, 1943–1951," *Journal of E-Media Studies* 5, no. 1 (2016), https://doi.org/10.1349/PS1.1938-6060.A.459.

25 *Television advertising revenue . . . two years* William H. Young and Nancy K. Young, *The 1930s (American Popular Culture Through History)* (Westport, Conn.: Greenwood Press, 2002).

25 *The NAB . . . to geographies* Frank Orme, "The Television Code," *The Quarterly of Film Radio and Television* 6, no. 4 (July 1, 1952): 404–13, https://doi.org /10.2307/1209951.

26 *Uncle Ben's Rice and M&Ms . . . time slot* John A. Martilla and Donald L. Thompson, "The Perceived Effects of Piggyback Television Commercials," *Journal of Marketing Research* 3, no. 4 (November 1966): 365–71, https://doi.org/10 .1177/002224376600300404.

27 *"M&Ms melt . . . hands"* Alison Alexander, Louise M. Benjamin, Keisha Hoerrner, and Darrell Roe, "'We'll Be Back in a Moment': A Content Analysis of Advertisements in Children's Television in the 1950s," *Journal of Advertising* 27, no. 3 (May 31, 2013): 1–9, https://doi.org/10.1080/00913367.1998.10673558.

27 *ten years after . . . spot commercials)* Alexander, Benjamin, Hoerrner, and Roe, "'We'll Be Back in a Moment.'"

27 *included manufacturers . . . larger businesses* John M. Lee, "Advertising: Piggyback Commercial Fight," *The New York Times*, January 8, 1964, https://www.nytimes .com/1964/01/08/archives/advertising-piggyback-commercial-fight.html.

28 *TV ad spending in the United States . . . Super Bowl* Brandon Katz, "Digital Ad Spending Will Surpass TV Spending for the First Time in US History," *Forbes*, September 14, 2016, https://www.forbes.com/sites/brandonkatz/2016

/09/14/digital-ad-spending-will-surpass-tv-spending-for-the-first-time-in-u
-s-history/?sh=64479e1b4207.

28 *broadcast TV viewership . . . and forty-nine* Nielsen, "The Nielsen Comparable
Metrics Report: Q4 2016," https://www.nielsen.com/wp-content/uploads/sites
/3/2019/04/q4–2016-comparable-metrics-report.pdf.

30 *"Once the blackout happened . . . nothing going on"* Angela Watercutter, "How
Oreo Won the Marketing Super Bowl with a Timely Blackout Ad on Twitter,"
Wired, February 4, 2013, https://www.wired.com/2013/02/oreo-twitter-super
-bowl/.

30 *teaser posters . . . "Mr. SquarePants will see you now"* Jess Denham, "Spongebob Squarepants Film Posters Spoof Fifty Shades of Grey Movie and Jurassic
World," *The Independent*, February 2, 2015, https://www.independent.co.uk
/arts-entertainment/films/news/spongebob-squarepants-movie-posters-spoof
-fifty-shades-grey-and-jurassic-world-10018046.html.

31 *Pepsi's video . . . approval of the protesters* Daniel Victor, "Pepsi Pulls Ad Accused
of Trivializing Black Lives Matter," *The New York Times*, April 5, 2017, https://
www.nytimes.com/2017/04/05/business/kendall-jenner-pepsi-ad.html.

32 *American Apparel's tone-deaf ad . . . $70 billion in damage* Steve Olenski,
"American Apparel's Hurricane Sandy Sale—Brilliant or Boneheaded?," *Forbes*,
October 31, 2012, https://www.forbes.com/sites/marketshare/2012/10/31
/american-apparels-hurricane-sandy-sale-brilliant-or-boneheaded/?sh=754d930
e5d75.

34 *Airbnb host created a listing . . . outcompeted its rival* Morgan Brown, "The
Making of Airbnb," *Boston Hospitality Review* 4, no. 1 (2016).

36 *Approximately 9 percent of the global population . . . overweight* Max Roser and
Hannah Ritchie, "Hunger and Undernourishment," *Our World in Data*, October
8, 2019, https://ourworldindata.org/hunger-and-undernourishment.

36 *according to the WHO . . . iodine deficiency* World Health Organization, "Assessment of Iodine Deficiency Disorders and Monitoring Their Elimination: A
Guide for Programme Managers," 3rd ed., 2007, World Health Organization,
http://apps.who.int/iris/bitstream/handle/10665/43781/9789241595827_eng
.pdf?sequence=1.

36 *About 740 million people had goiter* World Health Organization, "Goitre as a De-
terminant of the Prevalence and Severity of Iodine Deficiency Disorders in Populations," Vitamin and Mineral Nutrition Information System, 2014, https://apps
.who.int/iris/bitstream/handle/10665/133706/WHO_NMH_NHD_EPG_14
.5_eng.pdf?sequence=1&isAllowed=y.

36 *In 1924 . . . afterward* R. M. Olin, "Iodine Deficiency and Prevalence of Simple Goiter in Michigan," *Public Health Reports (1896–1970)* 39, no. 26 (June 24, 1924): 1568–71, http://www.jstor.org/stable/4577210.

36 *by the 1930s goiter . . . concerns* Data from two articles: David Bishai and Ritu Nabubola, "The History of Food Fortification in the United States: Its Relevance for Current Fortification Efforts in Developing Countries," *Economic Development and Cultural Change* 51, no. 1 (October 2002), https://doi.org/10.1086/345361; and Jeffrey R. Backstrand, "The History and Future of Food Fortification in the United States: A Public Health Perspective," *Nutrition Reviews* 60, no. 1 (January 1, 2002): 15–26, https://doi.org/10.1301/002966402760240390.

37 *UNICEF . . . world's population)* UNICEF, "Iodine," https://data.unicef.org/topic/nutrition/iodine/.

37 *In the 1990s Chile . . . occurred* Data from two articles: Gail G. Harrison, "Public Health Interventions to Combat Micronutrient Deficiencies," *Public Health Reviews* 32, no. 1 (June 2, 2010): 256–66, https://doi.org/10.1007/bf03391601; and Eva Hertrampf and Fanny Cortes, "Folic Acid Fortification of Wheat Flour: Chile," *Nutrition Reviews* 62, no. 1 (June 2004): S44–48, https://doi.org/10.1111/j.1753-4887.2004.tb00074.x.

37 *A randomized trial . . . 50 percent* T. H. Tulchinsky, D. Nitzan Kaluski, and E. M. Berry, "Food Fortification and Risk Group Supplementation Are Vital Parts of a Comprehensive Nutrition Policy for Prevention of Chronic Diseases," *European Journal of Public Health* 14, no. 3 (September 1, 2004): 226–28, https://doi.org/10.1093/eurpub/14.3.226.

37 *set of guidelines . . . experts* World Health Organization and Food and Agriculture Organization of the United Nations, *Guidelines on Food Fortification with Micronutrients*, eds. Lindsay Allen, Bruno de Benoist, Omar Dary, and Richard Hurrell (WHO, 2006).

38 *According to the Global Alliance for Improved Nutrition . . . fortify foods* Sharada Keats, "Let's Close the Gaps on Food Fortification—for Better Nutrition," Global Nutrition Report, January 28, 2019, https://globalnutritionreport.org/blog/lets-close-the-gaps-on-food-fortification-for-better-nutrition/.

38 *A study from 2010 . . . intake of iron* Victor Fulgoni and Rita Buckley, "The Contribution of Fortified Ready-to-Eat Cereal to Vitamin and Mineral Intake in the US Population, NHANES 2007–2010," *Nutrients* 7, no. 6 (May 25, 2015): 3949–58, https://doi.org/10.3390/nu7063949.

38 *in 2009 Nestlé . . . vitamin A* Nestlé, "Nestlé in Society: Creating Shared Value and Meeting Our Commitments 2017," 2017, https://www.nestle.com/sites/default

/files/asset-library/documents/library/documents/corporate_social_responsibility
/nestle-csv-full-report-2017-en.pdf.

39 *The story of M-Pesa . . . services* For more information, see these articles and
case studies: Nick Hughes and Susie Lonie, "M-PESA: Mobile Money for the
'Unbanked' Turning Cellphones into 24-Hour Tellers in Kenya," *Innovations:
Technology, Governance, Globalization* 2, no. 1–2 (April 2007): 63–81, https://doi
.org/10.1162/itgg.2007.2.1-2.63; Tavneet Suri and William Jack, "The Long-
Run Poverty and Gender Impacts of Mobile Money," *Science* 354, no. 6317 (December 9, 2016): 1288–92, https://doi.org/10.1126/science.aah5309; Isaac Mbiti
and David Weil, "Mobile Banking: The Impact of M-Pesa in Kenya," in *African
Successes, Volume III: Modernization and Development*, eds. Sebastian Edwards, Simon Johnson, and David N. Weil (Chicago: University of Chicago Press, 2016),
247–93; and Benjamin Ngugi, Matthew Pelowski, and Javier Gordon Ogembo,
"M-Pesa: A Case Study of the Critical Early Adopters' Role in the Rapid Adoption
of Mobile Money Banking in Kenya," *The Electronic Journal of Information Systems
in Developing Countries* 43, no. 1 (September 2010): 1–16, https://doi.org/10.1002
/j.1681-4835.2010.tb00307.x.

41 *The DfID granted about $20 million . . . existing services* Lisa Duke and Rajesh
Chandy, "M-Pesa & Nick Hughes," CS-11-010, London Business School, August 2018, https://publishing.london.edu/cases/m-pesa-nick-hughes/.

43 *In 2005 the informal sector constituted about 80 percent of the population* Kenya
National Bureau of Statistics, "Economic Survey 2005," 2005, https://www
.knbs.or.ke/?wpdmpro=economic-survey-2005-3.

43 *70 percent of the country's population lived in remote regions* World Bank, "Rural
Population (% of Total Population)," Data World Bank, 2018, https://data
.worldbank.org/indicator/SP.RUR.TOTL.ZS.

43 *80 percent of Kenya's population remained unbanked* E. Totolo, F. Gwer, and
J. Odero, "The Price of Being Banked," FSD Kenya, August 2017, https://
www.fsdkenya.org/blogs-publications/publications/the-price-of-being
-banked-2/.

44 *opening . . . per year* Kenya National Bureau of Statistics, "Economic Survey
2005."

44 *Within only two years of its launch . . . per month* Michael Joseph, "FY 2008/2009
Annual Results Presentation & Investor Update," Safaricom, 2009, https://www
.safaricom.co.ke/images/Investorrelation/2008-2009_results_announcement
_and_investor_update.pdf.

44 *It is estimated . . . different contexts* Vodafone, "M-PESA," Vodafone.com, ac-

cessed April 2020, https://www.vodafone.com/about-vodafone/what-we-do
/consumer-products-and-services/m-pesa.

45 *BBC profile . . . hefty markup* Will Smale, "The Mistake That Led to a £1.2bn
Business," *BBC News*, January 28, 2019, https://www.bbc.com/news/business
-46985443.

46 *He started to swap . . . with ties to the United Kingdom* See these two articles: Wise,
"The Wise Story," accessed April 2020, https://wise.com/gb/about/our-story; and
PwC, "Downright Disruptive Technology—We Meet TransferWise Co-Founder
Kristo Käärmann," *Fast Growth Companies* (blog), April 25, 2014, https://pwc
.blogs.com/fast_growth_companies/2014/04/downright-disruptive-technology
-we-meet-transferwise-co-founder-kristo-k%C3%A4%C3%A4rmann.html.

46 *It offered the real exchange rate . . . per transaction* See these two sources: Jordan
Bishop, "TransferWise Review: The Future of International Money Transfers Is
Here," *Forbes*, November 29, 2017, https://www.forbes.com/sites/bishopjordan
/2017/11/29/transferwise-review/?sh=34e4584419f0; and Wise, "Our Mission
to Zero Fees—an Update," Wise News, October 23, 2017, https://wise.com/gb
/blog/transferwise-drops-price-from-uk.

47 *An internal memo of Santander . . . "rate mark-ups"* Patrick Collinson, "Revealed: The Huge Profits Earned by Big Banks on Overseas Money Transfers,"
The Guardian, April 8, 2017, https://www.theguardian.com/money/2017/apr
/08/leaked-santander-international-money-transfers-transferwise.

48 *Almost a decade after its creation . . . every day* Wise (formerly TransferWise),
"Annual Report and Consolidated Financial Statements for the Year Ended 31
March 2019," 2019.

48 *In 2020 TransferWise was worth over $5 billion* Reuters Staff, "TransferWise
Completes $319 Million Secondary Share Sale at a $5 Billion Valuation,"
Reuters, July 28, 2020, https://www.reuters.com/article/transferwise-funding
-idUSL2N2EZ18V.

2: The Loophole

51 *In the year of that call, the average interest rate for credit card debt in Brazil was 323
percent per year* G1 Globo, "Brasil Tem Maior Juro do Cartão Entre Países da
América Latina, Diz Proteste," *G1 Economia*, July 17, 2012, http://g1.globo.com
/economia/seu-dinheiro/noticia/2012/07/brasil-tem-maior-juro-do-cartao
-entre-paises-da-america-latina-diz-proteste.html.

51 *The rate . . . went up to 875 percent* Pedro Peduzzi, "Juros Anuais do Cartão de
Crédito Chegam a Até 875%," *Agência Brasil*, March 14, 2021, https://agenciabrasil

.ebc.com.br/economia/noticia/2021-03/juros-anuais-do-cartao-de-credito
-chegam-ate-875.

51 *the second-highest rate. . . . in Peru* Banco Central de Reserva del Perú Ge-
rencia Central de Estudios Económicos, "Tasas de Interés," BCRPData, accessed April 2020, https://estadisticas.bcrp.gob.pe/estadisticas/series/mensuales
/tasas-de-interes.

51 *Even the Code of Hammurabi . . . silver-based loan* Robert P. Maloney, "Usury
and Restrictions on Interest-Taking in the Ancient Near East," *Catholic Biblical Quarterly* 36, no. 1 (January 1974): 1–20, https://www.jstor.org/stable
/43713641.

52 *The Merchant of Venice . . . practically impossible* William Shakespeare, *The Merchant of Venice*, ed. Laura Hutchings (Harlow, Essex, UK: Longman, 1994).

54 *the Cayman Islands—a country that houses more offshore companies than people*
Jacques Peretti, "The Cayman Islands—Home to 100,000 Companies and the
£8.50 Packet of Fish Fingers," *The Guardian*, January 18, 2016, https://www
.theguardian.com/us-news/2016/jan/18/the-cayman-islands-home-to-100000
-companies-and-the-850-packet-of-fish-fingers.

55 *defense of Arthur Ewert . . . horrific torture* Amelia Coutinho, "Arthur Ernst
Ewert," in *Centro de Pesquisa e Documentação de História Contemporânea do Brasil*, Fundação Getulio Vargas (FGV), accessed April 2020, http://www.fgv.br
/cpdoc/acervo/dicionarios/verbete-biografico/arthur-ernst-ewert.

56 *lawyer Sobral Pinto agreed to represent* Daniel M. Neves, "Como Se Defende
um Comunista: uma Análise Retórico-Discursiva da Defesa Judicial de Harry
Berger por Sobral Pinto," MSc Thesis, Universidade Federal de São João del-Rei,
2013, https://ufsj.edu.br/portal2-repositorio/File/mestletras/Daniel_Monteiro
_Neves.pdf.

56 *The act . . . and light* Presidência da República Casa Civil Subchefia para
Assuntos Jurídicos (Brazil), "Decreto Nº 24.645, de 10 de Julho de 1934," ac-
cessed April 2020, http://www.planalto.gov.br/ccivil_03/decreto/1930-1949
/D24645impressao.htm.

56 *He described how Ewert's treatment . . . human rights in the country* See these
two sources: Gabriel Giorgi, "El Animal Comunista," Hemispheric Institute,
accessed April 2020, https://hemisphericinstitute.org/en/emisferica-101/10-1
-dossier/el-animal-comunista.htm; and Neves, "Como Se Defende um Comunista."

58 *Malta allowed it only in 2011* Jake Wallis Simons, "Malta: Moment of Deci-

sion on Divorce," *The Guardian*, May 28, 2011, https://www.theguardian.com /lifeandstyle/2011/may/28/malta-divorce-referendum.

58 *Chile in 2004* Daniela Horvitz Lennon, "Family Law in Chile: Overview," Thomsom Reuters Practical Law, 2020, https://uk.practicallaw.thomsonreuters .com/9-568-3568?transitionType=Default&contextData=(sc.Default)&first-Page=true.

58 *Ireland in 1997* Rachael O'Connor, "On This Day in 1997, Ireland's Controversial Divorce Laws Came into Effect," *The Irish Post*, February 27, 2020, https:// www.irishpost.com/news/day-1997-irelands-controversial-divorce-laws-came -effect-180563.

58 *Argentina in 1987* Randall Hackley, "Divorce Is Now Legal in Argentina But, So Far, Few Couples Have Taken the Break," *Los Angeles Times*, July 12, 1987, https://www.latimes.com/archives/la-xpm-1987-07-12-mn-3473-story .html.

58 *Brazil in 1977* "Brazilian President Approves Bill Allowing Limited Right to Divorce," *The New York Times*, December 27, 1977, https://www.nytimes.com /1977/12/27/archives/brazilian-president-approves-bill-allowing-limited -right-to-divorce.html.

58 *the first to allow no-fault divorce was California* Herma Hill Kay, "An Appraisal of California's No-Fault Divorce Law," *California Law Review* 75, no. 1 (1987): 291–319, https://doi.org/10.2307/3480581.

58 *the last was New York, only in 2010* Post Staff Report, "NY Last State to Recognize 'No Fault' Divorce," *New York Post*, August 16, 2010, https://nypost.com /2010/08/16/ny-last-state-to-recognize-no-fault-divorce/.

58 *some countries granted . . . foreigners* Wendy Paris, "Destination Divorces Are Turning Heartbreaks into Holidays," *Quartz*, April 9, 2015, https://qz.com /377785/destination-divorces-are-turning-heartbreaks-into-holidays/.

58 *most jurisdictions honor legal instruments agreed to abroad* Rosenstiel v. Rosenstiel, 16 N.Y.2d 64, 262 N.Y.S.2d 86, 209 N.E. 2d 709 (N.Y. 1965), accessed April 2020, https://www.nycourts.gov/reporter/archives/rosenstiel.htm.

58 *Mexico became . . . 1940s–1960s* "Mexican Divorce—a Survey," *Fordham Law Review* 33, no. 3 (1965), https://ir.lawnet.fordham.edu/cgi/viewcontent.cgi ?article=1828&context=flr.

59 *divorce certificates were obtained via mail order* Marshall Hail, "Divorce by Mail," *Vanity Fair*, August 6, 2000, https://www.vanityfair.com/culture/1934 /03/increasing-divorce-rate.

59 *Approximately 500,000 couples . . . divorce* Katie Cisneros, "Quickie Divorces Granted in Juárez," *Borderlands* 13 (1995), https://epcc.libguides.com/c.php?g =754275&p=5406181.

59 *Elizabeth Taylor from Eddie Fisher* "Domestic Relations: The Perils of Mexican Divorce," *Time*, December 27, 1963, https://web.archive.org/web/20110218145406 /http://www.time.com/time/magazine/article/0%2C9171%2C870612%2C00 .html.

59 *Marilyn Monroe from Arthur Miller* "End of the Road for Monroe and Miller," *BBC News*, January 24, 1961, http://news.bbc.co.uk/onthisday/hi/dates/stories /january/24/newsid_4588000/4588212.stm.

59 *Paulette Goddard from Charlie Chaplin* "Paulette Wins Separation from Charlie Chaplin," *The Deseret News*, June 5, 1942, https://news.google.com/newspapers ?nid=336&dat=19420605&id=Bn0qAAAAIBAJ&sjid=plUEAAAAIBAJ &pg=3866,3989134&hl=en.

59 *until 1977 Brazilians . . . remarry* Instituto Brasileiro de Direito de Família, "A Trajetória do Divórcio no Brasil: A Consolidação do Estado Democrático de Direito," Jusbrasil, July 8, 2010, https://ibdfam.jusbrasil.com.br/noticias /2273698/a-trajetoria-do-divorcio-no-brasil-a-consolidacao-do-estado -democratico-de-direito.

59 *But by crossing the border into Bolivia . . . legal impediment* See these two articles: Rose Saconi and Carlos Eduardo Entini, "Divórcio Acabou Com O Amor Fora da Lei," *Estadão*, November 30, 2012, http://m.acervo.estadao.com.br /noticias/acervo,divorcio-acabou-com-o-amor-fora-da-lei-,8617,0.htm; and Laura Capriglione, "Para Os Filhos, 'Casa' Substituiu 'Lar,'" *Folha de São Paulo*, June 24, 2007, https://www1.folha.uol.com.br/fsp/mais/fs2406200718 .htm.

59 *couples worldwide got married . . . with no legal impediment* See these two sources: Marvin M. Moore, "The Case for Marriage by Proxy," *Cleveland State Law Review* 11, no. 313 (1962), https://core.ac.uk/download/pdf/216938329.pdf; and John S. Bradway, "Legalizing Proxy Marriages," *University of Kansas City Law Review* 21 (1953): 111–26, accessed April 2020, https://core.ac.uk/download/pdf /62563802.pdf.

59 *contemporary* For more information on contemporary proxy weddings, see Alan Travis, "Immigration Inspector Warns of Rise in Proxy Marriage Misuse," *The Guardian*, June 19, 2014, https://www.theguardian.com/uk-news/2014 /jun/19/immigration-proxy-marriage-misuse; and Jesse Klein, "Another Effect of Covid: Thousands of Double Proxy Weddings," *The New York Times*, De-

cember 15, 2020, https://www.nytimes.com/2020/12/15/fashion/weddings
/another-effect-of-covid-thousands-of-double-proxy-weddings.html.

60 *(in 2021, this meant 164 of the 195 countries in the world)* For an updated number, I suggest visiting the website of the Human Rights Campaign Foundation:
https://www.hrc.org/resources/marriage-equality-around-the-world.

60 *The first legislation . . . in the Netherlands* Government of the Netherlands, "Same-
Sex Marriage," Marriage, Registered Partnership and Cohabitation Agreements,
accessed April 2020, https://www.government.nl/topics/marriage-cohabitation
-agreement-registered-partnership/marriage-registered-partnership-and
-cohabitation-agreements/same-sex-marriage.

60 *many countries . . . the Dutch* Rosie Perper, "Countries Around the World
Where Same-Sex Marriage Is Legal," *Business Insider*, May 28, 2020, https://
www.businessinsider.com/where-is-same-sex-marriage-legal-world-2017-11
?r=US&IR=T.

60 *In Israel . . . Portugal* "World of Weddings: Same-Sex Couples in Israel Find
Legal Loophole to Recognize Marriages," CBS News, December 5, 2019, https://
www.cbsnews.com/news/world-of-weddings-israel-same-sex-couples-find-legal
-loophole-to-recognize-marriages/.

60 *Even though Israel . . . religious marriage* Aeyal Gross, "Why Gay Marriage
Isn't Coming to Israel Any Time Soon," *Haaretz*, June 30, 2015, https://www
.haaretz.com/opinion/.premium-gay-marriage-unlikely-in-israel-1.5374568.

60 *But even in Russia—a country . . . and LGBTQIA activists* For more information, see these two articles: Olga A. Gulevich, Evgeny N. Osin, Nadezhda A.
Isaenko, and Lilia M. Brainis, "Scrutinizing Homophobia: A Model of Perception of Homosexuals in Russia," *Journal of Homosexuality* 65, no. 13 (November 21, 2017): 1838–66, https://doi.org/10.1080/00918369.2017.1391017; and
Radzhana Buyantueva, "LGBT Rights Activism and Homophobia in Russia,"
Journal of Homosexuality 65, no. 4 (June 6, 2017): 456–83, https://doi.org/10
.1080/00918369.2017.1320167.

61 *The country's law . . . as married in Russia* Catherine Heath, "Family Law in the
Russian Federation: Overview," Thomson Reuters Practical Law, November 1,
2020, https://uk.practicallaw.thomsonreuters.com/4-569-5106?transitionType
=Default&contextData=(sc.Default)&firstPage=true.

61 *It doesn't mention . . . grant them the benefit* See these two articles: Lydia Smith,
"Russia Recognises Same-Sex Marriage for First Time After Couple Finds Legal Loophole," *The Independent*, January 26, 2018, https://www.independent.co
.uk/news/world/europe/russia-gay-marriage-samesex-couple-marriage-legal

-loophole-lgbt-rights-a8180036.html; and Patrick Kelleher, "Russian Authorities 'Accidentally' Recognise Queer Couple's Same-Sex Marriage Thanks to a Legal Loophole," *PinkNews*, June 23, 2020, https://www.pinknews.co.uk/2020/06/23/russia-same-sex-marriage-legal-loophole-family-code-tax-service-igor-kochetkov-fir-fyodorov/.

61 *Russia* Daria Litvinova, "Masked Men and Murder: Vigilantes Terrorise LGBT+ Russians," Reuters, September 24, 2019, https://www.reuters.com/article/russia-lgbt-crime-idUSL5N26A2IX.

61 *Poland* Lucy Ash, "Inside Poland's 'LGBT-Free Zones,'" *BBC News*, September 20, 2020, https://www.bbc.co.uk/news/stories-54191344.

61 *Uganda* Amnesty International UK, "Uganda's New Anti-Human Rights Laws Aren't Just Punishing LGBTI People," Amnesty International UK, Issues, Free Speech, May 18, 2020, https://www.amnesty.org.uk/uganda-anti-homosexual-act-gay-law-free-speech.

61 *Morocco* Human Rights Watch, "Morocco: Homophobic Response to Mob Attack," Human Rights Watch, July 15, 2015, https://www.hrw.org/news/2015/07/15/morocco-homophobic-response-mob-attack#.

63 *Safe abortions ... foreign bodies* World Health Organization, "Preventing Unsafe Abortion," Evidence Brief, September 25, 2020, https://www.who.int/news-room/fact-sheets/detail/preventing-unsafe-abortion.

63 *Data from the WHO ... unsafe conditions* J. Bearak, A. Popinchalk, B. Ganatra, A-B. Moller, Ö. Tunçalp, C. Beavin, L. Kwok, and L. Alkema, "Unintended Pregnancy and Abortion by Income, Region, and the Legal Status of Abortion: Estimates from a Comprehensive Model for 1990–2019," *Lancet Global Health* 8, no. 9 (September 2020): e1152–e1161, doi: 10.1016/S2214-109X(20)30315-6.

63 *Worldwide, about 22,000 people ... internal organs* Susheela Singh, Lisa Remez, Gilda Sedgh, Lorraine Kwok, and Tsuyoshi Onda, "Abortion Worldwide 2017: Uneven Progress and Unequal Access," Guttmacher Institute, March 2018, https://www.guttmacher.org/report/abortion-worldwide-2017.

63 *out of the average 60 million abortions ... and Latin America* Bela Ganatra, Caitlin Gerdts, Clémentine Rossier, Brooke Ronald Johnson, Özge Tunçalp, Anisa Assifi, Gilda Sedgh, et al., "Global, Regional, and Subregional Classification of Abortions by Safety, 2010–14: Estimates from a Bayesian Hierarchical Model," *The Lancet* 390, no. 10110 (November 2017): 2372–81, https://doi.org/10.1016/s0140-6736(17)31794-4.

64 *performing an abortion ... 30 percent of countries* Vinod Mishra, Victor Gaigbe-Togbe, and Julia Ferre, "Abortion Policies and Reproductive Health Around

the World," United Nations, Department of Economic and Social Affairs, Population Division, 2014, https://www.un.org/en/development/desa/population /publications/pdf/policy/AbortionPoliciesReproductiveHealth.pdf.

64 *Gomperts asked the captain . . . country apply The Vessel*, written and directed by Diana Whitten, Sovereignty Productions, 2014, film, https://vesselthefilm .com/.

64 *when a vessel is in international waters* "United Nations Convention on the Law of the Sea," UN Publication Sales no. *E.83.V.5*, 1983, https://www.un.org/depts /los/convention_agreements/texts/unclos/unclos_e.pdf.

65 *When combined, these pills . . . thousands of lives* Mary Gatter, Kelly Cleland, and Deborah L. Nucatola, "Efficacy and Safety of Medical Abortion Using Mifepristone and Buccal Misoprostol Through 63 Days," *Contraception* 91, no. 4 (2015): 269–73, https://doi.org/10.1016/j.contraception.2015.01.005.

70 *when the government . . . going silent* Kat Eschner, "The Story of the Real Canary in the Coal Mine," *Smithsonian Magazine*, December 30, 2016, https://www .smithsonianmag.com/smart-news/story-real-canary-coal-mine-180961570/.

71 *Through warrant canaries . . . while watching them* Canary Watch, "About Canary Watch," Canarywatch.org, accessed April 2020, https://canarywatch.org /about.html.

72 *under US freedom of speech laws . . . a warrant* "What Is a Warrant Canary?," *BBC News*, April 5, 2016, https://www.bbc.co.uk/news/technology -35969735.

72 *The case of Reddit . . . 2021* Sarah E. Needleman, "Reddit's Valuation Doubles to $6 Billion After Funding Round," *The Wall Street Journal*, February 8, 2021, https://www.wsj.com/articles/reddits-valuation-doubles-to-6-billion-after -funding-round-11612833205.

72 *Until 2014 . . . quiet compliance* Joon Ian Wong, "Reddit's Big Hint That the Government Is Watching You Is a Missing 'Warrant Canary,'" *Quartz*, April 1, 2016, https://qz.com/652570/no-more-warrant-canary-reddits-big-hint-that -it-got-a-secret-surveillance-order/.

73 *Swartz . . . plea bargain* John Schwartz, "Internet Activist, a Creator of RSS, Is Dead at 26, Apparently a Suicide," *The New York Times*, January 12, 2013, https:// www.nytimes.com/2013/01/13/technology/aaron-swartz-internet-activist-dies -at-26.html.

74 *the hashtag #icanhazpdf . . . the requester* Adam G. Dunn, Enrico Coiera, and Kenneth D. Mandl, "Is Biblioleaks Inevitable?," *Journal of Medical Internet Research* 16, no. 4 (April 22, 2014): e112, https://doi.org/10.2196/jmir.3331.

76 *With approximately half of its population living on less than $5.50 per day* Instituto Brasileiro de Geografia e Estatística, "Portal do IBGE," accessed April 2020, https://www.ibge.gov.br/.

76 *At the beginning of the outbreak . . . COVID-19 patients* João Paulo Charleaux, "A Diplomacia Paralela da Compra de Respiradores Pelo Maranhão," *Nexo Jornal*, April 21, 2020, https://www.nexojornal.com.br/expresso/2020/04/21/A -diplomacia-paralela-da-compra-de-respiradores-pelo-Maranh%C3%A3o.

76 *Local businesspeople . . . centralized plan* "Maranhão Comprou da China, Mandou Para Etiópia e Driblou Governo Federal Para Ter Respiradores," *Folha de São Paulo*, April 16, 2020, https://www1.folha.uol.com.br/colunas/painel /2020/04/maranhao-comprou-da-china-mandou-para-etiopia-e-driblou -governo-federal-para-ter-respiradores.shtml?utm_source=twitter&utm _medium=social&utm_campaign=comptw.

78 *instead of donating . . . local hospitals* For more information, see Charleaux, "A Diplomacia Paralela da Compra de Respiradores Pelo Maranhão," and "Maranhão Comprou da China."

81 *The anecdote . . . from others' illness* Charles Piller, "An Anarchist Is Teaching Patients to Make Their Own Medications," *Scientific American*, October 13, 2017, https://www.scientificamerican.com/article/an-anarchist-is-teaching-patients-to -make-their-own-medications/.

81 *The company . . . profit margins* Jana Kasperkevic and Amanda Holpuch, "EpiPen CEO Hiked Prices on Two Dozen Products and Got a 671% Pay Raise," *The Guardian*, August 24, 2016, https://www.theguardian.com/business/2016 /aug/24/epipen-ceo-hiked-prices-heather-bresch-mylan.

83 *In 2017, Sovaldi . . . treatment* Olga Khazan, "The True Cost of an Expensive Medication," *The Atlantic*, September 25, 2015, https://www.theatlantic.com /health/archive/2015/09/an-expensive-medications-human-cost/407299/.

84 *The Basel Convention . . . poor countries* "1989 Basel Convention on the Control of Transboundary Movements of Hazardous Wastes and Their Disposal," *Journal of Environmental Law* 1, no. 2 (1989): 255–77, https://doi.org/10.1093 /jel/1.2.255.

84 *over thirty years later . . . garbage dumps* Nikita Shukla, "How the Basel Convention Has Harmed Developing Countries," Earth.org, March 30, 2020, https:// earth.org/how-the-basel-convention-has-harmed-developing-countries/.

85 *dumping their e-waste . . . "secondhand products"* Peter Yeung, "The Toxic Effects of Electronic Waste in Accra, Ghana," Bloomberg CitiLab Environment,

May 29, 2019, https://www.bloomberg.com/news/articles/2019-05-29/the-rich
-world-s-electronic-waste-dumped-in-ghana.

85 *By 2016 . . . Ghana alone* C. P. Baldé, V. Forti, V. Gray, R. Kuehr, and P.
Stegmann, "The Global E-Waste Monitor 2017," Bonn/Geneva/Vienna:
United Nations University, International Telecommunication Union (ITU)
& International Solid Waste Association, 2017, https://collections.unu.edu
/eserv/UNU:6341/Global-E-waste_Monitor_2017__electronic_single
pages.pdf.

85 *When Greenpeace . . . ends meet* Kevin Brigden, Iryna Labunska, David San-
tillo, and Paul Johnston, "Chemical Contamination at E-Waste Recycling and
Disposal Sites in Accra and Korforidua, Ghana," Greenpeace Research Laboratories, August 2008, http://www.greenpeace.to/publications/chemical
-contamination-at-e-wa.pdf.

85 *Because of its . . . biblical cities* Clemens Höges, "How Europe's Discarded Comput-
ers Are Poisoning Africa's Kids," *Spiegel International*, December 4, 2009, https://
www.spiegel.de/international/world/the-children-of-sodom-and-gomorrah
-how-europe-s-discarded-computers-are-poisoning-africa-s-kids-a-665061.html.

3: The Roundabout

89 *"I came back . . . the streets"* Amit Madheshiya and Shirley Abraham,
"Tiled Gods Appear on Mumbai's Streets," Tasveer Ghar, a Digital Network
of South Asian Popular Visual Culture, accessed April 2020, http://www
.tasveergharindia.net/essay/tiled-gods-mumbai.html.

89 *Nearly half of Indian households . . . persists* Helen Regan and Manveena Suri,
"Half of India Couldn't Access a Toilet 5 Years Ago. Modi Built 110M Latrines—
But Will People Use Them?," CNN, October 6, 2019, https://edition.cnn.com
/2019/10/05/asia/india-modi-open-defecation-free-intl-hnk-scli/index.html.

90 *video on YouTube . . . water cannon* The Clean Indian, "Pissing Tanker," video,
YouTube, April 30, 2014, https://www.youtube.com/watch?v=aaEqZQXmx5M
&ab_channel=TheCleanIndian.

91 *an India-based production . . . "walk away from you"* Aur Dikhao, "#Dont
LetHerGo-Kangana Ranaut, Amitabh Bachchan & More Bollywood Comes
Together for 'Swachh Bharat,'" video, YouTube, August 10, 2016, https://www
.youtube.com/watch?v=jezSduqsRjs&ab_channel=AurDikhao.

91 *the roughly 80 percent of the country's population who practice Hinduism* Steph-
anie Kramer, "Key Findings About the Religious Composition of India," Pew

Research Center, September 21, 2021, https://www.pewresearch.org/fact-tank/2021/09/21/key-findings-about-the-religious-composition-of-india/.

92 *what feedback loops entail from a systems thinking perspective* For more information, see Donella H. Meadows, *Thinking in Systems: A Primer*, ed. Diana Wright (White River Junction, Vt.: Chelsea Green Publishing, 2008).

94 *This tune . . . their homes* Dan Barry and Caitlin Dickerson, "The Killer Flu of 1918: A Philadelphia Story," *The New York Times*, April 4, 2020, https://www.nytimes.com/2020/04/04/us/coronavirus-spanish-flu-philadelphia-pennsylvania.html.

94 *The Spanish flu . . . of the war* Cambridge University, "Spanish Flu: A Warning from History," film, YouTube, November 30, 2018.

94 *Philadelphia . . . (100,000, respectively)* Nina Strochlic and Riley D. Champine, "How Some Cities 'Flattened the Curve' During the 1918 Flu Pandemic," History and Culture, Coronavirus Coverage, *National Geographic*, March 27, 2020, https://www.nationalgeographic.com/history/article/how-cities-flattened-curve-1918-spanish-flu-pandemic-coronavirus.

95 *Why was Philadelphia . . . lower than that of Philadelphia* Barry and Dickerson, "The Killer Flu of 1918."

96 *In 2018 Professor Julia Gog . . . "each place"* Cambridge University, "Spanish Flu: A Warning from History."

96 *The United States devised a plan . . . potential dangers* Eric Lipton and Jennifer Steinhauer, "The Untold Story of the Birth of Social Distancing," *The New York Times*, April 22, 2020, https://www.nytimes.com/2020/04/22/us/politics/social-distancing-coronavirus.html.

96 *the United Kingdom Risk Register . . . dangers* Cabinet Office, National Security and Intelligence, and the Rt Hon Caroline Nokes, MP, "National Risk Register of Civil Emergencies—2017 Edition," Emergency Preparation, Response and Recovery, Government of the United Kingdom, September 14, 2017, https://www.gov.uk/government/publications/national-risk-register-of-civil-emergencies-2017-edition.

96 *In Bush's words . . . "control it"* Lipton and Steinhauer, "The Untold Story of the Birth of Social Distancing."

96 *Barack Obama's government . . . Directorate for Global Health Security and Biodefense* Abigail Tracy, "How Trump Gutted Obama's Pandemic-Preparedness Systems," *Vanity Fair*, May 1, 2020, https://www.vanityfair.com/news/2020/05/trump-obama-coronavirus-pandemic-response.

97 *the commission writing this playbook . . . transmission chains* Lipton and Stein-hauer, "The Untold Story of the Birth of Social Distancing."

97 *Glass and his colleagues . . . "antiviral drugs"* Robert J. Glass, Laura M. Glass, Walter E. Beyeler, and H. Jason Min, "Targeted Social Distancing Designs for Pandemic Influenza," *Emerging Infectious Diseases* 12, no. 11 (November 1, 2006): 1671–81, https://doi.org/10.3201/eid1211.060255.

98 *from 1.8 billion* US Department of Commerce, "Historical Estimates of World Population," United States Census Bureau, accessed April 2020, https://www.census.gov/data/tables/time-series/demo/international-programs/historical-est-worldpop.html.

98 *to 7.8 billion* US Department of Commerce, "US and World Population Clock," United States Census Bureau, accessed April 2020, https://www.census.gov/popclock/.

100 *Innovation management scholars call this bootlegging* For more information, see Paola Criscuolo, Ammon Salter, and Anne L. J. Ter Wal, "Going Under-ground: Bootlegging and Individual Innovative Performance," *Organization Science* 25, no. 5 (October 2014): 1287–305, https://doi.org/10.1287/orsc.2013.0856; and Charalampos Mainemelis, "Stealing Fire: Creative Deviance in the Evolution of New Ideas," *Academy of Management Review* 35, no. 4 (October 2010): 558–78, https://doi.org/10.5465/amr.35.4.zok558.

101 *Bootlegging has arguably resulted . . . a better alternative* Felix Hoffmann wrote the story about his bootlegging motivation in a footnote in a German encyclope-dia. This version has been disputed by others, who claim Hoffmann conducted this work under the direction of his colleague Arthur Eichengrün. For more information, see these two sources: W. Sneader, "The Discovery of Aspirin: A Reappraisal," *BMJ* 321 (7276) (2000): 1591–94, doi:10.1136/bmj.321.7276.1591; and the Science History Institute webpage on Felix Hoffmann, https://www.sciencehistory.org/historical-profile/felix-hoffmann.

101 *Klaus Grohe . . . biological weapon* Wolfgang Runge, *Technology Entrepreneur-ship: A Treatise on Entrepreneurs and Entrepreneurship for and in Technology Ventures* (Karlsruhe: Scientific Publishing, 1994).

101 *the first FDA-approved drug for the treatment of anthrax* Andrea Meyerhoff, Renata Albrecht, Joette M. Meyer, Peter Dionne, Karen Higgins, and Dianne Murphy, "US Food and Drug Administration Approval of Ciprofloxacin Hydrochloride for Management of Postexposure Inhalational Anthrax," *Clinical Infectious Dis-eases* 39, no. 3 (August 2004): 303–8, https://doi.org/10.1086/421491.

101 *Chuck House . . . "engineering duty"* George Andres, "Behind the Screen at Hewlett-Packard," *Forbes*, October 22, 2009, https://www.forbes.com/2009 /10/21/hewlett-packard-hp-phenomenon-opinions-contributors-book-review -george-anders.html?sh=7c3abe7d7862.

101 *Other bootlegged innovations . . . at Xerox* Claudia C. Michalik, *Innovatives Engagement: Eine empirische Untersuchung zum Phänomen des Bootlegging*, Deutscher Universität Verlag, Gabler edition (Wissenschaft, 2003).

102 *Innovation management studies . . . group efforts* For more information, see Criscuolo, Salter, and Ter Wal, "Going Underground," and Mainemelis, "Stealing Fire."

102 *3M and Hewlett-Packard . . . pursue their ideas* For more information, see these sources: Paul D. Kretkowski, "The 15 Percent Solution," *Wired*, January 23, 1998, https://www.wired.com/1998/01/the-15-percent-solution/; and Ernest Gundling and Jerry I. Porras, *The 3M Way to Innovation: Balancing People and Profit* (Tokyo and New York: Kodansha International, 2000).

103 *For more than three thousand years . . . raising pigs* "What Is India's Caste System?," *BBC News*, June 19, 2019, https://www.bbc.co.uk/news/world-asia -india-35650616.

111 *In their cosmological view . . . their land* Marcos Mondardo, "Insecurity Territorialities and Biopolitical Strategies of the Guarani and Kaiowá Indigenous Folk on Brazil's Borderland Strip with Paraguay," *L'Espace Politique* [online] 31, no. 2017–1 (April 18, 2017), https://doi.org/10.4000/espacepolitique.4203.

112 *In an open letter, written in Portuguese and posted on Facebook* Julia Dias Carneiro, "Carta Sobre 'Morte Coletiva' de Índios Gera Comoção e Incerteza," BBC Brasil, October 24, 2012, https://www.bbc.com/portuguese/noticias /2012/10/121024_indigenas_carta_coletiva_jc.

113 *activist Jacques Servin . . . relatively unscathed* Vincent Graff, "Meet the Yes Men Who Hoax the World," *The Guardian*, December 13, 2004, https://www .theguardian.com/media/2004/dec/13/mondaymediasection5.

114 *we can learn from Scheherazade, the legendary Persian queen* N. J. Dawood and William Harvey, *Tales from the Thousand and One Nights* (London: Penguin, 2003).

4: The Next Best

118 *the rise of electrical devices . . . "were built right into our walls"* International Electrotechnical Commission, "International Standardization of Electrical Plugs and Sockets for Domestic Use," IEC—Brief History, accessed April 2020, http://pubweb2.iec.ch/worldplugs/history.htm.

121 *Even the American giant 3M . . . face masks in March 2020* Reuters Staff, "3M Doubles Production of Respirator Masks amid Coronavirus Outbreak," Reuters, March 20, 2020, https://www.reuters.com/article/us-health-coronavirus-3m -idUSKBN2172RP.

122 *In March 2020 . . . across the country* Leila Abboud, "Inside the Factory: How LVMH Met France's Call for Hand Sanitiser in 72 Hours," *Financial Times*, March 19, 2020, https://www.ft.com/content/e9c2bae4-6909-11ea-800d -da70cff6e4d3.

122 *Hand sanitizer . . . the gel* Abboud, "Inside the Factory."

124 *Rocha founded CPCD . . . learning experiences* For more information, see the nonprofit's website: http://www.cpcd.org.br/.

124 *Rocha's approach . . . "raise a child"* "Cada Ação Importa," Universo Online (UOL), November 24, 2019, https://www.uol.com.br/ecoa/reportagens -especiais/tiao-rocha/#cada-acao-importa.

124 *96.7 percent of the children . . . were in a "critical state"* "Tião Rocha e Araçuaí Sustentável," Centro Popular de Cultura e Desenvolvimento (CPCD), ac- cessed April 2020, http://www.cpcd.org.br/portfolio/tiao-rocha-e-aracuai -sustentavel/.

126 *According to Interpol . . . inhabit the land* C. Nellemann and Interpol Environ- mental Crime Programme, eds., "Green Carbon, Black Trade: Illegal Logging, Tax Fraud and Laundering in the World's Tropical Forests," A Rapid Response Assessment, UN Environment Programme, GRID-Arendal (Birkeland, Nor- way: Birkeland Trykkeri AS, 2012).

126 *"didn't come . . . was already there"* Topher White, "What Can Save the Rain- forest? Your Used Cell Phone," TEDX CERN talk, posted September 2014, YouTube, March 15, 2015.

126 *He realized . . . in the act* White, "What Can Save the Rainforest? Your Used Cell Phone."

127 *expanded to ten countries on five continents* Cassandra Brooklyn, "Deep in the Rainforest, Old Phones Are Catching Illegal Loggers," *Wired*, February 17, 2021, https://www.wired.co.uk/article/ecuador-ai-logging-cellphones.

129 *About a third of the world's population . . . vaccines* World Health Organization and International Bank for Reconstruction and Development, "Tracking Uni- versal Health Coverage: 2017 Global Monitoring Report," World Bank, 2017, https://documents1.worldbank.org/curated/en/640121513095868125/pdf /122029-WP-REVISED-PUBLIC.pdf.

129 *about 9 percent of classified roads were paved in 2015* World Bank, "Combined

Project Information Documents / Integrated Safeguards Datasheet (PID/ ISDS)," Lake Victoria Transport Program, April 3, 2017, https://documents1 .worldbank.org/curated/en/319211491308886249/ITM00194-P160488-04-04 -2017-1491308883264.docx.

129 *it partnered . . . much-needed medical supplies* Zipline, "Put Autonomy to Work," accessed April 2020, https://flyzipline.com/how-it-works/.

130 *created a test bed . . . currently unfeasible* Jake Bright, "Africa Is Becoming a Testbed for Commercial Drone Services," *TechCrunch*, May 22, 2016, https://techcrunch.com/2016/05/22/africa-is-becoming-a-testbed-for -commercial-drone-services/.

131 *the cost of corruption . . . State of São Paulo* Federação das Indústrias do Estado de São Paulo (FIESP), "Corrupção: Custos Econômicos e Propostas de Combate," DECOMTEC, March 2010.

131 *As William Gibson . . . "evenly distributed"* Cyberpunk (Intercon Production, 1990), documentary.

134 *the NSA . . . engage in cryptography* Stephen Levy, *Crypto: How the Code Rebels Beat the Government, Saving Privacy in the Digital Age* (New York: Viking Penguin, 2001).

135 *in a 1976 article titled "New Directions in Cryptography"* Whitfield Diffie and Martin E. Hellman, "New Directions in Cryptography," *IEEE Transactions on Information Theory* 22, no. 6 (November 1976), https://ee.stanford.edu /~hellman/publications/24.pdf.

135 *very controversial . . . "is today"* Steve Fyffe and Tom Abate, "Stanford Cryptography Pioneers Whitfield Diffie and Martin Hellman Win ACM 2015 A. M. Turing Award," *Stanford News*, March 1, 2016, https://news.stanford.edu/2016 /03/01/turing-hellman-diffie-030116/.

136 *With this vision . . . diffusion of cryptography* Julian Assange, Jacob Appelbaum, Andy Müller-Maguhn, and Jérémie Zimmerman, *Cypherpunks: Freedom and the Future of the Internet* (New York and London: Or Books, 2012).

137 *Satoshi Nakamoto . . . financial system* Ying-Ying Hsieh, Jean-Philippe Vergne, Philip Anderson, Karim Lakhani, and Markus Reitzig, "Bitcoin and the Rise of Decentralized Autonomous Organizations," *Journal of Organization Design* 7, no. 1 (November 30, 2018), https://doi.org/10.1186/s41469 -018-0038-1.

138 *Hal Finney . . . later on* Andrea Peterson, "Hal Finney Received the First Bitcoin Transaction. Here's How He Describes It," *The Washington Post*, January 3, 2014, https://www.washingtonpost.com/news/the-switch/wp/2014/01/03

/hal-finney-received-the-first-bitcoin-transaction-heres-how-he-describes-it
/?noredirect=on.

138 *man from Florida . . . Papa John's pizzas* Michael del Castillo, "The Founder of Bitcoin Pizza Day Is Celebrating Today in the Perfect Way," *Forbes*, May 22, 2018, https://www.forbes.com/sites/michaeldelcastillo/2018/05/22/the -founder-of-bitcoin-pizza-day-is-celebrating-today-in-the-perfect-way/?sh =484dae5d9c45.

139 *Her path . . . more specifically, women's rights law* Lila Thulin, "The True Story of the Case Ruth Bader Ginsburg Argues in 'On the Basis of Sex,'" *Smithsonian Magazine*, December 24, 2018, https://www.smithsonianmag.com/history /true-story-case-center-basis-sex-180971110/.

140 *Sarah Grimké . . . "off our necks"* "Sarah Grimke," Elizabeth A. Sackler Center for Feminist Art, Brooklyn Museum, accessed April 2020, https://www .brooklynmuseum.org/eascfa/dinner_party/heritage_floor/sarah_grimke.

140 *In the 1960s . . . "precious few of them"* Ruth Bader Ginsburg, interview by Wendy Webster Williams and Deborah James Merritt, April 10, 2009, transcript, Knowledge Bank, Ohio State University Libraries, Columbus, Ohio, https://kb.osu.edu/bitstream/handle/1811/71376/OSLJ_V70N4_0805.pdf.

141 *At Rutgers . . . precedent for women, too* Thulin, "The True Story of the Case Ruth Bader Ginsburg Argues in 'On the Basis of Sex.'"

141 *Moritz was a bachelor . . . "doing so"* Thulin, "The True Story of the Case Ruth Bader Ginsburg Argues in 'On the Basis of Sex.'"

142 *The Ginsburgs . . . November 1972* Charles E. Moritz and Commissioner of Internal Revenue, Moritz v. CIR, 469 F. 2d 466 (United States Court of Appeals, Tenth Circuit 1972).

142 *RBG secured support . . . "the Constitution"* Cary Frankling, "The Anti-Stereotyping Principle in Constitutional Sex Discrimination Law," *New York University Law Review* 85, no. 1 (April 14, 2010), https://ssrn.com/abstract =1589754.

142 *the Ginsburgs' entire strategy . . . women the most* Franklin, "The Anti-Stereotyping Principle in Constitutional Sex Discrimination Law."

142 *On the opposing bench . . . all-male court* Thulin, "The True Story of the Case Ruth Bader Ginsburg Argues in 'On the Basis of Sex.'"

143 *On the Basis of Sex*, directed by Mimi Leder, written by Daniel Stiepleman (Focus Features, 2018), 2 hr.

143 *professor Jane Sherron De Hart . . . was, therefore, unconstitutional* Jane Sherron De Hart, *Ruth Bader Ginsburg: A Life* (New York: Alfred A. Knopf, 2018).

144 *Reed v. Reed* Reed v. Reed, 404 US 71 (1971), accessed April 2020, https://scholar
.google.co.uk/scholar_case?case=9505211932515131375&hl=en&as_sdt=6&as
_vis=1&oi=scholarr.

144 *This case . . . against women* Thulin, "The True Story of the Case Ruth Bader
Ginsburg Argues in 'On the Basis of Sex.'"

144 *Erwin Griswold appealed . . . sex-based references* Charles E. Moritz, Petitioner-
appellant, v. Commissioner of Internal Revenue, Respondent-appellee, 469
F.2d 466 (10th Cir. 1972), accessed April 2020, https://library.menloschool
.org/chicago/legal.

145 *An article RBG wrote . . . "to Abominable"* Ruth Bader Ginsburg, "The Need
for the Equal Rights Amendment," *American Bar Association Journal* 59, no. 9
(September 1973): 1013–19, https://www.jstor.org/stable/25726416.

5: The Workaround Attitude

152 *Freud details our innate tendencies . . . "dispute this assertion?"* Sigmund Freud,
Civilization and Its Discontents, ed. James Strachey, trans. Joan Riviere (London: Hogarth Press, 1963).

153 *"A man is a wolf to another man" . . . enforce rules* Thomas Hobbes, *On the Cit-
izen*, ed. Richard Tuck and Michael Silverthorne (New York: Cambridge University Press, 1998).

155 *In 1961 she covered Adolf Eichmann's trial in Jerusalem* Hannah Arendt, "Eichmann in Jerusalem—I," *The New Yorker*, February 8, 1963, https://www
.newyorker.com/magazine/1963/02/16/eichmann-in-jerusalem-i.

155 *a book on it* Hannah Arendt, *Eichmann in Jerusalem: A Report on the Banality of
Evil* (New York: Penguin, 1994).

155 *Arendt argued . . . murderous appetite* Arendt, "Eichmann in Jerusalem—I."

155 *Arendt coined . . . by rule followers* Judith Butler, "Hannah Arendt's Challenge
to Adolf Eichmann," *The Guardian*, August 29, 2011, https://www.theguardian
.com/commentisfree/2011/aug/29/hannah-arendt-adolf-eichmann-banality
-of-evil.

155 *Milgram experiments . . . conformed partially* Stanley Milgram, "Behavioral
Study of Obedience," *Journal of Abnormal and Social Psychology* 67, no. 4 (1963):
371–78, https://doi.org/10.1037/h0040525.

157 *Rules range from authoritative . . . and act* W. Richard Scott, *Institutions and
Organizations*, 2nd ed. (Thousand Oaks, Calif.: Sage Publications, 2001).

157 *Pierre Bourdieu puts it . . . "without saying"* Pierre Bourdieu, *Outline of a The-*

ory of Practice, trans. Richard Nice (Cambridge: Cambridge University Press, 1977).

158 *Douglass North . . . act in each circumstance* Douglass C. North, *Institutions, Institutional Change and Economic Perfomance* (Cambridge: Cambridge University Press, 1990).

158 *Although most rules . . . expected from each of us* Scott, *Institutions and Organizations.*

159 *Rules give us cognitive shortcuts . . . want them to or not* Amos Tversky and Daniel Kahneman, "Judgment Under Uncertainty: Heuristics and Biases," *Science* 185, no. 4157 (September 27, 1974): 1124–31, https://doi.org/10.1126/science.185 .4157.1124.

160 *In his book* Madness and Civilization . . . *discipline upon others* Michel Foucault, *Madness and Civilization: A History of Insanity in the Age of Reason* (New York: Vintage Books, 1964).

160 *Clennon King Jr. . . . "the Black Don Quixote"* Martin Luther King Jr., "To Governor James P. Coleman," June 7, 1958, accessed April 2020, http://okra .stanford.edu/transcription/document_images/Vol04Scans/419_7-June -1958_to%20James%20P%20Coleman.pdf.

161 *The problem Foucault raises . . . and inequity* Foucault, *Madness and Civilization.*

162 *richest twenty-six individuals hold wealth equivalent to that of the poorest 3.8 billion* "Public Good or Private Wealth?," Oxfam GB, January 2019, https://www .osservatoriodiritti.it/wp-content/uploads/2019/01/rapporto-oxfam-pdf.pdf.

163 *In* Discipline and Punish . . . *blame individuals for punishment* Michel Foucault, *Discipline and Punish* (Harmondsworth, UK: Penguin Books, 1979).

165 *"I ate his liver" . . . in* The Silence of the Lambs *The Silence of the Lambs*, directed by Jonathan Demme (Orion Pictures, 1991), 1 hr., 58 min. This quote is a screenplay adaptation of Thomas Harris's 1988 novel, *The Silence of the Lambs*. The excerpt from the book says "a big Amarone" instead of "a nice Chianti."

165 *Professor Ruth Wilson Gilmore . . . were left behind* Ruth Wilson Gilmore, *Golden Gulag: Prisons, Surplus, Crisis, and Opposition in Globalizing California* (Berkeley: University of California Press, 2007).

165 *Mafiosi, gangsters, and drug dealers . . . deviate from state laws* There are many studies on unlawful organizations. I suggest reading this book by Sudhir Venkatesh on his ethnography with drug dealers in Chicago: *Gang Leader for a Day: A Rogue Sociologist Takes to the Streets* (New York: Penguin Press, 2008).

167 *With his reputation . . . sport has ever seen* "Lance Armstrong: USADA Report

Labels Him 'a Serial Cheat,'" *BBC News*, October 11, 2012, https://www.bbc
.co.uk/sport/cycling/19903716.

168 *The first large-scale survey on cheating . . . academic dishonesty* William Bowers,
Student Dishonesty and Its Control in College (New York: Columbia University
Press, 1964).

168 *A study published in* Nature *in 2005 . . . a few get caught* Meredith Wadman,
"One in Three Scientists Confesses to Having Sinned," *Nature* 435, no. 7043
(June 2005): 718–19, https://doi.org/10.1038/435718b.

168 *Harvard professor Marc Hauser . . . were conducted* Nicholas Wade, "Harvard
Researcher May Have Fabricated Data," *The New York Times*, August 27, 2010,
https://www.nytimes.com/2010/08/28/science/28harvard.html.

168 *with this title . . . "Rhesus Monkeys"* M. D. Hauser, "Costs of Deception: Cheaters Are Punished in Rhesus Monkeys (Macaca Mulatta)," *Proceedings of the National Academy of Science* 89, no. 24 (1992): 12137–39, https://doi.org/10.1073
/pnas.89.24.12137.

169 *influential study . . . "of their own integrity"* Nina Mazar, On Amir, and Dan
Ariely, "The Dishonesty of Honest People: A Theory of Self-Concept Mainte-
nance," *Journal of Marketing Research* 45, no. 6 (2008): 633–44, https://doi.org
/10.1509/jmkr.45.6.633.

172 *In his "Letter from Birmingham Jail" . . . "respect for law"* Martin Luther King Jr.,
"Letter from a Birmingham Jail [King, Jr.]," April 16, 1963, accessed April 2020,
https://www.africa.upenn.edu/Articles_Gen/Letter_Birmingham.html.

174 *As American jurist and Harvard law professor Paul Freund . . . "the climate of the
era"* David Souter, Ruth B. Ginsburg, David S. Tatel, and Linda Greenhouse,
"The Supreme Court and Useful Knowledge: Panel Discussion," *Proceedings of
the American Philosophical Society* 154, no. 3 (September 2010): 294–306, https://
doi.org/10.2307/41000082.

6: The Workaround Mindset

176 *misrepresent Eshu . . . the devil* For more information on how the Catholic Church in Brazil demonized Eshu, I suggest reading: Reginaldo Prandi,
"Exu, de Mensageiro a Diabo. Sincretismo Católico e Demonização do Orixá
Exu," *Revista USP* 50 (August 30, 2001): 46, https://doi.org/10.11606/issn
.2316-9036.v0i50p46-63.

176 *He can both confuse . . . and possibilities* John Pemberton, "Eshu-Elegba: The
Yoruba Trickster God," *African Arts* 9, no. 1 (October 1975): 20, https://doi
.org/10.2307/3334976.

177 *Yoruba consider him the god . . . make things worse* Joan Wescott, "The Sculpture and Myths of Eshu-Elegba, the Yoruba Trickster: Definition and Interpretation in Yoruba Iconography," *Africa* 32, no. 4 (October 1962): 336–54, https://doi .org/10.2307/1157438.

178 *Our knowledge can curse us . . . not to know it* Chip Heath and Dan Heath, "The Curse of Knowledge," *Harvard Business Review*, December 2006, https://hbr .org/2006/12/the-curse-of-knowledge.

178 *appreciate that we don't know. . . . think we do know* For more on knowledge assumptions and deconstruction, see Sheila Jasanoff, *The Fifth Branch: Science Advisers as Policymakers* (Cambridge, Mass.: Harvard University Press, 1990).

178 *An old Yoruba tale . . . were both right* Judith Hoch-Smith and Ernesto Pichardo, "Having Thrown a Stone Today Eshu Kills a Bird of Yesterday," *Caribbean Review* 7, no. 4 (1978).

179 *"contradictory certitudes": the different (and often incompatible) diagnoses of reality* Steve Rayner, "Wicked Problems: Clumsy Solutions—Diagnoses and Prescriptions for Environmental Ills," First Jack Beale Memorial Lecture, University of South Wales, Sydney, Australia, July 25, 2006, James Martin Institute for Science and Civilization.

180 *what the poet John Keats called "negative capability"* Richard Gunderman, "John Keats' Concept of 'Negative Capability'—or Sitting in Uncertainty—Is Needed Now More than Ever," *The Conversation*, February 22, 2021, https:// theconversation.com/john-keats-concept-of-negative-capability-or-sitting-in -uncertainty-is-needed-now-more-than-ever-153617.

180 *Heath brothers called "forced prioritization"* Chip Heath and Dan Heath, *Made to Stick* (New York: Random House, 2010).

181 *"unknown unknowns" into "known unknowns"* These terms were used by US secretary of defense Donald Rumsfeld in a news briefing. They have since been used by various scholars to describe different dimensions of uncertainty; see, for instance, Andy Stirling, "Keep It Complex," *Nature* 468, no. 7327 (December 2010): 1029–31, https://doi.org/10.1038/4681029a.

181 *anthropologists who say that their aim is to "make the strange familiar and the familiar strange"* The origins of this expression are disputed. Some trace it back to T. S. Eliot's essay on Andrew Marvell; see T.S. Eliot, *Selected Essays* (New York: Harcourt Brace Jovanovich, 1978).

182 *navigate between . . . ("paralysis by analysis")* Ann Langley, "Between 'Paralysis by Analysis' and 'Extinction by Instinct,'" *MIT Sloan Management Review*,

April 15, 1995, https://sloanreview.mit.edu/article/between-paralysis-by-analysis-and-extinction-by-instinct/.

187 *paraphrase . . . thrown through the window* This brick analogy was in Brian Massumi's translator's introduction in Gilles Deleuze and Félix Guattari, *A Thousand Plateaus: Capitalism and Schizophrenia* (Minneapolis and London: University of Minnesota Press, 1987).

188 *these, Anil asserts, "aren't marginal minds"* Anil K. Gupta, *Grassroots Innovation: Minds on the Margin Are Not Marginal Minds* (Delhi: Penguin Random House, 2016).

188 *The expert's problem . . . from new angles* For more on differences between insiders and outsiders, see Roger Evered and Meryl Reis Louis, "Alternative Perspectives in the Organizational Sciences: 'Inquiry from the Inside' and 'Inquiry from the Outside,'" *Academy of Management Review* 6, no. 3 (July 1981): 385–95, https://doi.org/10.5465/amr.1981.4285776.

189 *John Steinbeck, "That's what makes . . . with numbers on it"* John Steinbeck, *The Grapes of Wrath* (New York: Viking, 1939).

189 *Behavioral economists . . . trouble letting it go* For more information, see Daniel Kahneman, Jack L. Knetsch, and Richard H. Thaler, "Experimental Tests of the Endowment Effect and the Coase Theorem," *Journal of Political Economy* 98, no. 6 (December 1990): 1325–48, https://doi.org/10.1086/261737; and Dan Ariely, *Predictably Irrational: The Hidden Forces That Shape Our Decisions* (New York: Harper Perennial, 2010).

190 *Range . . . there were many known unknowns* David Epstein, *Range: Why Generalists Triumph in a Specialized World* (New York: Riverhead Books, 2019).

190 *Organizations . . . as "bug bounty programs"* Suresh S. Malladi and Hemang C. Subramanian, "Bug Bounty Programs for Cybersecurity: Practices, Issues, and Recommendations," *IEEE Software* 37, no. 1 (January 2020): 31–39, https://doi.org/10.1109/ms.2018.2880508.

191 *Companies often . . . fresh eyes* There are many studies on balancing exploitation and exploration (sometimes referred to as ambidexterity) in organizational strategy. For more information, see James G. March, "Exploration and Exploitation in Organizational Learning," *Organization Science* 2, no. 1 (1991): 71–87, http://www.jstor.org/stable/2634940; and Charles A. O'Reilly and Michael L. Tushman, "Organizational Ambidexterity: Past, Present, and Future," *Academy of Management Perspectives* 27, no. 4 (November 2013): 324–38, https://doi.org/10.5465/amp.2013.0025.

191 *In Japan . . . same company* Ikujiro Nonaka and Johny K. Johansson, "Japanese Management: What About the 'Hard' Skills?," *Academy of Management Review* 10, no. 2 (April 1985): 181–91, https://doi.org/10.5465/amr.1985.4277850.

192 *embracing ambivalence and doubt* For more on embracing ambivalence and acting in situations of ambiguity, read this book on systems thinking: Peter M. Senge, *The Fifth Discipline: The Art and Practice of the Learning Organization* (New York: Doubleday, 1990).

192 *piecemeal improvements that may illuminate new possibilities* There are studies in different areas of knowledge on the value of partial activity in situations of ambiguity. See, for example, this prominent study in public administration: Charles E. Lindblom, "The Science of 'Muddling Through,'" *Public Administration Review* 19, no. 2 (1959), https://faculty.washington.edu/mccurdy /SciencePolicy/Lindblom%20Muddling%20Through.pdf.

193 *what they call "essential complexity" . . . task at hand* For more information on essential and accidental complexity, see F. P. Brooks, "No Silver Bullet Essence and Accidents of Software Engineering," *IEEE Computer* 20, no. 4 (April 1987): 10–19, https://doi.org/10.1109/mc.1987.1663532.

193 *Complex situations . . . no single solution at all* For more on complexity, see Stuart A. Kauffman, "The Sciences of Complexity and 'Origins of Order,'" *PSA: Proceedings of the Biennial Meeting of the Philosophy of Science Association* 1990, no. 2 (January 1990): 299–322, https://doi.org/10.1086/psaprocbienmeetp .1990.2.193076.

193 *the world's toughest challenges . . . come up short* For more on complex problems, I suggest reading literature on "wicked problems," starting with this seminal article: Horst W. J. Rittel and Melvin M. Webber, "Dilemmas in a General Theory of Planning," *Policy Sciences* 4, no. 2 (June 1973): 155–69, https://doi.org /10.1007/bf01405730.

194 *When Shango . . . "people think"* Migine González-Wippler, *Tales of the Orishas* (New York: Original Publications, 1985).

7: The Workaround Building Blocks

196 *Many of today's biggest challenges . . . contradictory—ways* For more information on messy organizations and wicked situations, see Russell Lincoln Ackoff, Herbert J. Addison, and Andrew Carey, *Systems Thinking for Curious Managers: With 40 New Management F-Laws* (Axminster, Devon, UK: Triarchy Press, 2010); and Steven Ney and Marco Verweij, "Messy Institutions

for Wicked Problems: How to Generate Clumsy Solutions?," *Environment and Planning C: Government and Policy* 33, no. 6 (December 2015): 1679–96, https://doi.org/10.1177/0263774x15614450.

198 *Abraham Maslow . . . "were a nail"* Abraham H. Maslow, *The Psychology of Science: A Reconnaissance* (South Bend, Ind.: Gateway Editions, 1966).

203 *feeling of fatalism, as if we are all paralyzed and doomed to fail* Mary Douglas, *Natural Symbols: Explorations in Cosmology* (Abingdon, UK: Routledge, 2003).

203 *Zambia's diarrheal death rate . . . that of Finland* I used data from UNICEF's data set of diarrheal death rates of all countries, available on the World Bank's website, to compare Finland and Zambia: https://data.worldbank.org/indicator/SH.STA.ORTH.

203 *Institute for Health Metrics and Evaluation . . . to approximately 500,000 deaths* Institute for Health Metrics and Evaluation, "Diarrhoea Prevalence, Rate, Under 5, Male, 2019, Mean," University of Washington, 2018, https://vizhub.healthdata.org/lbd/diarrhoea.

203 *making you realize . . . your ignorance* For more on the extent of our ignorance and how to make more factful analyses and decisions, see Hans Rosling, Ola Rosling, and Anna Rönnlund Rosling, *Factfulness: Ten Reasons We're Wrong About the World—and Why Things Are Better than You Think* (New York: Flatiron Books, 2018).

210 *the story of the three little pigs . . . through the chimney* Paul Galdone, *The Three Little Pigs* (New York: Seabury Press, 1970).

214 *United Nations High Commissioner for Refugees (UNHCR) . . . of displaced people* UN High Commissioner for Refugees, "Figures at a Glance," UNHCR, accessed April 2020, https://www.unhcr.org/uk/figures-at-a-glance.html.

220 *Alice asking the Cheshire Cat . . . "get SOMEWHERE"* Lewis Carroll, *Alice in Wonderland and Through the Looking Glass* (New York: Grosset and Dunlap, 1946).

8: The Workaround in Your Organization

221 *"I always . . . case in court?"* Will Schwalbe, *The End of Your Life Book Club* (New York: Knopf, 2012).

223 *it's often impossible for them to plan their way out of complex problems* For more information, see Senge, *The Fifth Discipline*; Rittel and Webber, "Dilemmas in a General Theory of Planning;" Ackoff, Addison, and Carey, *Systems Thinking for Curious Managers*; and Ney and Verweij, "Messy Institutions for Wicked Problems."

224 *studies in psychology . . . not going to college* For an example of these studies, see Thomas Gilovich and Victoria Husted Medvec, "The Experience of Regret: What, When, and Why," *Psychological Review* 102, no. 2 (1995): 379–95, https://doi.org /10.1037/0033-295x.102.2.379.

224 *Ian McEwan, "At moments" . . . voice of reason* Ian McEwan, *Solar* (London: Jonathan Cape, 2010).

224 *Laurence J. Peter . . . "undecided about them"* Laurence J. Peter, *Peter's Almanac* (New York: William Morrow, 1982).

225 *Systems change practitioners . . . "mission accomplished"* This idea has been re-produced by many systems change practitioners, and it has been used by some philanthropic organizations in the social impact space, such as the Omidyar Foundation. For more information, read Peter Serge, Hal Hamilton, and John Kania, "The Dawn of System Leadership," *Stanford Social Innovation Review* 13, no. 1 (2015), https://doi.org/10.48558/YTE7-XT62.

225 *Instead of fixating . . . the problem disappear* Roy Steiner, "Why Good Intentions Aren't Enough," Medium, Omidyar Network, May 12, 2017, https://medium .com/omidyar-network/why-good-intentions-arent-enough-698b161435f0.

226 *Unlike organizations . . . ascribing ownership* For more information, see Steven Levy, *Hackers: Heroes of the Computer Revolution* (Sebastopol, Calif.: O'Reilly, 2010); and Eric S. Raymond, ed., *The New Hacker's Dictionary* (Cambridge, Mass.: MIT Press, 1991).

226 *balance the need for accountability . . . future strategy* eWeek editors, "Python Cre-ator Scripts Inside Google," interview of Guido van Rossum by Peter Coffee, eWeek, March 6, 2006, https://www.eweek.com/development/python-creator -scripts-inside-google/.

227 *Overemphasizing ownership . . . and individuals* For more information, see Eric S. Raymond, "The Cathedral and the Bazaar," *First Monday* 3, no. 2 (March 2, 1998), https://doi.org/10.5210/fm.v3i2.578; and Eric S. Raymond, "Home-steading the Noosphere," *First Monday* 3, no. 10 (October 5, 1998), https://doi .org/10.5210/fm.v3i10.621.

228 *In 1996 researchers Roy Baumeister . . . ate the chocolaty goodness* Roy F. Baumeis-ter, Ellen Bratslavsky, Mark Muraven, and Dianne M. Tice, "Ego Depletion: Is the Active Self a Limited Resource?," *Journal of Personality and Social Psychology* 74, no. 5 (1998): 1252–65, https://doi.org/10.1037//0022-3514.74.5.1252.

229 *Pivoting . . . you hadn't anticipated* For more information on pivoting, see John W. Mullins and Randy Komisar, *Getting to Plan B: Breaking Through to a Better Business Model* (Boston: Harvard Business School Publishing, 2009).

230 *directions of scale (up, deep, or out)* I reinterpreted the distinction between "scale up," "scale deep," and "scale out" from Michele-Lee Moore, Darcy Riddell, and Dana Vocisano, "Scaling Out, Scaling Up, Scaling Deep: Strategies of Non-Profits in Advancing Systemic Social Innovation," *Journal of Corporate Citizenship* 2015, no. 58 (June 1, 2015): 67–84, https://doi.org/10.9774/gleaf.4700 .2015.ju.00009.

231 *Scaling deep means establishing stronger ties . . . in the context* For more on scaling with stronger ties, see Cynthia Rayner and François Bonnici, *The Systems Work of Social Change: How to Harness Connection, Context, and Power to Cultivate Deep and Enduring Change* (Oxford: Oxford University Press, 2021).

232 *aid organizations* For a critical view of the impact of aid, see Dambisa Moyo, *Dead Aid: Why Aid Is Not Working and How There Is a Better Way for Africa* (New York: Farrar, Straus and Giroux, 2009).

232 *"hero"-like entrepreneurs . . . white messiahs* For more on hero-like social entrepreneurs, see these three sources: Alex Nicholls, "The Legitimacy of Social Entrepreneurship: Reflexive Isomorphism in a Pre-Paradigmatic Field," *Entrepreneurship Theory and Practice* 34, no. 4 (July 2010): 611–33, https://doi.org /10.1111/j.1540-6520.2010.00397.x; P. Grenier, "Social Entrepreneurship in the UK: From Rhetoric to Reality?," in *An Introduction to Social Entrepreneurship: Voices, Preconditions, Contexts*, ed. R. Zeigler (Cheltenham, Gloucester, UK: Edward Elgar, 2009); and A. Nicholls and A. H. Cho, "Social Entrepreneurship: The Structuration of a Field," in *Social Entrepreneurship: New Models of Sustainable Change*, ed. A. Nicholls (Oxford: Oxford University Press, 2006).

232 *sometimes make things worse* For more information on the unintended consequences of entrepreneurial efforts, see Robert K. Merton, "The Unanticipated Consequences of Purposive Social Action," *American Sociological Review* 1, no. 6 (December 1936): 894, https://doi.org/10.2307/2084615.

233 *professor Herminia Ibarra . . . experience taught us* Herminia Ibarra, *Act Like a Leader, Think Like a Leader* (Boston: Harvard Business Review Press, 2015).

234 *it means that our sense-making processes . . . your reactions* Herminia Ibarra, "Provisional Selves: Experimenting with Image and Identity in Professional Adaptation," *Administrative Science Quarterly* 44, no. 4 (December 1999): 764, https://doi.org/10.2307/2667055.

235 *Steve Rayner . . . "damn well work"* Rayner, "Wicked Problems."

235 *Donald Winnicott . . . complex world* D. W. Winnicott, "The Theory of the Parent-Infant Relationship," *International Journal of Psycho-Analysis* 41 (1960):

585–95, https://icpla.edu/wp-content/uploads/2012/10/Winnicott-D.-The
-Theory-of-the-Parent-Infant-Relationship-IJPA-Vol.-41-pps.-585–595.pdf.

237 *culture of pragmatism* To learn more about pragmatism as a school of thought
in the social sciences, see these two articles: N. A. Gross, "Pragmatist Theory
of Social Mechanisms," *American Sociological Review* 74, no. 3 (2009): 358–79;
and J. Whitford, "Pragmatism and the Untenable Dualism of Means and Ends:
Why Rational Choice Theory Does Not Deserve Paradigmatic Privilege,"
Theory and Society 31 (2002): 325–63.

239 *Malcolm Gladwell wrote . . . "service of perfection"* Malcolm Gladwell, "The
Real Genius of Steve Jobs," *The New Yorker*, November 6, 2011, https://www
.newyorker.com/magazine/2011/11/14/the-tweaker.

239 *attempting to explore* better *paths . . . the* right *path* For more information, see
Sidney G. Winter, "Purpose and Progress in the Theory of Strategy: Comments
on Gavetti," *Organization Science* 23, no. 1 (February 2012): 288–97, https://doi
.org/10.1287/orsc.1110.0696; Teppo Felin, Stuart Kauffman, Roger Koppl, and
Giuseppe Longo, "Economic Opportunity and Evolution: Beyond Landscapes
and Bounded Rationality," *Strategic Entrepreneurship Journal* 8, no. 4 (May 21,
2014): 269–82, https://doi.org/10.1002/sej.1184; and Lindblom, "The Science
of 'Muddling Through.'"

240 *Adam Grant . . . launch flopped* Adam Grant, *Originals: How Non-Conformists
Move the World* (New York: Viking Penguin, 2016).

240 *Bill Gates . . . Microsoft failed* Grant, *Originals*.

241 *Leadership is not an innate ability . . . hedge our bets* For more on leaders as individuals acting in situations of uncertainty, see Hongwei Xu and Martin Ruef,
"The Myth of the Risk-Tolerant Entrepreneur," *Strategic Organization* 2, no. 4
(November 2004): 331–55, https://doi.org/10.1177/1476127004047617; Joseph
Raffiee and Jie Feng, "Should I Quit My Day Job?: A Hybrid Path to Entrepreneurship," *Academy of Management Journal* 57, no. 4 (August 2014): 936–63,
https://doi.org/10.5465/amj.2012.0522; Grant, *Originals*; and Ibarra, *Act Like
a Leader, Think Like a Leader*.

242 *Gianpiero Petriglieri . . . or disturb* G. Petriglieri, "The Psychology Behind
Effective Crisis Leadership," *Harvard Business Review*, Crisis Management,
April 22, 2020, https://hbr.org/2020/04/the-psychology-behind-effective
-crisis-leadership.

242 *Russel Ackoff, "manage messes well"* Russell L. Ackoff, "The Art and Science
of Mess Management," *Interfaces* 11, no. 1 (February 1981): 20–26, https://doi
.org/10.1287/inte.11.1.20.

242 *New Zealand's Prime Minister Jacinda Ardern . . . social cohesion* For more information, see Uri Friedman, "New Zealand's Prime Minister May Be the Most Effective Leader on the Planet," *The Atlantic*, April 19, 2020, https://www.theatlantic.com/politics/archive/2020/04/jacinda-ardern-new-zealand-leadership-coronavirus/610237/.

242 *Brazilian president Jair Bolsonaro . . . alone manage it* For more information, see "The Guardian View on Bolsonaro's Covid Strategy: Murderous Folly," editorial, *The Guardian*, October 27, 2021, https://www.theguardian.com/commentisfree/2021/oct/27/the-guardian-view-on-bolsonaros-covid-strategy-murderous-folly.

243 *what management scholars call "robust action"* For more information, see these two sources: John F. Padgett and Christopher K. Ansell, "Robust Action and the Rise of the Medici, 1400–1434," *American Journal of Sociology* 98, no. 6 (1993): 1259–1319, http://www.jstor.org/stable/2781822; and Amanda J. Porter, Philipp Tuertscher, and Marleen Huysman, "Saving Our Oceans: Scaling the Impact of Robust Action Through Crowdsourcing," *Journal of Management Studies* 57, no. 2 (2020): 246–86, https://doi.org/10.1111/joms.12515.

244 *Robust action suggests three forms of engagement . . . identify new opportunities* Fabrizio Ferraro, Dror Etzion, and Joel Gehman, "Tackling Grand Challenges Pragmatically: Robust Action Revisited," *Organization Studies* 36, no. 3 (February 24, 2015): 363–90, https://doi.org/10.1177/0170840614563742.

246 *open innovation strategies . . . rivals* Henry W. Chesbrough, *Open Innovation: The New Imperative for Creating and Profiting from Technology* (Boston: Harvard Business School Press, 2006).

247 *process of co-creation* For more information on co-creation, see C. K. Prahalad and Venkat Ramaswamy, "Co-Creation Experiences: The Next Practice in Value Creation," *Journal of Interactive Marketing* 18, no. 3 (January 2004): 5–14, https://doi.org/10.1002/dir.20015.

247 *group decisions . . . "groupthink"* There are many studies on the dangers of conformity and undesirable group behaviors in psychology and behavioral economics. See this seminal study: Irving L. Janis, *Victims of Groupthink* (Boston: Houghton Mifflin, 1972).